The Ramsey East Branch

by
Peter Paye

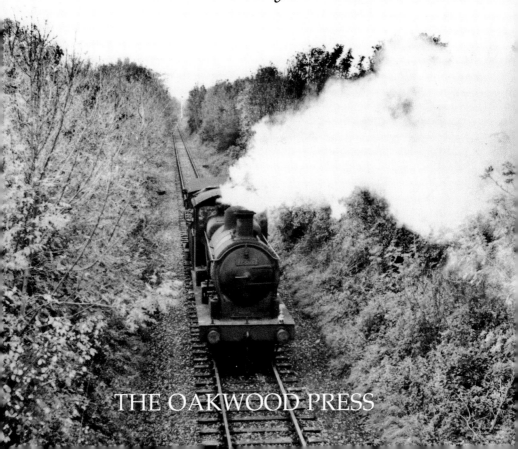

THE OAKWOOD PRESS

Published by Oakwood Press, an imprint of Stenlake Publishing Ltd, 2018

British Library Cataloguing in Publication Data
A Record for this book is available from the British Library
ISBN 978 0 85361 451 7

Printed by Claro Print, Unit 2, Kirkhill House, 81 Broom Road East, Glasgow,
G77 5LL

By the same author and published by Oakwood Press:

The Snape Branch (2005)
The Hadleigh Branch (2006)
The Jersey Eastern Railway (2007)
The Framlingham Branch (2008)
The Wisbech & Upwell Tramway (2009)
The Bishop's Stortford, Dunmow and Braintree Branch (2010)
The Mellis & Eye Railway (2012)
The Aldeburgh Branch (2012)
The Hayling Railway (2013)
The Ely & St Ives Railway (2014)
The Axminster & Lyme Regis Light Railway (2015)
The Saffron Walden Branch (2017)

Title page: If there was no traffic to take to Warboys and it was a fine day arrangements were made quite unofficially for the engine to propel the brake van from Somersham to Warboys, which according to local staff saved shunting time. On one such occasion 'J17' class 0-6-0 No. 65528 fitted with a small 2,640 gallon tender propels her brakevan near Park Hall Road overbridge. In the background, almost hidden by the trees is Somersham up branch fixed distant. *Dr I.C. Allen*

Rear cover: The 1 inch to 1 mile Ordnance Survey map of 1920 showing the Ramsey East branch (reproduced to scale). *Crown Copyright*

Note:
Much of the rolling stock used on the Ramsey East branch was also used on many other ex-Great Eastern Railway branches. For this reason, plans published in the author's earlier titles have not been repeated in this volume.

Oakwood Press, 54-58 Mill Square, Catrine, KA5 6RD,
Tel: 01290 551122   *Website:* www.stenlake.co.uk

Contents

	Introduction	5
Chapter One	The Advent of the Railway	6
Chapter Two	Independent Days	29
Chapter Three	GN & GE Joint line ownership	47
Chapter Four	Grouping to Closure	59
Chapter Five	The Route Described	81
Chapter Six	Permanent Way, Signalling and Staff	98
Chapter Seven	Timetables and Traffic	109
Chapter Eight	Locomotives and Rolling Stock	139
Appendix One	Lengths of Platforms, Sidings, etc.	179
Appendix Two	Bridges	180
Appendix Three	Level Crossings	182
	Acknowledgements	183
	Bibliography	183
	Index	184

'J17' class 0-6-0 No. 65562 waiting to depart from Ramsey East with the RCTS 'Fensman' Railtour on 24th July, 1955. *Author's Collection*

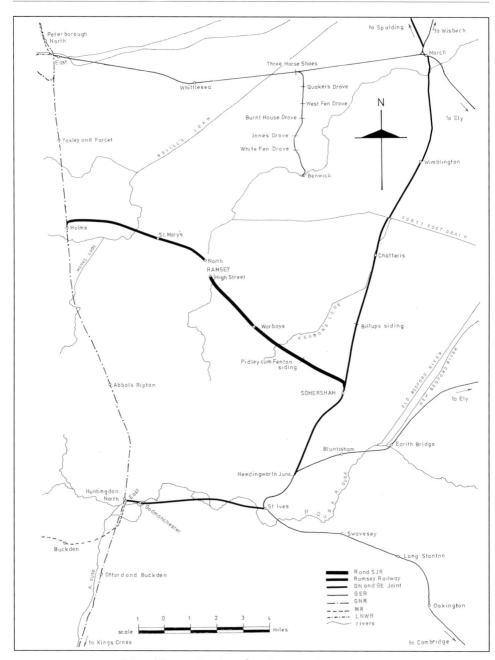

Map of Ramsey East branch and surrounding railways.

Introduction

The Ramsey High Street branch was a relative latecomer to the East Anglian railway scene. Many abortive attempts were made to link the town of Ramsey with the main line network, initially as a through route and then after the opening of the Ramsey Railway in 1863, by continuing the line through to the Great Eastern Railway (GER) system. Traffic potential, however, was questionable and once the GER had acquired control of the Holme to Ramsey line from under the nose of the Great Northern Railway (GNR) by purchasing most of the shares of the smaller company to prevent their rivals using the line to gain access into East Anglia, the main line Directors showed little interest in building a railway east of Ramsey.

The Ramsey & Somersham Junction Railway (R&SJR) was subsequently promoted by local businessmen to provide the necessary link but the failure to obtain financial backing from either the GNR or GER delayed effective progress for almost a decade. It finally required four Acts of Parliament and 14 years from conception to the birth of the seven mile railway (1875-1889), which was worked from the outset by the GER. Failure to connect with the Holme branch at Ramsey however virtually sealed the Ramsey High Street branch to a domiciled fate. After absorption by the Great Northern & Great Eastern Railway Joint Committee in 1897 and before the widespread use of the motor vehicle, the line enjoyed good business and provided an essential service to this rural area of Huntingdonshire.

Unfortunately the branch came too late and did little to encourage the growth of the community, although brickyards helped increase freight revenue from the turn of the century. By the 1920s the halcyon days of passenger services were drawing to a close, for receipts from the sparsely populated area were poor and except for St Ives market day, the train ran with few passengers. At Grouping the London & North Eastern Railway re-titled Ramsey High Street to Ramsey East but little attempt was made to enhance trade, and it was of no surprise therefore that the passenger service was withdrawn during the depressed days of 1930 when the company was seeking economies.

Freight services remained intact until after World War II when roads improved and traffic turned to the internal combustion engine for door-to-door service. Ramsey East closed for goods in 1956 when traffic was concentrated at Ramsey North, leaving the eastern end of the branch reduced to the status of a siding between Somersham and Warboys. Further displacement of traffic rendered this truncated section unremunerative and the branch was closed entirely in 1964.

An attempt has been made at tracing the history of the line. Details have been checked with documents that are available, but apologies are offered for any errors which might have occurred.

Peter Paye,
Bishop's Stortford

Note: The railway spelling of Whittlesea (with an 'a') instead of the geographical spelling of Whittlesey, has been used throughout the text for clarity.

Chapter One

The Advent of the Railway

Ramsey, a typical Fen island town on the western extremity of the rich East Anglian farming area, has for almost three centuries relied almost entirely for its prosperity on crops grown in the peaty alluvial soil. The name is said to be derived from two English words, Ram and Eie or Eye, which compounded means Island of the Ram. The origins of the town of Ramsey stem from the foundation of an Abbey in AD 969 by Ailwyn of Eold. The Benedictine Abbey, built above the flood plain on one of the many fen islands was dedicated to Our Lady, St Benedict and All Holy Virgins, and was initially staffed by a prior and 12 monks. By the 12th century the establishment was one of the largest and richest in the country, and had gathered a small community adjacent to the Abbey. The following century a market town had developed and in 1247, Henry III granted authority for the holding of an annual fair. Soon after the Reformation most of the magnificent abbey buildings were destroyed, whilst in 1665 the town was devastated by the plague when over 400 people died from the infection, thought to have been conveyed from London in cloth tailored for a coat. Disaster struck again in the 18th century when the town suffered two extensive fires, which destroyed the timber and thatch buildings.

Despite these setbacks, by the early 19th century the town was one of the four largest communities in the old administrative county of Huntingdon, with its centrepiece the remains of the Abbey House dating from the 13th century. With the drainage of the fens, engineered by the Dutchman Sir Cornelius Vermuyden, the surrounding land was drained utilizing both wind and steam power, after which smallholdings and farms were established on the newly acquired soil. Unfortunately, Ramsey had relied almost entirely on waterways for connection to the outside world and at one time the thoroughfare, Great Whyte, was a navigable channel through the town centre. The drainage of the soil brought about the re-routing of such waterways and although barges and lighter traffic continued to provide cheap conveyance for goods, it was slow and laborious. Road systems connecting Ramsey with St Ives, Huntingdon and Peterborough were slow to materialize and often during wet and wintry weather the routes were impassable because of deep ruts and flooding.

The town of Ramsey was by the 1840s suffering the effects of the agricultural depression of the previous decades and a correspondent reported the town being in a dreadful state with the poor nearly 'all out of work'. The advent of the railways and the various proposed schemes would at least offer the community far quicker transportation of produce from the area to London and provincial markets, and in return bring commodities required by the townsfolk, at a speed which was impossible by waterway or cart track. Unfortunately, the initial provision of railways in the area left Ramsey isolated.

After many abortive schemes to build a railway linking London and York, success finally came in 1846 when the genesis of the Great Northern Railway was conceived. Surviving many trials and tribulations the Bill received the

Royal Assent on 26th June, 1844 with a capital of £5,600,000 and borrowing powers of £1,868,000. The first contracts for the Peterborough to Maiden Lane section were awarded in November 1848 but progress was relatively slow, despite the use of between five thousand and six thousand men on the scheme. Funds were scarce and major works including nine tunnels, Welwyn viaduct and the three-mile crossing of the treacherous Whittlesey Mere, effectively delayed opening until 7th August, 1850, followed by the extension into King's Cross on 14th October, 1852. The GNR route by-passed Ramsey six miles to the west at Holme, where a station was provided as a railhead for the district.

Meanwhile to the east the Eastern Counties Railway (ECR) had been active in building railways into East Anglia. The Northern & Eastern Railway (N&ER) had linked Stratford with Bishop's Stortford by 16th May, 1842 and the following year sought powers to extend the 10 miles to Newport. In an agreement dated 23rd December, 1843 the N&ER was taken over by the ECR on a 999-years lease with effect from 1st January, 1844. The line was subsequently extended from Bishop's Stortford through Newport and Cambridge to Brandon to join up with the Norfolk Railway line from Norwich on 30th July, 1845. In the same year the ECR was granted powers to build a branch from Chesterton, just north of Cambridge, to St Ives. This line was opened to traffic on 17th August, 1847, the same day as the Ely and Huntingdon Railway opened its section of line from St Ives to Huntingdon (Godmanchester after 1882). In 1844 the company had also promoted a route from Ely to Peterborough via March and this line was opened to goods from 9th December, 1846, and for passenger traffic from 14th January, 1847.

The railway routes in the area were augmented by the Wisbech, St Ives & Cambridge Junction Railway, authorized in 1846 to join the towns mentioned, its main aim being to carry cattle and corn from St Ives market to the port of Wisbech. The line was opened north of March on 3rd May, 1847 and finally connected up with existing railways at St Ives on 1st February, 1848. The ECR, in its takeover bid for East Anglian railways, had absorbed the smaller company before the opening of the southern section and in its first year of operation conveyed grain valued at £33,820 between the Huntingdonshire town and the Cambridgeshire port. Once again to the detriment of the area, the town of Ramsey was by-passed seven miles to the east, where a railhead station was provided at Somersham.

The first of many abortive schemes to place Ramsey on the railway map was made as early as 1845 when plans were submitted for a line connecting Huntingdon with Wisbech, from a junction facing south off the then proposed London and York Railway in the parish of Great Stukeley, and passing by way of Warboys to Chatteris, March and on to Wisbech. To counteract such proposals and in an effort to strengthen its territorial rights in the area, the ECR proposed to construct a branch from the proposed Wisbech, St Ives & Cambridge Junction Railway at Somersham to Ramsey. The necessary plans for the Eastern Counties Extension Railway, running for a distance of 6 miles, 5 furlongs and 9 chains were submitted to the Clerk of the Peace for Huntingdon on 30th November, 1846 and the House of Commons Bill Office on 23rd December. Having nullified each other's claims to the territory around Ramsey, both parties abandoned their proposals after encountering vehement opposition from local landowners. The original scheme was allowed to lapse, whilst the latter was rejected in the 1847 session of Parliament.

Some 13 years elapsed before further efforts were made to place Ramsey on the railway map, when proposals were published on 9th November, 1859 for the Somersham, Ramsey & Holme Railway, commencing 10 chains north of the Eastern Counties, Somersham station and passing through the parishes of Pidley-cum-Fenton, Warboys, Wistow, Bury, Ramsey, Upwood, Wood Walton and Connington to terminate at a junction with the Great Northern Railway at Holme station. The plans showing the route, following much the same path as the later branch lines, were deposited at the Private Bill Office of the House of Commons on 23rd December, 1859. The cost of the line was estimated at £60,000, with an additional £15,000 for purchase of land and legal expenses. The company was empowered to enter into a working agreement with the ECR or GNR or both. It was confidently forecast that the proposed line would carry thriving passenger traffic, as it served an area with a combined population of 14,000 people, whilst substantial goods traffic was also envisaged with the transit of corn, potatoes, coal, iron, timber, bricks and artificial manures. The promoters forecast the new railway would provide better communication than the existing fen waterways, where routes were circuitous and slow. A petition was lodged against the Bill by the Middle Level Drainage Commissioners, pending confirmation of sureties for the protection of the navigation, but this was withdrawn on 27th March, 1860.

At the beginning of April the Somersham and Holme Railway Bill was placed in the list of unopposed schemes. Despite this, difficulties were experienced raising capital. The proposed contractors, Simpson and Walker of Park Farm, Ely had offered to take capital of £25,000, some of it in shares, whilst other parties had promised to subscribe a total of £20,000. The undertaking could take advantage of borrowing powers of £26,600 but this at best left a deficit of £3,400. Approaches were made to both the ECR and GNR for financial support but both declined to assist in any way and the promoters were faced with the inevitable, of abandoning the scheme. Undeterred by the failure of successive schemes to link Ramsey with the main line, local businessmen again attempted to engender support for their own railway. Such backing was evidently available, for on 7th November, 1860 plans were published for a railway commencing at a junction with the GNR, five chains north of Holme station and terminating in a field belonging to Thomas Darlow, 50 yards south-west of Ramsey gasworks. The plans were duly submitted to the Clerk of the Peace for Huntingdonshire on 30th November, 1860 and with the Parliamentary Bill Office on 23rd December.

The Ramsey Railway Act (24 and 25 Vict. cap. cxciv) incorporated on 22nd July, 1861 authorized the company to build a line from the GNR at Holme to Ramsey. Two years were allowed for the compulsory purchase of land and three years for the completion of works. To finance construction, the statute sanctioned the company to raise £30,000 by £10 shares with additional borrowing powers of £10,000. The Board of Directors was Arthur Ballantyne, Chairman, Thomas Darlow and John Poulter. (The full story of this line is given in the forthcoming companion volume *The Ramsey North Branch.*) Encouraged by progress, and after a public meeting at Ramsey, the Directors decided on a possible extension of the railway from Ramsey via Warboys and the Hursts to St Ives. Sir Charles Fox, the company Engineer was duly asked to arrange the necessary surveys with a view to presenting a Bill to Parliament for the 1862-63 session. During the late summer and autumn Fox made preliminary surveys for the extension and reported no untoward opposition to the scheme. By March 1862 he had completed the fieldwork and returned to concentrate on the construction of the authorized line to Holme.

The ECR having by this time leased or taken over the working of most major railways in East Anglia, was determined to serve Ramsey with its own line and independent of any GNR influence. Before positive action was taken the ECR together with the Eastern Union, Newmarket and Norfolk railways amalgamated to form the Great Eastern Railway. The Act sanctioning amalgamation, the Great Eastern Railway Act 1862 (25 and 26 Vict. cap. ccxxiii), received the Royal Assent on 7th August but took effect retrospectively from July 1862.

The new company continued the work initiated by the ECR and plans were duly drawn up for a railway from Chatteris, leaving the St Ives to March line at or near the 83 mile post and passing through the parishes of Chatteris, Doddington, Warboys, Wistow, Bury and Ramsey to terminate at an end-on junction with the authorized line of the Ramsey Railway in or near a field in the occupancy of Thomas Darlow, at a point 50 yards from the gasworks at Ramsey. The GER (Chatteris and Ramsey) proposals dated 10th November, 1862, were duly deposited with the Clerks of the Peace at Cambridge, Wisbech and Huntingdon on 29th November, and submitted to the Private Bill Office on 23rd December, 1862.

The rival scheme, mooted at an open meeting held at Ramsey in July 1861, was the Ramsey & St Ives Railway. This proposed line also commenced from a junction with the authorized Ramsey Railway in field No. 54 on the deposited plans and terminated at a junction with the GER St Ives to March line at or near the coal depot occupied by Thomas Coote Ltd, north of St Ives station. The railway was to pass through the parishes of Ramsey, Bury, Wistow, Warboys, Old Hurst, Wood Hurst and St Ives. The plans dated 18th November, 1862, were also submitted to the Parliamentary Private Bill Office on 23rd December, the same day as the GER scheme.

The GER authorities took great exception to this rival scheme, whilst the Ramsey Railway Directors in turn objected to the Chatteris connection. Within a month, however, the Bishopsgate Directors were showing an interest in the St Ives route, as it would save unnecessary expenditure if that scheme were adopted and the Chatteris scheme abandoned. Negotiations commenced with the Ramsey Railway Board, but as the local company had entered into a working agreement with the GNR, the authorities at King's Cross were highly suspicious of the GER approach. Unable to find adequate financial backing from the GNR, the Ramsey & St Ives promoters sought help from the GER. After lengthy discussion it was agreed the Chatteris scheme would be abandoned and on 5th March, 1863 the GER Secretary advised the St Ives promoters that the company would advance a sum not exceeding £30,000 if the

Act passed. Edward Fellowes, Chairman of the Ramsey Railway and of the Ramsey & St Ives scheme, then approached the GNR for similar financial assistance but assured of traffic from Ramsey the King's Cross Directors turned down the application on 30th April, 1863. The Ramsey & St Ives scheme was subsequently withdrawn at the Parliamentary Committee stage whilst the Chatteris scheme was rejected in the same session. As a result of the rapid advancement of the Holme to Ramsey line, the Ramsey Railway Board again decided to try and extend their line eastwards, despite the failed St Ives scheme. Sir Charles Fox was again called upon to survey a route, this time from Ramsey to Somersham. The eminent engineer must have been puzzled, especially as all other proposals had failed but between his commitments to the Ramsey Railway and other schemes he duly conducted the survey. Meanwhile construction of the authorized Ramsey Railway continued steadily and the branch was opened to traffic on 22nd July, 1863. Under the agreement between the two companies, the GNR initially worked the line for a period of seven years.

Within months of the abandonment of the Ramsey to St Ives scheme, plans were again resurrected by a third party for powers to build a railway 9 miles, 4 furlongs and 3½ chains in length over almost the same course from St Ives to Ramsey. Commencing from a junction off the March line, 650 yards north of St Ives station and passing through the parishes of St Ives, Wood Hurst, Old Hurst, Warboys, Wistow and Bury, the proposed line was to terminate by a junction with the Ramsey Railway near Ramsey station. The plans dated 10th November, 1863 were deposited with the Clerk of the Peace at his office in Huntingdon on 28th November, 1863 and with the Private Bill Office at the House of Commons on 24th December, in readiness for the 1864 session but nothing came of the proposals.

In the meantime Sir Charles Fox had completed his survey of the line to Somersham. By now the GER authorities were highly suspicious of any attempt to build a railway east of Ramsey into their territory, which might allow the GNR access into East Anglia. It was thus imperative that a blocking action be effected and in early March 1864, the company announced preliminary plans to build an alternative line from Somersham to Ramsey. Good fortune was on their side, for with the publication of the plans to build a line from Somersham to Ramsey, the Ramsey Railway Directors became alarmed at the effect such a railway would have on their existing line. Approaches were made to the GNR directors for monetary assistance to block the scheme and initially on 24th March, £600 was granted to assist with Parliamentary Committee costs but was then withdrawn. When the unwillingness of the GNR became known, the GER authorities approached Edward Fellowes, the Ramsey Railway Chairman and suggested a compromise. The Ramsey Railway was obviously unable to finance any extension to Somersham, whilst the GER wished to safeguard their territory. A satisfactory solution was a takeover of the minor company. The absorption of the Ramsey Railway by the GER, however, required an Act of Parliament to which the GNR would obviously object. After protracted negotiations the GER achieved the next best thing by offering to purchase, for the sum of £40,000, all the shares of the Ramsey Railway Co. and to transfer them to a GER nominated holding. The main line company, however, was itself in financial difficulties and had to borrow the £40,000 from the Union Bank. Thus unbeknown to the GNR authorities, all except 122 shares of the Ramsey Railway were purchased in April 1864, and the acquisition by the GER was all but absolute.

In 1864 the Lancashire & Yorkshire and Great Eastern Junction Railway envisaged a line connecting Bluntisham, on the Ely to St Ives Railway, with Ramsey and Peterborough via Somersham, Pidley, Warboys, Ramsey and Yaxley but nothing came of the ambitious scheme. Having all but taken over the Ramsey Railway, the GER Board decided once again to apply for full control and on 8th November, 1864 published proposals for the takeover of the line. At the same time the company announced its proposed railway linking Somersham with Ramsey, thereby protecting its territory from any infiltration by the GNR. Surveyed by Charles R. Chaffins with Robert Sinclair as Engineer, the line followed almost the same route as the final branch. Commencing north of Somersham station, 25 chains or thereabouts west of the then 77 mile post, the line terminated by a junction with the Ramsey Railway, 12 chains or thereabouts north of School Ground Drove, where the same was crossed on the west by the said railway. The GER plans for the 7 miles, 7 furlongs and 8 chains line leaving the St Ives to March line on a 2 furlongs 25 chains radius curve, were duly deposited with the Clerk of the Peace for Huntingdonshire on 29th November, 1864 and the Private Bill Office on Christmas Eve. Following objections by the GNR the plans for outright purchase of the Ramsey Railway were thwarted in March 1865, at the Committee stage in the Commons, but in recompense authority was granted for the advancement of the Ramsey to Somersham scheme.

The Great Eastern Railway (Ramsey Branch) Act 1865 (28 Vict. cap. lxii) was passed on 2nd June, 1865 authorizing the company to construct a railway commencing at a junction with the St Ives and March railway in the parish of Somersham, and terminating at an end-on junction with the Ramsey Railway in the parish of Ramsey in the county of Huntingdon. The GER was empowered to provide level crossings over public road No. 19, drove road No. 31 in the parish of Pidley-cum-Fenton, drove road No. 7 in the Warboys parish and drove roads Nos. 8 and 14 in the parish of Wistow and drove road No. 5 and public road No. 17 in the parish of Bury. In addition, at road No. 17 in the parish of Pidley-cum-Fenton and Nos. 8 and 14 in the parish of Wistow, the company was to construct a road under the railway having clear headroom of 10 feet. Three years were allowed for the compulsory purchase of land and five years for the completion of works. Any construction over the Bedford Level required the authority and approval of the Middle Level Commissioners. To finance the construction the GER was authorized to create shares or stock not exceeding £52,000, together with borrowing powers of £17,300 once all the capital was subscribed and half actually paid up. By the Great Eastern Railway (Additional Powers) Act 1866 (29 and 30 Vict. cap. cclv) passed on 23rd July, 1866, the company received Parliamentary authority to make certain alterations to the levels proposed in the original Act.

Despite the authority to build a railway from Somersham, the GER Board was highly suspicious the GNR might still use the line from Holme to extend

ANNO VICESIMO OCTAVO

VICTORIÆ REGINÆ.

****

Cap. lxii.

An Act to authorize the *Great Eastern* Railway Company to make a Railway from their *Saint Ives and March* Railway at *Somersham* to the *Ramsey* Railway at *Ramsey* in the County of *Huntingdon*. [2d *June* 1865.]

WHEREAS by the "*Great Eastern* Railway Act, 1862," the *Great Eastern* Railway Company (herein-after called "the Company") were formed by the Amalgamation of several previously existing Companies, and the Acts relating to those Companies respectively were consolidated and amended : And whereas other Acts have since been passed relating to the Company : And whereas a Railway from the *St. Ives and March* Railway of the Company in the Parish of *Somersham* in the County of *Huntingdon* to the *Ramsey* Railway in the Parish of *Ramsey* in the same County would be of public Advantage, and the Company are willing (if authorized by Parliament) to make such Railway : And whereas the Object aforesaid cannot be effected without the Authority of Parliament : May it therefore please Your Majesty that it may be enacted ; and be it enacted by the Queen's most Excellent Majesty, by and with the Advice and Consent of the Lords Spiritual and Temporal,

25 & 26 Vict. c. ccxxiii.

[*Local.*]   9 *L*   and

beyond Ramsey towards Ely and thus jeopardize their monopoly in East Anglia. However, no progress was made on the new line and because of monetary problems, the GER subsequently allowed the powers of the 1865 Act to lapse. Edward Fellowes, Chairman of the Ramsey Railway, later Lord de Ramsey, vehemently protested when the GER announced the plans of abandonment, as he foresaw his own line losing possible traffic. Fellowes complained to the GER Board in April 1869 that the GNR was neglecting the line to Holme but was told in no uncertain terms that it was the responsibility of the Ramsey Railway Directors to enforce the GNR as user to paint the stations. The GER subsequently included the submission for abandonment in its Bill to Parliament, which received the Royal Assent as the Great Eastern Railway (General Powers) Act 1870 on 20th June, 1870. After referring to the GER involvement in the majority holding of the Ramsey Railway with £30,000 share capital and £10,000 borrowing powers, authority was duly given for the abandonment of the construction of the railway from Somersham to Ramsey authorized in the GER (Ramsey Branch) Act of 1865.

In the meantime Edward Fellowes, as Chairman of the Ramsey Railway, had constantly pressed the GER management for complete takeover of his railway. At a meeting on 31st March, 1870, the Directors noted his concerns and advised that if he and his followers wished to pursue the making of a railway from Ramsey to Somersham then they were required to produce two-thirds of the cost for a cheaply built line before the GER would pay the remainder. On 14th April Fellowes signed an agreement with the GER withdrawing opposition to a Holme, Ramsey and Somersham scheme provided the GER was fully involved and would work the new line. Any future Bill to build the line to the GER was to include the clause that the Ramsey Railway would meet half the costs, the other half being raised by the GER. When the GNR declined to work the Ramsey Railway in July 1870 and wanted an increase above the 60 per cent of gross receipts, the GER was in no position to take up its promise. Delicate negotiations followed to maintain a service on the branch and three months later a truce was agreed when the percentage paid varied between 50 and 70 per cent, depending on the level of traffic receipts. The GNR continued to work the Holme to Ramsey line whilst the GER authorities negotiated for full takeover of the undertaking.

Thus having defended its territory from invasion by the GNR via Ramsey, the GER was left in the peculiar position of having an isolated railway on its hands. The GER and GNR companies initially entered discussions on the future of the line in May 1874. Terms were finally agreed on 15th December, 1874, involving the Ramsey Railway, maintenance of the GER Shepreth branch by the GNR, and the GER granting running powers to the GNR to Victoria Park and North Woolwich. The terms of agreement were subject to Parliamentary approval and as a result the GER General Powers Act 1875 (38 and 39 Vict. cap. cxxxiv), which received the Royal Assent on 19th July, 1875, included the dissolution of the Ramsey Railway and the vesting of the line in the GER. It was immediately leased to the GNR retrospectively from 1st July, 1875, on payment of two per cent per annum on the agreed authorized capital of £43,000. This dividend was to increase at the rate of one quarter per cent annually to a maximum payment

CHAPTER ccxii.

An Act to incorporate a Company for making a Railway from the Holme and Ramsey Railway at Ramsey to the Great Eastern Railway at Somersham ; and for other purposes.

A.D. 1875.

[13th August 1875.]

WHEREAS the making of the railway herein-after described from the Holme and Ramsey Railway at Ramsey to the Great Eastern Railway at Somersham would be of public and local advantage :

And whereas the persons in this Act named, with others, are willing at their own expense to construct the railway, and are desirous of being incorporated into a company for the purpose :

And whereas it is expedient that the Company, and all other companies and persons lawfully using their railway, should be empowered to work into and use the stations of the Holme and Ramsey Railway Company, and to use the railway of that Company, and also to work into and use the Somersham and Saint Ives stations of the Saint Ives and March Railway, and so much of the said railway as lies between the point of junction of the proposed railway at Somersham and Saint Ives and the booking and other offices, buildings, works, and conveniences connected therewith :

And whereas plans and sections showing the lines and levels of the railways authorised by this Act, and also books of reference containing the names of the owners and lessees, or reputed owners and lessees, and of the occupiers of lands required or which may be taken for the purposes or under the powers of this Act, were duly deposited with the clerk of the peace for the county of Huntingdon, and are herein-after respectively referred to as the deposited plans, sections, and books of reference :

And whereas the purposes of this Act cannot be effected without the authority of Parliament :

[*Local.–212.*]   A   1

of 3¾ per cent per annum. The GNR was to bear the cost of any work on the railway, subject to the approval of the GER, and after 21 years the GER would repay the GNR a fair valuation of the works executed.

The GER, fully engaged ratifying the purchase of the Ramsey Railway, showed little enthusiasm for resurrecting proposals to link Ramsey with the St Ives to March line and so it was left to local interested parties to secure powers to build a railway east of the town, and this was submitted for authorization in the same session of Parliament. The Bill was presented on 9th February, 1875, and read for the first time in the Commons on 11th February. The Royal Assent was finally given on 13th August, 1875 to the Ramsey and Somersham Junction Railway Act 1875 (38 and 39 Vict. cap. ccxii). The statute authorized the company to construct a railway 7 miles 3 furlongs or thereabouts in length situated wholly in the county of Huntingdon, commencing in the parish of Ramsey by a junction with the Holme & Ramsey Railway 8 chains or thereabouts west of the booking office at Ramsey station. The line was to terminate in the parish of Somersham by a junction with the St Ives to March line of the Great Eastern Railway, 14 chains or thereabouts north of the booking office at Somersham station. Three years were allowed for the compulsory purchase of land and five years for the completion of works. The Act authorized the raising of £50,000 in £10 shares and borrowing powers of £16,666, once all the capital shares were taken, and £25,000 actually paid up. Level crossings were authorized over drove road No. 27 in the parish of Bury, drove roads Nos. 8 and 14 in the parish of Wistow and public road No. 7 in the parish of Warboys.

As the railway was to pass over the waters of the Middle Level, all construction and maintenance of earthworks, bridges and drainage were to be made to the approval and satisfaction of the Middle Level Commissioners. Every cut, drain or watercourse crossed required the provision of single span bridges allowing enough clearance for navigation if necessary. All works were to be executed to the satisfaction of the engineer appointed by the Middle Level Commissioners. Under powers of the Act, the Ramsey & Somersham Junction Co. had running powers over the Holme & Ramsey line to Holme station and over the GER system between Somersham and St Ives. The route of the proposed line crossed property belonging to Lord de Ramsey, the Duke of Manchester, Sir Henry Pelly, the Revd G. Hill, John Hall, the Master and Fellows of St John's College Cambridge, George Wilson and Mrs Ann Mahan and passed through the parishes of Ramsey, Bury, Wistow, Warboys, Pidley-cum-Fenton and Somersham.

The initial Directors of the company were George Campion, Alfred Fuller and Thomas Smith Mawdesley, whilst the Engineer was George Hopkins of Parliament Street London SW, Solicitors Serjeant and Sons of Ramsey and the Secretary Frederick Serjeant, who had also been the Secretary of the Ramsey Railway. Having obtained the Act, the Directors for almost three years found extreme difficulty raising capital to build the line. The company, unable to find adequate local backing entered into correspondence with both the GER and GNR for financial assistance but met with complete rebuff from both Boards. Finally on 17th January, 1878 George Hopkins again wrote on behalf of the Somersham Railway Board asking for a meeting with the GER Directors. The

Board considered the application on Friday 25th January and requested the company Law Clerk to arrange a meeting to consider the proposals for the railway. Following a GER Directors' visit to St Ives on 18th May, 1878, the Town Clerk reported a rumour that the GER and GNR would not construct the Ramsey to Somersham extension for which Parliamentary powers existed. He was adamant that the extension was essential as trade formerly enjoyed between Ramsey and St Ives now went by water to Peterborough. Henry Oakley, the GNR General Manager, who had received a copy of the correspondence commented that neither the GNR or the GER companies had considered the question but asked Birt, the GER General Manager, of the latest position in the matter as he was of the opinion 'such short lines were very costly to work - a tramway system might answer the purpose'. The GER Board considered the matter on 23rd May but decided no immediate action was necessary.

Later F.R. Serjeant, Secretary of the R&SJR, suggested in a letter to the GER Board that the GNR and GER should jointly own the line and work the traffic once construction was completed. Charles Parkes (Chairman of the GER) was requested to negotiate with the Ramsey Board and subsequently had several meetings in an attempt to negotiate a scheme suitable and acceptable to both parties. Parkes was reminded that the GER Board had offered to subscribe £30,000 towards an earlier undertaking in 1863 and possibly work the line at cost price. Unfortunately, no offer was forthcoming and it was realised that the time allowed for the purchase of land and construction of the line, as specified in the 1875 Act, had almost expired. The lack of finances had meant that no land had been acquired, in fact nothing had been done to develop the railway, and the Secretary was requested to advise the Parliamentary Agents to present an application to Parliament for a Bill seeking an extension of time for purchase of land and completion of works. After an uneventful passage through both houses, the Ramsey and Somersham Junction Railway Act 1878 (41 and 42 Vict. cap. cxliii) was passed on 4th July, 1878, authorizing the company to extend the time allowed for the purchase of land by two years and completion of works to three years from 13th August, 1878.

For many years the GER had attempted to forge a link with railway companies in the North of England but at every turn the GNR objected and in return sought powers to gain access to East Anglia. Frustrated the GER commissioned Sir John Hawkshaw to examine possible routes to the North independent of the GNR. Two of these routes south of Lincoln envisaged using the Somersham to Ramsey corridor. The first commenced from the GER at Long Stanton and ran via Somersham, Warboys and Ramsey thence to Peterborough, Bourne and Sleaford where it would run alongside the planned GNR route to Lincoln. The second proposal again commenced at Long Stanton and ran via Somersham, Warboys, Ramsey, Whittlesea and thence to Thorney, Crowland, Spalding, Donnington and Sleaford to Lincoln. After a further confrontation in 1878, when the GNR obtained powers to build a Spalding to Lincoln extension and the GE Northern Extension plans were rejected, Parliament added a rider to the effect that the GER ought to have access to the North. The possible costly duplication of lines was fortunately avoided when the GNR dropped its demands for running powers to Norwich, Yarmouth and Lowestoft, and proposed a joint line to the North commencing at Huntingdon. The GER authorities agreed to the proposals and on 3rd July, 1879 the Great Northern & Great Eastern Joint Committee was authorized, the Board formed by five Directors from each company. The new joint railway ran on existing lines from Huntingdon to St Ives, with running powers thence over the GER to Needingworth Junction, then from Needingworth Junction to March South Junction, March Whitemoor Junction to Spalding, the authorized Spalding to Lincoln section, completed in August 1882, and then via GNR lines to Gainsborough and on to Black Carr Junction just south of Doncaster.

The R&SJR Directors again wrote to the GER Board in July 1880, reminding them of the earlier offer of financial assistance to purchase land and for the construction of the line, urging that the main line company was morally obliged to uphold the offer. The matter was raised at the GER Board meeting on 18th August, 1880, when the Secretary reported that although the GER owned the Holme to Ramsey railway it had been leased to and worked by the GNR for 21 years at 3¾ per cent. The route followed by the R&SJR had originally been mooted in the 1860s, when monetary assistance was offered, but authority for construction was not obtained until 1865 when the GER had obtained an Act of Parliament. The idea was later abandoned and the Directors of the R&SJR had resurrected the scheme. Parkes had initially offered a financial subscription of £25,000 to £30,000 and a working agreement at cost price. These arrangements had been superseded by the GE Northern Extension Act, which itself had run into difficulties because of the high price of tenders submitted for construction. After considerable discussion the GER Directors were reluctant to offer any assistance as it was thought it would cost the company £50,000, which was considered excessive for such a minor railway. The Board concluded that if the offer of subscription was taken up it should be jointly, half by the GER and half by the GNR, in which case arrangements could be made to offset costs by selling the GNR half shares in the Holme to Ramsey line and making the Ramsey to Somersham railway a jointly-owned line.

The matter was raised at a special committee of the GER Board on 20th August, 1880, when it was confirmed that if the GNR purchased half of the Ramsey Railway, the Joint Committee should consider working the Somersham to Ramsey line. Parkes also later explained to the GN&GE Joint Committee the reasoning of the GER Board and suggested both main line companies considered the position of the proposed line and the former Ramsey Railway. After due investigation, and another meeting on 14th September, Parkes raised the matter at a subsequent meeting of the Joint Committee on 8th November and suggested a junction between the two railways to form a through route between the GNR main line and the GER. The GNR representatives reported back to their Board but were far from enthusiastic and in a terse letter dated 14th December, 1880, A. Fitch, the Secretary, advised that the GNR Directors were not disposed to take any share in the construction of the proposed line.

Once again the R&SJR Directors were doomed to disappointment. After five years of inactivity since the passing of the Act, the feeling in the district was that the railway would never be constructed. With all these trials and tribulations the time allowed to purchase the necessary land for the railway in the 1878 Act was also almost expired. For the second time the Parliamentary Agents placed the necessary documentation in the Private Bill Office for an extension of time Bill. The Bill received the Royal Assent on 8th April, 1881, as the Ramsey and Somersham Junction Railway Act 1881 (44 Vict. cap. xii) authorizing the company to again extend the time limited for the compulsory purchase of land, two years from 13th August, 1881 and for the completion of works, three years from the same date.

During an inspection of the railway between 11th and 13th July, 1881, by the former GER Chairman, Lightly Simpson, General Manager William Birt and four others, a visit was made to Somersham, where it was agreed provision would be made for a crossover to enable an up train to go direct to the goods yard. Other improvements authorized, included the raising in height of both platforms and extension at each end. Langley, the Engineer, was asked to action the improvements and charge expenditure to the Joint Committee. The work was completed by May 1882 and Major F.A. Marindin conducted the official Board of Trade (BoT) inspection on 22nd June. He found the new connections and interlocking were worked from Somersham signal box containing a 29-lever frame, with 24 working and five spare levers. The only requirement was for the provision of an electrical repeater for the down distant signal, whilst ground disc signals were to be substituted for semaphore signals worked by Nos. 10 and 11 levers. All other interlocking was correct and Marindin authorized use of the new connections, subject to early completion of the outstanding work.

With little action and almost total silence from the boardroom at Bishopsgate, the R&SJR Board was desperate for assistance. F.R. Serjeant wrote to the GER Directors on 4th September, 1882, stating that the time had arrived when it was absolutely necessary for steps to be taken to construct the line from Somersham to Ramsey. The local company Board were anxious to know what assistance the main line company would give and, in the absence of correspondence, requested the GER Directors to receive a deputation. The GER Secretary replied on 3rd October that the Board was prepared to accept the deputation and subsequently a meeting was held on 24th October, 1882. Amongst those attending for the Somersham Company were Alfred Fuller, Chairman, Captain Fellowes, Mr Warren, Mayor of St Ives, and Messrs Cooke, Knight and Serjeant. After all topics had been raised the GER General Manager was requested to write to the GNR regarding the line. Birt subsequently met Henry Oakley of the GNR, who was adamant that his company would neither approve of nor assist the R&SJR in any way, as the new line would drain traffic from the GNR at Holme.

On 1st December, 1882 the GNR Directors were advised by their General Manager that following his meeting with Mr Birt, he learned that the GER was morally bound to subscribe half of the capital of the proposed railway, estimated at £35,000. As the full cost of construction was in the region of £70,000, Birt was again asking if the GNR would subscribe the other half. The GNR Directors were, however, totally committed to refusal and instructed the General Manager to advise the GER that they would not assist in any way with the construction of the R&SJR line as they saw no economic prospects for the proposed railway. Early in 1883 the GER Board advised the R&SJR Directors that they could not assist with the financing of the construction of the railway but offered to assist the Somersham company by arranging a working agreement subject to the necessary Parliamentary approval. Two years had almost elapsed since the 1881 Act authorizing the extension of time, but with the continuing inactivity the local company was again forced to reapply to Parliament for yet another extension of time.

The Ramsey and Somersham Junction Railway Act 1883 was passed on 2nd August, 1883 (46 and 47 Vict. cap. cl). Powers for the compulsory purchase of land was extended for two years from 13th August, 1883, and completion of works for three years from the same date. Clause 7 of the statute authorized the company to enter into a working agreement with the GER. The Act also granted powers to stop up the road or lane numbered 37 in the Bury parish.

No advance was made for another 2½ years until it was realized the conveyance of horse and cattle traffic was on the increase at Somersham. With additional traffic also expected from the proposed railway, it was decided to extend the horsebox siding a distance of 82 ft at a cost of £40. The Joint Line Committee gave authority on 18th June, 1885 and work was completed in March of the following year.

The R&SJR Directors were still desperately seeking financial assistance to achieve their goal and in May and June 1885, Thomas Cooke of St Ives wrote to the GER Board on behalf of the promoters asking the main line company to subscribe £10,000 towards the undertaking and, as per the Act of Parliament, make an agreement to work the line when completed, for 50 per cent of the gross receipts. In return the R&SJR Directors were agreeable to two GER Directors being appointed to the Board of the Somersham Company. The letters were passed to the GN&GE Joint Committee for action but after the full history of the project was discussed the offer was declined.

The R&SJR Directors were at last realising that no financial backing would be forthcoming from either the GER, or the GNR or indeed the Joint Committee. However, over the intervening years capital had been steadily accruing and in August 1885 the Board decided to raise the money for their railway independently of any outside body. To this end the three Directors took a vast gamble and purchased the majority of the shares, offering few to outside parties. Thus heartened, F. Serjeant, the Secretary and solicitor, was requested in October 1885, to negotiate the purchase of the required land. By March 1886 most of the property had been obtained and tenders were sought for the construction of the railway.

Because of local family ties, the civil engineering firm of John Mowlem was approached. Their involvement in railway construction included, from 1870, the laying of the vast London Tramway system whilst early in 1886 they secured the contract for building the Bournemouth Junction & Parkstone & Poole Railway for the London & South Western Railway. The R&SJR Directors formally signed the contract with Mowlem in early May 1886, and by the 10th the contractor's men were surveying the ground of the proposed line. The *Hunts Guardian* reporting on Friday 14th May, 1886 was wildly optimistic over the progress of the work.

We are informed the new railway from Ramsey to Somersham is to be commenced immediately. The distance is eight miles and the country is not difficult for construction. It is thought that if all goes well the line will be open by Christmas. It is understood the station at Ramsey is to be built near the cricket ground. [The report concluded] the railway will be a great boon in the town - it will contact with the Great Eastern Railway and bring it into closer contact with Cambridge.

On 8th July, 1886 the R&SJR Board requested permission for Mowlem's to install an additional siding at Somersham so that equipment and materials for the new line could be delivered by rail and then carted to the work site. At a meeting of the Joint Line Committee on 19th August, 1886, a letter from Serjeant & Son of Ramsey gave notice that the R&SJR required to commence the laying of the physical junction near Somersham. No objections were raised and the company was duly granted permission subject to the normal easement payment of £100, but no immediate action was taken. During initial excavations on the course of the new railway near Somersham, a seam of gravel was discovered on land belonging to George Wilson and Hopkins, the Engineer, and Mowlem's site engineer considered the gravel to be suitable for ballasting the railway and subsequently saved the company £1,200.

Progress on the construction was satisfactory and on 23rd July, 1887, the R&SJR Secretary optimistically advised the GER Board that the railway was nearing completion and it was expected the line would open for traffic in the autumn. The communication, which was also sent to the Joint Committee Directors, also asked if the GN&GE would work the line and if so on what terms. They also suggested a takeover. 'If the company wished to purchase the undertaking on fair terms, my Directors would be disposed to entertain the proposals'. The letter concluded by advising that the railway was constructed with 'heavy permanent way, 80 lbs per yard steel rails and with goods sheds, weighbridges and other conveniences suitable for carrying large quantities of goods traffic'.

Neither the GER authorities nor the Joint Committee were impressed by the correspondence but agreed to seek the thoughts of the GNR Directors on taking over the line. At the Joint Committee meeting on 20th October, 1887, Henry Oakley, General Manager of the GNR, advised that he had conferred with William Birt, the General Manager of the GER but before reporting to his Board wanted to know the views of the Committee as to whether the former Ramsey Railway should be included in any arrangements. Unfortunately, at the meeting on 15th December, 1887, the Joint Line Committee again deferred a decision on working the Ramsey to Somersham line, as it was thought the Holme to Ramsey line should be included in any agreement.

Construction work on the railway proceeded without incident until Monday 18th January, 1888 when Charles Mess, a navvy working on earthworks, caught his hand between the side of a tipping wagon and a loading board. His hand was crushed but he was quickly conveyed to Ramsey for treatment. On 19th April, 1888 the Joint Committee agreed to the construction of the physical junction at Somersham, originally requested on 16th August, 1886, provided all expenses were borne by the local company and paid in advance before work commenced. The contractor's men annoyed some of the local residents by blocking the locally-known Potters Lane and two footpaths near Ramsey whilst laying the permanent way. Edward Darlow complained to the Board of Trade on 11th June, 1888 but, as the blockage was only of a temporary nature, he was advised the subject was a matter for the local authority to settle.

Work on the connection between the R&SJR and the GN&GE Joint line at Somersham Junction began in May 1888 and by 16th June the portion on the Joint line property was completed. Two weeks later the junction was made and through running was possible, although ballasting was far from complete. Ballasting and packing was however completed on the entire line by the second week of August, when the Engineer advised that the line was ready for inspection. F.R. Serjeant duly notified the Board of Trade on 21st August, 1888 and again on 10th September.

Major F.A. Marindin conducted the BoT inspection on 12th September, 1888. He noted the new line was single track over a distance of 6 miles 64 chains, although land had been purchased and bridges built for double track. The width of the formation was 17 ft in cuttings and 18 ft on embankments. No embankment was above 8 ft in height, whilst the two cuttings near Warboys were 14 ft and 16 ft in depth. The Major found that the railway was straight for the greater part of its length with the sharpest curve at Somersham Junction of 26 chains radius, whilst the steepest gradient was a mere 1 in 100. Of the three overbridges on the line with brick abutments and brick arches, Marindin found the one with the greatest span was of 28 ft. There were also six small underbridges of which two were returned as culverts. The inspector found all had brick abutments, two with brick arches of 20 ft span, three with wrought iron triangular girders, the greatest having a 14½ ft span whilst the remaining spans were of timber construction. There were also two brick culverts. The works were well constructed and Marindin reported the wrought-iron girders and wooden rail bearers were of sufficient theoretical strength after testing. The south abutment of the culvert at 2 miles 62 chains had settled a little and the inspector required this to be kept under surveillance, whilst all other culverts were satisfactory. The operation of points and signals at stations were controlled from signal boxes, that at Ramsey having a 24-lever frame, with 21 working and three spare levers, and at Warboys a 16-lever frame, with 14 working and two spare levers. At Pidley siding, a small signal box was provided containing a nine-lever frame. Somersham Junction signal box had a 23-lever frame with 19 working and four spare levers.

Marindin then reported on the large number of crossings on the line and the complexity of what was required, and what in fact had been provided. Under the 1875 Act, level crossings were to be provided where the railway crossed the public road No. 7 in the Wistow parish, two drove roads, Nos. 8 and 14, in the same parish and over the drove road No. 27 in the Bury parish. At No. 7 a lodge had been built and gates provided, whilst at No. 27 a bridge had been constructed but at crossings Nos. 8 and 14 no lodges had been built or gates erected to protect the public. Similarly at drove road No. 19, which crossed the railway at Pidley public siding, a lodge and gates had been provided as the road was shown by the R&SJR as public but prior to the inspection was notified as a private road. With regard to the other drove road crossings at 2 miles 44 chains,

5 miles 37 chains and 6 miles 11 chains the inspector commented: 'The whole of these drove roads are much the same in character and the question is whether they should be considered private or public'. Marindin noted that most led from a public road running more or less parallel to the railway, to cross the line to maintain access to fen farmlands. None of the roads was properly metalled, neither were they maintained by public authority and most led to more than one smallholding. One in fact led to no less than 10 small pockets of land. Except where crossing lodges were provided, ordinary field gates guarded the crossings, and this was acceptable to the local road authority. Marindin concluded,

I should think if the usual chains and padlocks were fitted to these gates and keys given to all farmers having the use of the several drove crossings, it would not be necessary to insist on the erection of lodges, provided the R&SJ Company give an undertaking to add them to the list of public roads if any of the roads showed an increase in use.

At Warboys the company had purchased land on which to make at some future date an additional approach to the station. The inspector remarked that if the road was made it might possibly lead to the drove roads at 4 miles 66 chains or 5 miles 44 chains being used by a greater volume of traffic, and if this were the case he insisted on the company providing a crossing keeper's lodge.

At the conclusion of his inspection Marindin advised the Engineer of a considerable number of deficiencies. The line was devoid of mileposts and these were required to be placed. Padlocks were to be provided for all field gates and clocks were to be positioned at Ramsey and Warboys stations and in the signal boxes. At Ramsey No. 11 facing points were deemed to be dangerous and required removal, whilst No. 7 gate lock lever at Pidley siding required connecting up with the crossing gates. At Warboys, the inspector insisted on the slewing of the line at the north end of the station to provide a better lead to the facing points for up trains. At Somersham Junction, Nos. 15 and 22 levers required interlocking, whilst a signal for up road trains was necessary to protect the level crossing at 3 miles 30 chains. Oil lamps and red warning targets or discs were also required for this crossing and also the gates at 2 miles 04 chains. Marindin also required the easing of all levers in frames of all signal boxes as they were stiff to work.

In the absence of an engine turntable at Ramsey, the inspector stipulated all trains were to stop at Warboys, as locomotives would be working bunker or tender first in one direction. The R&SJR Directors had failed to notify the BoT the method of working and Marindin was notified on the day of inspection that no working arrangements had in fact been made with either the GNR or GER. He concluded that because of the lack of any such agreement and the incompleteness of the works the railway could not be opened for traffic. At the end of his report Major Marindin commented:

There is no junction from the new line to the existing line from Holme Junction on the Great Northern Railway also terminating at Ramsey. This small country town has therefore two terminal stations half a mile apart and the public will be put to considerable inconvenience by this state of affairs. It seems to me that such a thing should not be sanctioned, arising as it does simply from the opposition of one railway company to another, but as Parliament has thought fit to do so, I presume the Board of Trade have no powers in the matter.

The syndicate that owned the majority of the shares immediately arranged for Mowlem's to carry out the remedial work and Serjeant advised the BoT on 26th December, 1888 that work was completed. The opening was, however, still some way off for the company was to endure lengthy negotiations with the GNR, GER and the Joint Committee before a working agreement was finally settled.

The impending opening of the new line to Ramsey and a substantial increase in the amount of goods traffic expected to be imported and exported from Ramsey, Warboys and Pidley siding was of concern to the local goods manager. It was expected the additional flow, as well as an increase in traffic at Somersham, would necessitate an additional clerical post to handle the paperwork. The existing goods office attached to the goods shed at Somersham was considered far too cramped and authority was given on 15th October, 1888 for the provision of a new goods office at a cost of £40. The building was completed in July 1889.

At a meeting of the GN&GE Joint Committee on 17th January, 1889 Oakley and Birt were requested to agree terms for the working of the Ramsey & Somersham Junction Railway. After prolonged discussion between the two and their chief officers an arrangement was reached, and the R&SJR Directors were duly notified of the proposals at the end of February, the Joint Committee being advised on 4th March, 1889 and both the GN&GE Directors the following day.

1   The Great Eastern Railway to work the Ramsey and Somersham Junction Railway for a period of five years from 1889 at 70 per cent of the gross receipts.

2   The loss on working expenses, if any, to be borne equally by the Great Northern and Great Eastern Railway companies.

3   The Great Eastern Railway to compete in the interests of the Ramsey and Somersham Company in opposition to the Great Northern Railway in the same mode as the Great Northern and Great Eastern compete against each other at Spalding, Sleaford and Lincoln.

4   The division of traffic on and off the Ramsey and Somersham Junction Railway to be by mileage and ordinary terminals.

5   The Great Eastern to hand over to the Great Northern their mileage earnings of traffic passing between Ramsey and the Great Northern and Great Eastern Joint line, less remaining expenses at 30 per cent.

6   The loss to the Great Northern Company by reason of the Great Eastern Company opening to Ramsey and carrying the Ramsey Company traffic, to be contributed to by the Great Eastern out of any amount the Great Eastern Company may derive from such traffic, after deducting the terminal and working expenses at the rate of 50 per cent. Such loss whatever it may be to be ascertained yearly.

7   The Ramsey and Somersham Company to be charged easement over the Joint line near Somersham at the sum of £100 annually.

George Hopkins, the R&SJR Engineer, acknowledging the offer of the GER to work the line on 2nd March, 1889, asked if Birt would see Scotter of the GNR to conclude matters on their behalf. In the same month tenders for the construction of a new station master's house at Somersham produced six replies and the cheapest of these was accepted from J. Saint & Sons of St Ives quoting a cost of £378.

In the spring of 1889 news regarding the opening of the line was rife, and on Saturday 1st April the *Hunts County Guardian* reported, 'Various rumours respecting the opening of the new line have been around lately - we understand on good authority that arrangements for working the line have been made and we may expect the opening shortly'. The following week the paper incorrectly predicted the railway would open for traffic on 1st May, 1889. On 4th May it reported, 'in about another fortnight we may see carriages laden with passengers steam out of the new station premises', but, as before, the prophesy was false.

On 7th May the Joint Committee discussed the question of the rate quoted in clause 1 of the working agreement. The R&SJR Directors thought 70 per cent was rather high and after discussion the Chairman agreed to lowering the rate to 65 per cent if traffic carried on the line was up to and including £10 per mile per week, and 60 per cent if the earnings were over £10 per mile per week.

The first official train to work across the line ran on Saturday 25th May, when a special formed of an engine and three coaches, conveyed several GER Directors to inspect the railway. On arrival at Somersham at 2.00 pm, a stop was made to allow Serjeant and Fuller to join the train, which then made a leisurely journey to Ramsey stopping at various points to permit an inspection of installations. A detailed tour of the facilities at the terminus was made before the GER Directors returned to Somersham at 3.40 pm. Although not officially announced at the time, it was hoped the visit would finally secure the working agreement for the GER to work the line.

The R&SJR Directors announced that expenditure incurred on building the railway to 30th June, 1889 amounted to:

	£	s.	d.
Purchase of land	13,252	7	4
Construction	45,000	0	0
Parliamentary expenses	6,000	0	0
Interest in advance	1,873	9	4
General expenses	33	7	3
Total	66,159	3	11

Construction of the Ramsey and Somersham line had required the purchase of 86 acres of land and the company was fortunate that in many cases landowners had released the portion of their property at agricultural rates of £40 per acre. Some land purchases, however, required the payment of much larger sums of money but only in one instance was arbitration necessary, when the final accepted exchange rate between landowner and the railway company reached £240 per acre.

Further predictions that the Ramsey and Somersham line would open on 1st July, 1889 proved unfounded, for the date came and went and still the railway remained dormant. A general meeting of shareholders at the offices of the Company Engineer at Westminster on the morning of Monday 29th July, 1889, met to approve and agree the working agreement between the R&SJR and GER. Charles Parkes at the 54th meeting of GER shareholders held the following day told the assembly that the agreement for operating the new line was initially for five years from 1st July, 1889. The terms were for the GER to take 60 per cent of the gross receipts if traffic exceeded £10 per mile per week or 65 per cent if traffic was under £10 per mile per week, the remaining 35 or 40 per cent being passed to the local company. The arrangements received the approval of the GER Board and shareholders and the agreement, dated 29th July, 1889, was signed by Frederick R. Serjeant for the R&SJR and J. Hadfield the Secretary of the GER. Thomas Whittall, Clerk to the Railway & Canal Commission, also countersigned the document on 9th September, 1889. The GN&GE Joint Committee also approved of the agreement regarding the use of Somersham station and running powers to St Ives on 29th July, 1889, the document being signed by Frederick R. Serjeant on behalf of the R&SJR, J. Hadfield for the GER and Andrew Fairbairn, a Director of the GN&GE Joint Committee.

At the beginning of August 1889, the GER authorities advised the BoT that the R&SJR line would be worked by the Train Staff and Train Ticket method of working together with full block signalling, confirmed by certificate on 3rd September, with all trains stopping at all stations until an engine turntable was provided at Ramsey High Street. On 16th August, Courtney Boyle on behalf of the BoT advised the local Directors of the GER statement and then requested the R&SJR officials to negotiate with the main line company on two outstanding issues. Of these the Board of Trade required the R&SJR to signify their willingness to erect lodges for crossing keepers at the various drove crossings if so required by the BoT, whilst all trains were required to stop at Warboys until an engine turntable was provided at Ramsey. When such undertakings were agreed and signed by the Chairman and Secretary of both companies the BoT would sanction the opening of the line. Within four days of receiving the letter both companies duly agreed and signed the additional clauses.

Rumours concerning the railway were again rife at the end of August and the *Hunts County Guardian* announced the railway would open on Monday 2nd September, 1889 but once again the prophecy proved false. During the first two weeks of September the contractor employed 60 men to bring the permanent way up to the required standard. The original ballast excavated locally near Somersham was found to be inadequate and 50 wagons of ballast were brought in by the GER Civil Engineer to rectify the deficiencies in the trackbed.

On Friday 13th September, 1889, the GER sent a train across the branch with equipment and furniture for the stations, signal boxes and goods sheds. Work on the station master's house at Warboys was incomplete and the new appointee had to lodge in the village for a short while before he could take up residence. Such was the short notice given of the intended opening of the new railway that GER staff were only advised on 14th September that the line would definitely open for traffic on Monday 16th September. Prior to the opening staff were transferred to the branch stations, station master Perry being promoted from Earith Bridge on the Ely to St Ives branch to take charge at Ramsey High Street, as the new station was to be titled. The terminus of the branch from Holme retained the title of Ramsey.

Articles of Contract made the Twenty-ninth day of July One thousand eight hundred and eighty-nine **between** THE RAMSEY and SOMERSHAM JUNCTION RAILWAY COMPANY (hereinafter called " The Somersham Company ") of the one part and THE GREAT EASTERN RAILWAY COMPANY (hereinafter called " The Great Eastern Company ") of the other part

WITNESSETH that the Somersham Company and the Great Eastern Company Do hereby mutually Covenant and agree with each other in manner expressed in the several Clauses hereinafter contained that is to say :—

1. THE following words and expressions in these articles shall have the several meanings hereby assigned to them (that is to say) the term "Somersham Railway" shall comprehend the Railway of the Somersham Company in the County of Huntingdon and the Lands Stations Sheds Sidings Turntables Junctions pumps cisterns water supply and all other the works appurtenances and conveniences thereof The term "Engines" shall comprehend all locomotive engines and tenders in good working order and condition and the term "Carrying Stock" shall comprehend all descriptions of Carriages for the Conveyance of Passengers and all luggage and break vans wagons boxes and trucks for the conveyance of animals goods minerals and things whatsoever The term traffic shall comprehend all passengers goods animals minerals and things whatsoever and the conveyance thereof respectively and Local Traffic and Foreign Traffic The term "Local Traffic" means traffic which arises and ends on the Somersham Railway The term "Foreign Traffic" comprehends all other traffic including traffic which arises or ends at the Somersham Station The term "Tolls" shall comprehend all Tolls Rates charges and other payments from time to time during the term payable or due to the Somersham Company for and in respect of traffic whether Local or Foreign

2. THE Great Eastern Company shall as and from the date hereof for the residue of the term of Five years computed from the 1st day of July 1889 at their own expense and on payment to the Somersham Company of such sums as are provided for by these articles and subject to the conditions of these presents manage and work the Somersham Railway and receive the Tolls arising in respect thereof Provided that if the Somersham Company shall at or before the expiration of the second year of the term apply to the Great Eastern Company to revise the terms of working and the Great Eastern Company shall refuse so to do the Somersham Company upon giving six months' notice in writing shall be at liberty to terminate this Agreement at the end of the third year of the said term

3. AT all times during the continuance of the said term the Great Eastern Company shall at their own expense work use manage and regulate the Somersham Railway and the traffic thereof in a proper and safe manner and shall use their utmost reasonable endeavours so to use manage and regulate the trains and tolls as that the traffic of the Somersham Railway shall be developed and increased to the utmost reasonable extent and if at any time it appears to the Somersham Railway Directors that a better system might be adopted by the Great Eastern Company or that the arrangement and conduct of such trains and tolls are not perfectly adapted to develope or increase the traffic or any part thereof or that the traffic or any part thereof suffers from want of a sufficient supply of Engines or carrying stock or from neglect on the part of the Great Eastern Company or their Directors Officers or Servants the Somersham Company may from time to time give notice to the Great Eastern Company of such additions alterations or arrangements as in the opinion of the Somersham Directors would remedy the evil PROVIDED ALWAYS that if at any time or times the Somersham Company give such notice as aforesaid or otherwise complain of the manner in which the traffic is worked or in any respect of the mode in which this Agreement is carried out and the Directors of the two Companies differ thereon the matter in difference and the proper mode of remedying the evil in respect of which such notice or complaint may have been given or made shall be referred to Arbitration.

54131

After almost 30 years of various proposals and 14 years from sanctioning, the railway between Somersham and Ramsey finally opened for traffic on Monday 16th September, 1889. 'U13' class 2-4-0 No. 382 and rolling stock worked down light from Somersham late the previous day to form the first official train from Ramsey High Street departing at 8.10 am. The *Cambridge Chronicle* reported that the opening of the line caused 'considerable interest' with many townsfolk of Ramsey turning out to witness the event but the day proved something of an anti-climax. The *Huntingdon Post* reported 'there was mutual agreement amongst those present that the railway was a boon to the district' but there was 'no flag bedecked station or rousing cheers and only one solitary handkerchief was waved' as the train departed with a complement of 84 passengers. A number of people stood at the lineside to wave the train on its way to Warboys, where the reception was in complete contrast to that at Ramsey. Both platforms at the intermediate station were crowded with spectators and intending passengers, whilst many of the older inhabitants of the village, some of whom had never seen a train, were brought to the station in carts and waggons by benevolent farmers of the district and seated on chairs on the platforms for a 'grandstand' view. No less than 127 people joined the train at Warboys bringing the total number of passengers on the initial run to 211.

Station master Evans duly supervised the departure and the train continued past Pidley-cum-Fenton siding to the cheers of farm workers. More onlookers waved greetings as the train rounded the curve into Somersham station where the platforms were thronged with people. As it halted to more enthusiastic cheers, station master Whiteman greeted the passengers and crew. Amongst those who travelled on the inaugural train were the Chairman of the R&SJR, Alfred Fuller, with his family and other leading dignitaries. J. Wimbolt, district engineer, J. Platt, Cambridge district locomotive superintendent, Mr Roper, district goods manager and Mr Norton, district superintendent, represented the GER.

On the opening day Somersham station handled 45 trains from the Joint Line and the Ramsey High Street branch, and dealt with over 1,000 passengers; 540 tickets being issued at Somersham, Warboys and Ramsey High Street for travel on the branch trains. Individual ticket totals issued at Ramsey High Street for departures on the first day were 8.10 am - 84, 10.00 am - 60, 11.05 am - 5, 12.04 pm - 12, 1.51 pm - 19, 3.09 pm - 24, 4.23 pm - 20 and 6.54 pm - 22, many of the passengers booking through to St Ives for the market. The following day 246 tickets were issued from Ramsey High Street and 130 from Warboys. The articles of contract between the R&SJR and the GER was published on 29th July, 1889 confirming the document signed by Fred J. Sergeant for the Somersham company and J. Hadfield for the GER and countersigned by Thomas Whittall clerk to the Railway & Canal Commission on 9th September, 1889.

At the time of opening of the R&SJR to traffic, the Board was formed of Alfred Fuller, Chairman and fellow Directors George Burt JP of Purbeck House, Swanage and J.J. Freeman of 2 Poet's Corner. Westminster, London SW. Freeman was in fact the major shareholder and held £43,000 of the £50,000 share holding. No shares were ever offered or issued to the public and the trio forming a syndicate held all the shares. Frederick R. Serjeant remained in office as Secretary.

Gradient profile

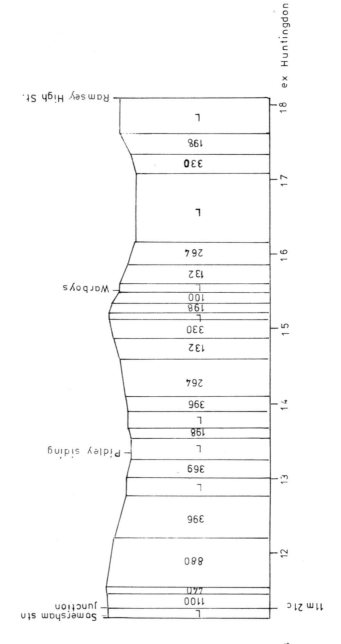

Chapter Two

Independent Days

On 17th September, 1889 the GER General Manager reported to his Traffic Committee that the Somersham to Ramsey High Street line had opened the previous day, worked by the GER as agreed with the R&SJR and sanctioned by the Board on 5th March. The opening of the new railway resulted in additional lamp trimming and the lamp room at Somersham was found to be totally inadequate for the extra responsibilities. The Joint Committee quickly agreed to the provision of a new lamp room on 17th October, 1889 costing £37, work being completed the following summer.

In October 1889 a new connection with the down loop line of the Ramsey branch was completed at Somersham Junction and during inspection on 4th November, Major General C.S. Hutchinson examined the full signalling arrangements at the station. He found that the new connection with the down loop line of the Ramsey High Street branch was worked by properly interlocked levers in the existing Somersham Junction signal box, containing a 23-lever frame with 21 working and two spare levers. As a result of the inspection Hutchinson required certain alterations. Nos. 5 and 6 levers were to be painted in some other distinct colour than red, as they could be mistaken for signal controlling levers. The number 13 was to be added to the lettering on lever No. 16, and subject to these requirements receiving attention the inspector was of the opinion the new works could be used. Whilst at Somersham, Hutchinson was asked by railway officials to look at some of the alterations planned in Somersham Station signal box to obviate delays at the adjacent public road level crossing. He advised a number of changes: No. 8 lever being freed from No. 28 home signal provided it interlocked with No. 29 distant signal; No. 8 lever was also to be freed from Nos. 12, 13 and 18 levers provided it was interlocked with Nos. 14 and 19 disc signals, and with a lever yet to be brought into use for working a disc signal at the down end of No. 12 crossover road. Hutchinson was also of the opinion that the wicket gates of the level crossing at the up end of the platform should be controlled from the signal box. He concluded, 'it would contribute to safety if a footbridge for the use of the public using the highway, as well as for connection between the platforms, were provided at this level crossing and the wicket gates abolished'.

The GER General Manager reported to the Traffic Committee on 19th November that during October, the first complete month of working, the earnings from the R&SJR were £5 5s. 6d. per mile of railway per week, or the equivalent to 11d. per train mile. The following month receipts showed a fall to £4 19s. 3d. and 10d. respectively. Compared with the average for GER secondary and branch lines of 1s. 6d. per train per mile, the figures were not encouraging. Subsequent figures showed no improvement during December at 10d. per train per mile, whilst traffic receipts from the opening to 31st December 1889 were:

A view taken at Ramsey High Street soon after the opening day for passenger traffic. 'Little Sharpie' 2-4-0 No. 47 stands with the three-coach branch train in front of the engine shed, which has yet to be begrimed with smoke and soot. The engine crew are standing proudly on the running plate of No. 47, whilst a selection of station staff pose in the foreground, including station master Francis Perry on the right. The tender of the 2-4-0 is fitted with a backplate to protect the footplate crew when running tender first across the branch, a requirement necessitated by the absence of a turntable at both Somersham and Ramsey High Street. The water tank for locomotive supplies is unusually mounted on the roof of the engine shed. Note also the goat, possibly the station mascot!

Author's Collection

	£	s.	d.
Passenger	167	19	6
Parcels	14	2	7
Goods	317	12	10
Coal	13	15	3
Cattle	1	8	10
Total	*514*	*19*	*0*

Additional land purchases costing £256 12s. 2d., together with interest of £329 8s. 10d. and general expenses of £35 6s. 8d. brought the total expended on the railway for the year ending 31st December, 1889 to £66,980 11s. 7d. Shares issued totalling £50,000 and a mortgage of £10,000, left the R&SJR syndicate with a deficit of £6,980 11s. 7d. and the company attempted to clear this by issuing £6,666 of four per cent debentures.

Traffic receipts during the early months of 1890 showed no improvements, and were paltry when compared with the earnings from the Essex lines, opened from Shenfield to Wickford in 1888 and Wickford to Southminster and to Southend in 1889, both of which ran through areas of greater population, shown in brackets.

January	10d.	per train per mile	(1s. 11d.)
February	11d.	per train per mile	(2s. 0d.)
March	10d.	per train per mile	(2s. 0d.)
April	10d.	per train per mile	(2s. 8d.)
May	10d.	per train per mile	(3s. 1d.)
June	8d.	per train per mile	(3s. 0d.)
The average being	10d.	per train per mile	(2s. 5d.)

Receipts for the half-year ending 30th June, 1890 showed an upward trend especially on goods and cattle.

	£	s.	d.
Passenger	215	0	0
Parcels	23	8	4
Goods	511	11	9
Coal	27	17	8
Cattle	14	9	7
Total	*792*	*7*	*4*

Of the £1,307 16s. 6d. received since the opening of the line to traffic, working expenses as per the agreement were deducted at 65 per cent.

	£	s.	d.
Working expenses to GER (65 per cent)	850	1	8
Government duty		11	2
Rent for use of Somersham station	39	13	2
Tithes, rates and taxes	7	3	2
Auditor's fees	5	5	0

leaving a balance to net revenue of £405 2s. 4d.

With the opening of the branch the increasing number of passengers using Somersham station were forced to cross the railway by foot crossing at the south

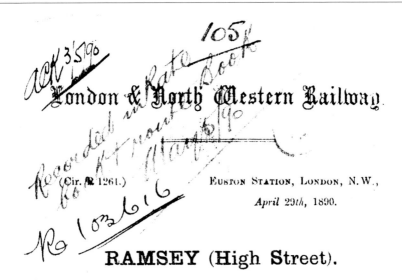

London & North Western Railway.

(Cir. R 1261.)　　　　　EUSTON STATION, LONDON, N.W.,

April 29th, 1890.

RAMSEY (High Street).

The Great Eastern Company have opened a Goods Station at Ramsey, and the Rates now in force with Ramsey (G. N.) will apply.

The route will be the same as for St. Ives.

To arrive at the distance

Miles.　Chains.

add　1　　0　to St. Ives' distance, if route is *via* Peterboro';

„　12　44　„　if route is *via* Cambridge or *via* Camden and Stratford.

F. HARRISON,
Chief Goods Manager.

PLEASE ACKNOWLEDGE
TO RUGBY

Warboys station, soon after the opening of the branch with a 'Little Sharpie' 2-4-0 standing at the down platform with a Somersham to Ramsey High Street train. To the left is the station master's house whilst in the background is Warboys Road overbridge No. 2310 and in the distance Longlands overbridge No. 2309. Warboys signal box to the right; the points in the left foreground lead to the goods yard. *Author's Collection*

Adams '61' class 0-4-4T No. 64 built by Neilson & Co. in 1875 shunting a van and two open wagons from the up loop towards the goods yard at Warboys, soon after the opening of the line. Note the cleanliness of the brickwork on all buildings including the goods shed except where the top of the opening has been blackened by smoke from the engines. The high fence backing on the platform is unusual whilst ornate oil lamps provide illumination during the hours of darkness. The ballast covers the sleepers except where permanent way staff knocked in the keys by the chairs. *Huntingdon Record Office*

RAMSEY & SOMERSHAM JUNCTION RAILWAY.

Offices:—HIGH STREET, RAMSEY, HUNTS.

Directors.

ALFRED FULLER, Esq., Ramsey, *Chairman.*
GEORGE BURT, Esq., J.P.
J. J. FREEMAN, Esq.

Engineer.

GEORGE HOPKINS, Esq., C.E., 30, Parliament Street, London.

Solicitors.

SERJEANT & SON, Ramsey, Hunts.

Secretary.

F. R. SERJEANT, Esq., Ramsey.

REPORT of the DIRECTORS,

To be submitted to the Shareholders at the Ordinary General Meeting to be held at 30, Parliament Street, Westminster, on Friday, the 29th August, 1890.

---

1. The Directors submit herewith their Report and Statement of Accounts for the Half-year ending 30th June, 1890.

2. Since the last Report the Directors have issued the remainder of the Debenture Stock (£6,666) at 4 per cent. per annum.

3. The gross receipts, as per accounts furnished by the Great Eastern Railway Company, from 16th September to 31st December, 1889, were £515 9s., and for the half-year ending 30th June, 1890, £792 7s. 6d., together £1,307 16s. 6d.; deducting from this sum the agreed working and other expenses, leaves a net revenue of £405 2s. 4d. at 30th June, 1890.

By order of the Board,

F. R. SERJEANT,
Secretary.

HIGH STREET, RAMSEY,
20th August, 1890.

Ramsey & Somersham Railway Directors Report, 29th August, 1890.

end of the station. To obviate possible accidents and to placate the public wishing to cross the line, tenders were invited on 5th August, 1890 for the provision of a footbridge to connect the platforms and also provide a public right of way. The contract was duly awarded to J. Westwood who tendered a price of £344 3s. 6d., providing the work was completed by 1st November, 1890. The footbridge later became No. 2302 at 11 miles 06 chains from Huntingdon.

Earnings from the new line after an uncertain start gradually increased, although the GER average for branch and secondary lines of 1s. 6d. per train mile was never achieved. Monthly averages for the second half of 1890 after falling initially, showed a marked improvement as a result of increased goods and coal traffic; comparable earnings from Essex lines in brackets.

July	9d.	per train per mile	(3s. 5d.)
August	10d.	per train per mile	(4s. 4d.)
September	1s. 0d.	per train per mile	
October	1s. 3d.	per train per mile	(2s. 3d.)
November	1s. 1d.	per train per mile	(1s. 11d.)
December	1s. 2d.	per train per mile	

By 31st December, 1890 the total expended on the railway was £82,342 14s. 5d., whilst receipts for the half-year were:

	£	s.	d.
Passenger	291	19	9
Parcels	32	7	2
Goods	630	3	9
Coal	40	8	10
Cattle	6	2	7
Total	*1,001*	*2*	*1*

from which the GER received £650 14s. 4d. with an additional £25 for the use of the facilities at Somersham. Surplus land near Somersham and Pidley was sold to adjacent landowners for £250. After a promising start, the 1891 earnings per train per mile declined rapidly much to the concern of the GER authorities. Earnings during the first half of the year compared with the new Essex lines were:

January	1s.	4d.	(1s.	9d.)
February	1s.	2d.	(1s.	11d.)
March	1s.	3d.	(2s.	2d.)
April		11d.	(2s.	1d.)
May		9d.	(2s.	3d.)
June		8d.	(3s.	1d.)
July		9d.	(3s.	9d.)

The dangers of trespassing on railway property was all too evident when on 31st March, 1891 a local man named Andrews, using the branch line as a walking route, was killed by a passenger train near Warboys, his body being found on the track by a platelayers the following morning.

The receipts for the year fluctuated considerably before falling away in the second half of 1891:

Half year ending	30th June, 1891			31st December, 1891		
	£	s.	d.	£	s.	d.
Passenger	245	2	1	311	5	1
Parcels	44	19	7	47	0	2
Goods	681	19	0	446	17	3
Coal	28	18	10	40	15	9
Cattle	19	16	5	10	14	6
Total	1,020	15	11	856	12	9

From these returns the GER received a total of £1,220 6s. 3d. working expenses together with £50 for the use of Somersham station. By 31st December, 1891, £82,456 0s. 11d. had been expended on the railway. To save costs the half-yearly meeting of shareholders was held from February 1892 in the office of the railway's Engineer at 2 Poet's Corner, Westminster, London SW and the office rented by the company at High Street, Ramsey was closed, and the lease surrendered.

Receipts for the two six-monthly periods of 1892 showed a slight increase over the previous year:

Half year ending	30th June, 1892			31st December, 1892		
	£	s.	d.	£	s.	d.
Passenger	267	9	5	374	2	1
Parcels	50	19	6	50	11	9
Goods	702	1	2	447	5	7
Coal	31	7	1	9	10	11
Cattle	19	1	10	39	6	8
Total	1,070	19	0	920	17	0

The decline in goods receipts over the year was partially offset by a welcome increase in passenger revenue.

On and from 1st January, 1893, second class accommodation was withdrawn from the branch train services. Alfred Fuller, Chairman of the R&SJR, owned considerable property in the area around Warboys and during the spring of 1893 was developing a portion of land near the railway, west of the station on the south side of the line, as an extension of a brickfield originally established in 1886. He subsequently approached the GER to provide rail access to the brickworks. The GER Traffic Committee was advised by the Engineer on 1st August, 1893 that the cost of installing a siding and making the connection with the main line would be £450 on land belonging the Fuller, and £340 on R&SJR land. Fuller was willing to pay the costs on his land but the R&SJR had no funds available for its portion of the works. The Traffic Committee decided that by clause 9 of the working agreement, provision was made for the GER, with the consent of the R&SJR Directors, to finance additional works. The consent of the Ramsey Directors was duly obtained and authority to install the siding at a cost of £340 on railway land was approved, subject to the GER receiving in return interest payable at a rate of four per cent per annum, with the R&SJR being under obligation to recoup the original sum after the termination of the working agreement due to expire on 1st July, 1894. The siding was installed early in 1894.

In the meantime the GER Board had learned of the results of working the two Ramsey branches, under which they received 65 per cent of the earnings from the Somersham route and in turn compensated the GNR for traffic abstracted from the Holme to Ramsey line, whilst the GNR compensated the GER for any loss incurred in working the line. From the opening of the Somersham line on 16th September, 1889 to 1st June, 1892 the General Manager estimated the GER owed the GNR £1,536 for abstraction of traffic whilst the GNR owed the GER £3,785 as a share of the loss on the R&SJR line.

In early December 1893, the 7.17 am Somersham to Ramsey goods train was involved in an accident at Pidley-cum-Fenton siding. On a dark and wet morning the relief porter in charge of the siding opened the level crossing gates as usual but completely overlooked the fact that after the first up road goods train that morning had called at the siding to pick up wagons, he had left the points in the main single line set for the siding. The engine driver, equally at fault, failed to notice the down home signal at danger and was aghast to find his locomotive lurching over the points and into the siding. Despite making an emergency brake application the engine collided with two wagons standing by the buffer stops, demolishing one vehicle and badly damaging the other. The locomotive was also damaged and was unable to move under its own power. The branch service was suspended until later in the day when the line was cleared by the Cambridge breakdown crane and staff, and a relief engine obtained.

Traffic receipts for 1893 showed a slight upturn on the previous year and goods revenue during the second half was particularly encouraging.

Six months ending	30th June, 1893			31st December, 1893		
	£	s.	d.	£	s.	d.
Passenger	266	17	7	288	5	1
Parcels	62	18	11	38	11	8
Goods	672	19	6	800	6	4
Coal	30	16	6	35	7	10
Cattle	17	11	1	10	11	5
Total	1,051	3	7	1,173	2	4

From these totals the GER received £1,451 18s. 7d.

The continuing operating losses incurred working the Somersham to Ramsey High Street branch were a constant source of concern to both the GER as operators and their GNR counterparts at King's Cross. Birt reported on 2nd February, 1894 that by the agreement of July 1889, the GER had undertaken for a period to work the line at 65 per cent on earnings up to £10 per mile per week and 60 per cent at anything over and above that figure. The actual receipts had never in fact reached £10 per mile per week, and were actually only about £6 per mile per week. At about the same time the GER had entered into an agreement with the GNR whereby they would share any resultant operational losses. The losses incurred working the line from the opening to traffic on 16th September, 1889 to 30th June, 1893 amounted to £9,658, and the company had claimed half that amount from the GNR as per the agreement. The agreement was due to expire the following July and Birt explained that he had been in communication with Sir Henry Oakley, who had replied that the GNR were not interested in renewing the agreement, thus leaving the GER with the full liability. This was totally unacceptable and the two parties took steps to reach formal agreement as to the future of the fenland branch.

After a preliminary meeting held at King's Cross on 2nd August, 1894, officers were asked to fully investigate the operation of the Ramsey High Street line with a view to effecting economies. At a reconvened meeting on 24th September, the GER was represented by H.G. Drury, assistant superintendent, together with Messrs Poulter and Glaze, whilst Messrs W.J .Grindling and Alexander attended for the GNR. Drury explained to the group that a small amount could be saved by dispensing with the post of lad porter at Ramsey High Street and the post had in fact been withdrawn. After discussion it was agreed that the signal box at Pidley-cum-Fenton could be closed, the signalman manning the box was paid 18s. 0d. per week, less 2s. 0d. per week for the rent of the crossing house. Approval was given for the signalman's position to be withdrawn and replaced by a porter-in-charge for the goods siding, who would be responsible for attending to the level crossing gates in addition to his normal duties. For this additional task the man appointed would occupy the crossing cottage rent free. Drury advised that the alterations when implemented would effect an annual saving of £77. The agreed establishment at stations after alterations was

Ramsey High Street	Station master, 1 lad clerk, 1 signalman, 1 porter.
Warboys	Station master, 1 lad clerk, 1 signalman, 1 porter.
Heath Grove	1 gate keeper.
Pidley-cum-Fenton	1 porter-in-charge.

The GNR representatives had earlier mooted that considerable savings might be effected if the line was worked by one engine instead of two and Drury submitted a proposed timetable showing how this could be achieved:

Present service for 1894
Down	*Up*
7 passenger	7 passenger
1 passenger Mondays-only	1 passenger Mondays-only
2 goods	2 goods

Proposed service
4 passenger	5 passenger
2 mixed	2 goods
1 goods	1 goods Mondays-only when necessary
1 goods Mondays-only when necessary	

After further discussion the meeting recommended that if joint working of the branch was to commence, the locomotive superintendents of the GNR and the GER should consult and agree the annual fixed charge for the hire of the locomotive working the railway, on the basis of the proposed timetable as well as agreeing payment for any additional mileage. Finally the question of the locomotive water supply was discussed. Drury told the assembly that the water at Ramsey High Street was inadequate for engine purposes and unless alternative supplies were obtained at the terminal or a new supply provided at Somersham, it would be necessary for the branch engine to run light to St Ives and back for replenishment, if water was short at Ramsey. The R&SJR had been charged a total of £45 in 1892 and £100 in 1893 for light engine running between Somersham and St Ives. The meeting instructed both locomotive superintendents to investigate and give their recommendations as quickly as possible.

On 3rd October, 1894, the GER Directors heard from General Manager Birt that it was proposed to jointly purchase the Ramsey and Somersham line. The proposal also involved the Holme to Ramsey line. Up to 30th June, 1894 the net amount of traffic abstracted from the Holme and Ramsey line was £2,648, and the GER was asking the GNR for their share of the loss incurred working the Ramsey to Somersham line. He reminded the Directors that the GER had purchased the Holme to Ramsey line for £43,000 and then leased it to the GNR. The lease was due to expire on 1st July, 1896, and the amount earned was £1,612 10s. 0d. in total. A proposal had originally been made to connect the two railways but the general opinion was it would 'now cost more than any savings, which could reasonably be expected from coupling up the lines'. The net earnings from the Ramsey and Somersham line was £780 per annum, equal to £1 3s. 0d. per mile per annum, while the authorized subscription totalled £66,666 (£50,000 share capital and £16,666 loan liability). The value of new traffic passing on the GER line on or off the Ramsey to Somersham branch was £4,773, and the cost of working the line £5,306 leaving a loss of £533.

At the meeting of the GN&GE Joint Committee on 18th October, 1894, Sir Henry Oakley reported that the agreement whereby the GER worked the R&SJR had expired at the end of June 1894 but by arrangement between the General Managers of both companies it had been agreed the GER would continue to work the line until the end of the year. Despite all efforts to improve traffic, gross receipts had never exceeded £2,000 per annum and it was not practicable to reduce the annual working expenses below £2,700, leaving an annual working deficit of £700. After considerable debate the committee decided to open negotiations to purchase the railway on reasonable terms and requested both the GN and GE General Managers to commence negotiations. As the GER worked the line, William Birt agreed to actually negotiate with the R&SJR Directors.

In the meantime revenue had showed a welcome increase in the first half of 1894 but then declined in the autumn:

Six months ending	30th June, 1894			31st December, 1894		
	£	s.	d.	£	s.	d.
Passenger	276	0	3	292	7	4
Parcels	47	11	3	46	0	7
Goods	859	18	5	705	18	4
Coal	44	17	0	40	17	5
Cattle	15	2	0	6	7	4
Total	*1,243*	*8*	*11*	*1,091*	*11*	*0*

Although the passenger traffic had showed a slight upturn, this was more than offset by the disappointing loss of goods and cattle traffic. The GER working expenses from these returns totalled £1,522 18s. 2d.

Birt reported to his Directors on 6th February, 1895 regarding the proposed reduction of train services on the Somersham to Ramsey line using one engine only. The existing services were worked by one locomotive full time and one part time. The driver and fireman would be on duty from 8.10 am to 8.00 pm, exclusive of the half-hour they required on duty for preparation and disposal of the locomotive, before and after the run. By eliminating the use of the partially-employed engine and making one or two reductions in staff it was possible to make net annuals savings of £500. The earnings from the line were approximately £2,500 and the expenditure £3,000.

On 22nd February, 1895 Mr Grindling, representing Sir Henry Oakley, belatedly wrote to Patrick Stirling the GNR locomotive engineer at Doncaster enclosing a copy of the minutes of the meeting held on 24th September, 1894 and asked him to contact James Holden, his counterpart at Stratford, to agree the fixed charges for the hire of engines on the Ramsey High Street branch. Oakley advised that the GER had in the past charged the R&SJR at a rate of 7*d*. per train mile for passenger traffic and 10*d*. for goods traffic, with an additional 5*d*. per mile in respect of light engine running between Somerham and St Ives when water was required. The annual cost on this basis totalled £1,400. Grindling also advised Stirling of the proposed timetable compiled by the GER for introduction on 1st March, 1895 and concluded:

> In fixing the price, bear in mind that for the last train of the day the engine will come from Somersham to St Ives and back to take the GE corn traffic to London, and as the GE will pay the mileage over the GN and GE Joint line, that payment will have to be taken into consideration when fixing the rate for the Somersham line. It appears a fair charge for the branch engine would be £1,000 per annum.

H.G. Drury wrote to Grindling on 26th February that because of the worsening situation at Ramsey, it was now necessary for the branch engine to run light twice daily to St Ives for water and Stirling was duly advised of this fact the following day.

Without further consultation the revised timetable was introduced from 1st March, 1895, with one engine working the branch services. James Holden wrote from Stratford on 13th March that the GER was willing to provide locomotive power to the Ramsey High Street branch on the basis of the new timetable at £1,050 per annum, with an additional charge for light engine running at 7½*d*. per mile. A breakdown of the estimated costs of working the Ramsey and Somersham Junction Railway for 12 months as shown in the new timetable was:

Train	Between	Trains per day	Miles	Days	Miles	Rate per mile	Total £	s.	d.
Passenger & mixed	Ramsey & Somersham	10	7	311	21,770	7*d*.	634	19	2
Goods	Ramsey & Somersham	4	7	311	8,708	10*d*.	362	16	8
Empty engine	Somersham & St Ives	2	11	311	3,421	7½*d*.	71	5	5
Grand total							1,069	1	3

The GNR authorities, however, disagreed and requested a reduction in charges. Holden again wrote to Stirling on 27th March agreeing to revise charges to £1,000 and 7½d. per mile for light running, provided the 5.40 pm passenger train from Somersham to St Ives and return was booked as a Joint Line train.

Patrick Stirling passed the information to Oakley at King's Cross the following day and on 1st April the General Manager wrote to the GER stating that the details were not favourable when compared with the charges for 1893. In that year the train mileage totalled 43,503, which equated to 7.8d. per mile. The new timetable showed only about 28,000 miles or a reduction of a third, to which Holden's suggestion fixed the payment at 8.5d. per mile. In addition the GER was to get free mileage Somersham to St Ives equal to £100 per annum, normally charged for their train mileage over the Joint line. Oakley was adamant, no additional mileage was to be requested or paid, unless a second locomotive or additional staff were required to operate the line, which defeated the object of the exercise. Stirling was again requested to seek more favourable terms from Holden.

Eleven days later agreement over payments for locomotive power was finally reached and a memorandum dated 27th April, 1895, confirming the decision of 11th April signed by James Holden for the GER and Patrick Stirling for the GNR, advised that the Somersham and Ramsey High Street timetable for March 1895 provided a service, between the hours of 8.10 am and 7.02 pm, of six trains on weekdays from Ramsey to Somersham and return, and one train from Somersham to Warboys and return. To provide this service it was agreed the GER would be paid at the rate of £1,000 per annum for locomotive power, with 7½d. per mile for any mileage incurred running additional services. These rates would cover any light engine running for water or any other purposes and all payments were to date from 1st March, 1895. The agreement was subject to three calendar months notice of termination by either party from the first day of any month.

Whilst Stirling and Holden were wrangling over the motive power charges, William Birt continued negotiations with the R&SJR Directors for the takeover of their line by the Joint Committee. On 15th April, 1895 he reported that after consulting with Sir Charles Cotter, representing the Ramsey & Somersham Company, the line could be purchased for £35,000 free of any liability. He considered this a bargain, as the authorized share capital of the company was £50,000 with additional loan liability of £16,666. The half-yearly accounts showed the capital account to be overdrawn by £15,800 making the capital expended on the whole scheme as £82,466. The Joint Committee, well aware that the local Directors were keen to have their financial millstone removed, asked Birt to make a counter offer of £30,000 for the complete undertaking, including excess lands and to be free of mortgage or debenture debts, annual rent charges and any other liabilities. The GER General Manager informed the R&SJR Directors of the offer in May and subsequently reported back to the Joint Committee on 18th July, 1895, that the revised offer had been accepted, subject to the additional sum of £340 being made available for the construction of a siding at Warboys. So keen were the R&SJR Directors to dispose of their railway that they urged the Joint Line Committee to obtain powers for the purchase in the next session of Parliament. This was acceptable to the GN&GE Committee, although the R&SJR were to be held responsible for paying their proportion of costs.

The Great Eastern Railway,
Locomotive Carriage & Waggon Department.
Stratford, E.

TELEGRAPHIC ADDRESS
"EASTDEN, LONDON".

11th April 1895

Working of Ramsey & Somersham Branch

Memorandum of agreement between Mr James Holden of the Great Eastern Railway, of the one part, and Mr Patrick Stirling of the Great Northern Railway of the other part, on the day of April 1895.

The Somersham and Ramsey time-table for March 1895 provides for a train service, between the hours of 8:10 a.m. and 7:2 p.m, of six trains on week days from Ramsey to Somersham and return, and one train on week days from Somersham to Warboys and return. It is hereby agreed that the Great Eastern Railway Company shall be paid, from 1st March 1895, at the rate of £1000 per annum for providing Locomotive power for working this train service.

It is further agreed that any train mileage run in addition to the above train service shall be paid for at the rate of 7½ per train mile. This agreement to be terminable by three calendar months notice on either side from the 1st day of any month.

signed   for James Holden   Locomotive Engineer of Great Eastern Railway
                John Shearsmith Moore

Memorandum of agreement between James Holden, Locomotive Engineer of the GER and Patrick Stirling, Locomotive Engineer of the GNR regarding the working of the Ramsey and Somersham Junction Railway.

Whilst all attention had been centred on the economic working of the branch and possible purchase of the undertaking, Major G.W. Addison had visited Warboys on 8th March, 1895 to inspect the new sidings and connections authorized in 1893. He found the new goods siding had a trailing connection into the up loop line whilst the safety points had been placed 35 ft nearer to the main line than shown on the working plan. Two new disc signals were provided to signal train movements into and out of the siding, and these together with the points were worked from the existing signal box containing a 17-lever frame with all levers in use. Addison found all interlocking correct except that No. 2 lever should have locked No. 7 lever, and subject to early rectification he officially sanctioned use of the new works.

The placing of the proposed purchase in a GN&GE Bill to Parliament was impracticable and it was reported on 15th October, 1895 that arrangements had been made for the necessary powers of purchase to be made in the next GNR Bill. The Joint Line solicitor duly advised that the debts of the R&SJR including debentures totalled £33,000 and a proportion of the purchase price would be used to pay off the debenture in full, leaving a balance to other creditors of 16s. in the pound, whilst ordinary shares would have no return.

Oakley reported to his GNR Directors on 20th October, 1895 the terms of the proposed purchase of the R&SJR by the Joint Committee. The GER would work the train service as a matter of convenience, receiving in return 30 per cent of the receipts with the remaining 70 per cent divided into moieties, whilst other expenses were to be borne in equal proportions. Part of the arrangement would involve the GNR renewing the lease of the Holme to Ramsey line from the GER for a further 21 years from 1st January, 1896. These terms were agreed on 14th December, 1895 and signed by J. Darby Secretary, and J.J. Freeman and John Mowlem Burt, Directors of the R&SJR, and Reginald Capel, Director for the GN&GE Joint Committee.

The early months of 1895 were disappointing, for the R&SJR receipts reduced even further by poor passenger returns. These results were completely offset by the second half receipts, which were the highest since the railway opened to traffic, resulting from an upsurge in goods traffic conveyed.

Six months ending	30th June, 1895			31st December, 1895		
	£	s.	d.	£	s.	d.
Passenger	231	3	9	266	15	0
Parcels	43	7	1	39	0	4
Goods	727	10	9	1,095	3	1
Coal	39	5	8	46	5	9
Cattle	8	18	10	4	1	11
Total	1,050	6	1	1,451	6	1

From these receipts the GER deducted a total of £1,630 8s. 6d. for working expenses.

Early in 1896 John Darby, the R&SJR Secretary, moved to 23 Abingdon Street, London SW1 and future company meetings were held at that address. At a special general meeting the GER Directors resolved unanimously for the Bill to grant a further lease of the Ramsey Railway to the GNR and to vest the R&SJR

CHAPTER cxxxviii.

An Act to confer further powers upon the Great Northern A.D. 1896.
Railway Company to empower the Great Eastern Rail- ——
way Company to grant a further lease of their Ramsey
Railway to that Company to vest in the Great Northern
and Great Eastern Joint Committee the undertaking of
the Ramsey and Somersham Junction Railway Company
and for other purposes. [20th July 1896.]

WHEREAS it is expedient that the Great Northern Railway
Company (in this Act called "the Company") should be
authorised—

To make and maintain the railways and works herein-after
described;

To abolish certain level crossings of their railway and otherwise
to deal with certain roads and footpaths connected with their
undertaking; and

To purchase and acquire additional lands and easements for the
purposes of their undertaking:

And whereas by the Great Northern Railway Act 1892 (herein- 55 Vict.
after referred to as "the Act of 1892") the Company were c. cxxi.
authorised to construct amongst other railways certain railways in
that Act called "Extensions of Leen Valley Railway" and it is
expedient that the Company be authorised to abandon certain
portions of such railways:

And whereas by the Great Northern Railway Act 1891 the 54 Vict.
Company were authorised to construct amongst other railways a c. xix.
railway (in that Act referred to as "Railway No. 11") at Keighley
in the west riding of the county of York and it is expedient that
the time limited for the completion of the said railway should be
extended:

And whereas it is expedient that the powers of the Company 56 & 57 Vict.
for the compulsory purchase of lands in the parish of Saint Mary c. xcviii.

[*Price 2s. 3d.*] A 1

in the GN&GE Joint Committee. The GNR presented its Bill to Parliament and after a smooth and unopposed passage through both Houses, the statute received the Royal Assent on 20th July, 1896, as the Great Northern Railway Act 1896 (59 and 60 Vict. cap. cxxxviii) empowering the GN&GE Joint Line Committee to purchase the Ramsey & Somersham Junction Railway for £30,340. The purchase was to be under the terms agreed between the R&SJR, the GNR, the GER and GN&GE Joint Committee on 14th December, 1895, with completion by 1st January, 1897. The Act stipulated the purchase money was to be used to clear debts, outstanding mortgage and arrears of interest, which totalled £33,171.

The final traffic receipts issued by the local company was for the six months ending 30th June, 1896, after which the GER furnished the totals until the line was absorbed into the GN&GE Joint undertaking from 1st January, 1897.

	£	s.	d.
Passenger	207	18	8
Parcels	60	2	5
Goods	932	6	2
Coal	38	9	8
Cattle	3	0	7
Total	*1,241*	*17*	*6*

An inspection before completion of the purchase of the railway, found that a road in the parish of Pidley-cum-Fenton, which the R&SJR had included in its construction plans, had not been made. The cost estimated by the GER Engineer was £566 and subsequently this sum was deposited in the bank in the joint names of the GNR Solicitor and Mr Freeman the GER Solicitor. However, the road in question, which led off a drove road, was found to be in a better condition than the main road. The accommodation work was considered unnecessary and therefore there was no necessity to carry out the improvements. The estimate of the purchaser's engineer had been 2s. 6d. per yard which was considered excessive. It was thought 1s. 0d. per yard would suffice and thus reduce expenditure from £200 to £100.

The legalities involving the purchase of the R&SJR took some months to complete. The GN&GE Joint Committee were advised on 9th October, 1896 that agreement for purchase was being finalized for completion by the appointed date. On the first day of the New Year the R&SJR ceased to exist and became a branch line owned by the Joint Committee. The £30,340 purchase money was exchanged and on 6th January, 1897 the GNR General Manager reported the completion of the takeover to his Directors. At the time of absorption the Chairman of the R&SJR was George Campion, whilst his fellow Directors were Alfred Fuller and Thomas Smith Mawdesley.

Somersham station, view facing towards the junction in the 1890s. Beyond the down platform is the original goods shed and at the north end of the up platform, Somersham Station signal box which was abolished in 1931. *Author's Collection*

Railway staff and passengers at Ramsey High Street in GN&GE days. Driver Charles Steel and guard James Jeffreys are second and third from the left. Charles Lambert, a future engine cleaner at Ramsey High Street shed is the infant on his mother's knee. Note the ornate arched windows in the station building. *C. Lambert*

Chapter Three

GN&GE Joint line ownership

New ownership brought little change to the Ramsey High Street branch, which continued to operate purely as a feeder into the March-St Ives-Cambridge line at Somersham. Nevertheless gradual improvements were made after the GN&GE Joint Committee had carried out a detailed evaluation in the early months of 1897. Increasing traffic and the problems of shunting and storage of wagons at Warboys necessitated the installation of one additional siding in the goods yard. This was authorized on 8th April, 1897, at a cost of £350 and installed later in the summer of the same year. In the same month alterations were made to the staffing at both Ramsey High Street and Warboys stations where assistant adult clerks were appointed in place of the previously-employed lad clerks.

The Joint Committee received little praise for these minor improvements and local farmers and growers complained that the goods yard access roads were full of ruts, which required repairing before the winter months. Evidently the remedial work was completed before the onset of adverse weather, for no subsequent complaints were recorded. After the general improvements, few changes were made in the ensuing months. However, an increase in the branch train service necessitated the appointment of an additional guard on the establishment. Passenger receipts were still at a mediocre level and, in order to save staff costs, it was decided in January 1898, that the appointee at Ramsey would be a porter/guard, and when not working trains the man could be gainfully employed on station duties. Similarly at Warboys when the signalman's post became vacant a porter/signalman was appointed in his place. Half of the wages cost was borne by the GER and the other half by the GN&GE Joint Committee.

The increase in goods traffic registered at Ramsey in 1898 brought with it additional documentation, and as the booking clerks at the station were also responsible for goods and parcels work it became necessary to appoint an additional post. To save costs the Joint Line Committee recommended the employment of a lad clerk to exclusively handle the goods invoicing and accounts.

In the same year to the north-east of Ramsey the GER opened a goods branch from Three Horse Shoes, on the March to Peterborough line, through to the village of Benwick. After years of petitioning by local landowners and farmers the company had received Parliamentary approval on 30th May, 1895 and the line, with sidings at roughly half- mile intervals, was opened in two stages from Three Horse Shoes to Burnt House Drove on 1st September, 1897 and thence to Benwick on 2nd August, 1898. The branch generated new traffic from the district it served but had little impact on the Ramsey High Street to Somersham line, where traffic continued to increase.

The Regulation of Railways Act 1889 amongst other things required the interlocking of points and signals on all lines, and although the signalling and points at Somersham Junction, Warboys and Ramsey High Street conformed to the statute, only the points and signals were interlocked at Pidley siding. Thus the crossing gates were not interlocked with the protecting signals and the latter could

A rather poor photograph of Pidley-cum-Fenton siding in the early 1900s with a Ramsey High Street to St Ives goods train hauled by a 'Y14' class 0-6-0 halted by the small signal box. Pidley-cum-Fenton siding was located between Somersham and Warboys at 2 miles 20 chains from the junction and was essentially provided for the use of local farmers and growers for the loading of vegetable and fruit traffic and later for sugar beet. Inwards traffic included coal and coke and fertilizer. A small amount of livestock was also handled. The signal box on the down side of the line was provided with a 9-, later 10-lever McKenzie & Holland Tappett frame with 4 in. centres with all levers working. Just before Grouping it was replaced by a ground frame, the hut being later resurrected as a waiting shelter at Mill Road Halt on the Elsenham & Thaxted Light Railway. In addition to the driver and fireman standing on and by the locomotive, the guard is to the right of the engine buffer beam, with the goods foreman by the signal box door, the shunter by the hut and a lad in the yard by the wagons on the siding.

Huntingdonshire Record Office

Instructions for shunting Pidley-cum-Fenton siding from the GER Appendix to Working Timetable 1910.

Pidley-cum-Fenton Siding, about midway between Somersham Junction and Warboys Station.

The Goods Trains appointed to call at this Siding are so noted in the Monthly Working Time Tables.

This is a Block Telegraph Signal Station, and the Trains stopping at the Siding are to be protected by the Fixed Signals under the Block Telegraph Regulations. The Signalman on duty will be responsible for seeing that the Trucks standing in the Siding are kept inside the Catch Points.

The Warboys Station Master must satisfy himself that these Instructions are duly carried out.

be pulled off whilst the gates were open for the road and across the railway. This was totally unacceptable for the safety of the line and authority was given on 20th October, 1898 for the remedial interlocking work to be carried out at a cost of £39.

At the end of September 1898 application was received from Alfred James Bateman, the owner of a brickfield located near the railway between Somersham and Pidley siding, for a connection and siding to his works. The Engineer estimated the cost at £455 on Joint Committee property and £380 on the brick company land. Bateman subsequently agreed to the costs, and authority was given on 30th October for the work to proceed without delay, provided the traffic superintendent could agree the best method of working the traffic to and from the siding. Arrangements were finalized with Bateman in January 1899 but after work had commenced it was found necessary to purchase an additional strip of land, 30 ft wide, parallel to the railway to accommodate the shunt siding at an additional cost of £155. The estimate was then revised to £610 on railway land and £255 on the brick company's property, and authority for the revised expenditure of £865 was approved on 20th April, 1899. The guarantee of 10 per cent by the brick company on works on railway property was adjusted accordingly.

The locomotive water supply at Ramsey shed continued to cause problems and necessitated the branch locomotive in costly light running from Somersham to St Ives and back for replenishment. It was subsequently agreed on 19th January, 1899 to provide a water supply at the junction station, where work including the sinking of a well and provision of storage tank and pump was estimated at £660. Work at the station was completed in July, with Ransome & Rapier supplying the cast-iron tank at a cost of £117.

The expected upturn in passenger receipts at Warboys never materialized and the decision of April 1897 was reversed in January 1899, when to save costs a lad clerk was re-appointed at Warboys in place of the adult clerk who was transferred away. After complaints by the Warboys station master of cramped accommodation in the station house, authority was given by the Joint Committee on 20th April, 1899 for alterations and improvements to be made at an estimated cost of £20, the work being completed early the following year. Parcels and goods traffic handled at Warboys continued to fluctuate and there was a considerable upsurge of traffic by the winter of 1899/1900, especially with the daily arrivals and departures for the brick sidings. The duties involved in loading vans and shunting wagons were considered too much for the lad porter on the establishment and authority was subsequently given on 1st May, 1900 for the lad porter's post to be abolished and replaced by an adult porter.

Installation of the new siding serving Bateman's brickworks between Somersham and Pidley siding was completed by April 1900. Although brought into use almost immediately, the BoT inspector Lieutenant P.G. Von Donop did not examine the new works until 6th June, 1900. He found the points and signals associated with the connection, which was trailing for up trains, were worked from a five-lever ground frame, locked and released by the key on the Train Staff for the Somersham to Warboys section. Von Donop found the interlocking was correct and officially sanctioned use of the siding.

Goods facilities installed by the R&SJ were satisfactory for the first few years of operation but on takeover the GN&GE Joint Committee found that the increase

BATEMAN'S SIDING, with Points facing Down Line.
Between Somersham Junction and Pidley Siding, on the Ramsey Branch, situate about
1¼ miles from Somersham Junction.
    The Points are controlled by "Annetts" Patent Lock, the key of which is attached to the Somersham
and Warboys Single Line Train Staff.
                    WORKING OF BATEMAN'S BRICK SIDING.
    When there are two guards in charge of a train working this siding, the head guard must work the
ground locking frame, and will be responsible for seeing that the trucks are placed inside the catch points, and
that the points are replaced and locked in their proper positions before handing the train staff back to the
driver. The key of the locking frame hut to beobtained from the Somersham Station Master before proceeding
to Ramsey.
    The Somersham Station Master is responsible for seeing that these instructions are strictly carried out.
    The traffic will be worked on up-trains only, as shewn in the Joint Working Time Book.

GN&GE Joint line instructions regarding the working of Bateman's siding.

in traffic was steadily outgrowing the infrastructure. After several complaints by local traders and farmers regarding delays to traffic caused by the inadequacies of the loading dock at Warboys, authority was given on 18th October, 1900 for the dock to be extended. Work carried out by the GER was completed the following spring. Following the improvements made to the station house at Warboys, the station master at Somersham complained of the complete lack of washing facilities for himself and his family. After investigation the authorities agreed and authorized the spending of £40 on an additional washhouse on 18th October, 1900. The work was completed six months later, although the estimate was well exceeded, for the total expenditure was £190.

Perishable and valuable parcels traffic handled at Somersham was steadily increasing and by 1900 was a source of embarrassment for the railway company, as there was a total lack of suitable lock-up facilities at the station. To obviate further problems, authority was given on 19th July for a small wooden structure to be erected as a tranship lock-up shed at a cost of £17. The shed was completed on 17th January, 1901.

By 1902 traffic handled in the goods yard at Warboys was still increasing and the GN&GE Committee were somewhat concerned by the possible loss of revenue because of the absence of a cart weighbridge. On 16th October, 1902 the Committee authorized the provision of a weighbridge at an estimated cost of £180. Earlier in the year the GER locomotive engineer requested the renewal of bridges on the system to allow for an axle weight of 20 tons instead of the existing 17 tons or less. The costs of upgrading were considerable and in order to reduce expenditure a number of branches including the Somersham to Ramsey High Street branch were excluded as it was considered unlikely that any of the heaviest GER locomotive classes would ever be required to operate the services.

After 13 years of constant use the approach road to Pidley-cum-Fenton siding was in a decidedly poor state, especially in wet weather. The Sweeting Estate, which offered much traffic to the railway, constantly complained about the condition of the road and in 1902 matters came to a head. The Joint Committee finally authorized, on 16th October, 1902, the extension of the approach road and repair and widening to 25 ft, for the accommodation of Sweeting's Trustees traffic, at a cost of £570. Provision had originally been made in the agreement entered into with the R&SJR, but the obligation to maintain the roadway had been nullified when the Joint Committee purchased the local company in 1897. In order to meet the costs of the upkeep of the approach road and other roads, the Somersham company prior to takeover had deposited £566 in Parr's Bank and authority was sought to use this money to offset maintenance. After deliberation, the accountant informed the Joint Committee that it was agreeable to wind up the affairs of the R&SJR by withdrawing the entire £566, together with £65 8s. 4d. interest earned to 30th January, 1902, to finance the repair and making up of the road. The Board readily agreed to this course of action at their meeting on 15th January, 1903, and the work was subsequently completed the following June.

In the same year improvements were made to upgrade the main line through Somersham including a bridge renewal programme. A contract to provide the ironwork for bridge No. 2301 at 11 miles 04 chains from Huntingdon was awarded to Hill Smith on 15th December, 1903 at a cost of £57 10s. 0d.

The increasing lengths of goods trains handled on the branch proved an operating inconvenience in the years after the turn of the century. Lack of space was particularly prevalent at Ramsey High Street, where considerable shunting had to take place before the locomotive could be released from its train. To obviate such problems, authority was given on 18th July, 1907 to extend the loop line to enable the locomotive to run-round the longer formations. Estimated to cost £350, the work was completed the following March, when the loop was extended from 410 feet to 594 feet in length. The new works were officially inspected by Lieutenant Colonel P.G. Von Donop on 8th March, 1908 when he found the single running line on the up side of the station had been slightly realigned, while the connection from it leading to the up siding had been moved further from the platform. The position of some signals had been altered accordingly but no alterations had been made to the interlocking in the signal box. The inspector found the arrangements satisfactory and sanctioned use of the new works.

Torrential rain and gale force winds brought havoc and flooding to many parts of East Anglia on 26th August, 1912. A number of routes on the GER were closed as embankments were washed away or water flooded the permanent way. Services on the Ramsey High Street branch were suspended for over 24 hours after swollen rivers overflowed, filling the dykes and flooding the railway between Warboys and the terminus. Services resumed on 27th August.

The outbreak of World War I on 4th August, 1914 found the GER, GNR and the GN&GE Joint Committee with other British railway companies under Government control. The services continued to run to pre-war timetables as passengers travelled on business or pleasure. Soon after the commencement of hostilities farmers were urged to increase the production of vegetables and fruit, to offset the deficit of imported foodstuffs caused by enemy action against shipping. The growers of Huntingdonshire, like their counterparts all over the country, rallied to the call. As a result a considerable number of additional wagon loads and, on occasions, freight trains ran across the branch to clear the traffic. As the war years progressed hay traffic increased as fodder and bedding for horses was required by the many military establishments in London and East Anglia. The Ramsey High Street branch was not as strategically placed as many other East Anglian lines and few military exercises were conducted in the

Somersham station, junction for the Ramsey High Street branch from the south *c.*1908. In the foreground is Chatteris Road level crossing and at the far end of the up side platform, the original Station signal box, abolished in 1931. *Author's Collection*

Somersham station 75 miles 73 chains from Liverpool Street via Clapton, and 11 miles 07 chains from Huntingdon East on the GN&GE Joint line, facing south viewed from Somersham Station signal box in 1911. To the left is the 260 ft-long up platform and on the right the down platform of similar length. The main station building on the down side included ladies' waiting room, general waiting room, station master's office, booking hall and office, gentlemen's toilet and coal store. The up side building constructed of brick, housed the ladies' and general waiting rooms. Ornate canopies fronted both buildings and platform lighting was by gas lamps. Footbridge No. 2302 at 11 miles 06 chains spanned the line at the south end and connects the platforms. Beyond the station is Chatteris Road level crossing with gates open for rail services whilst in the distance is Colne Road level crossing with gates across the railway. *GERS/Windwood 1504*

General view of Somersham station and goods yard facing south in 1911. To the left is the up siding serving the cattle dock and loading dock, then the up and down GN&GE Joint main line from Huntingdon to March. The extensive goods yard is served by the shed road beside the down main line and back or coal road serving the coal grounds. In the distance on the up side of the railway is Somersham Station signal box and beyond that the station.   *GERS/Windwood 1509*

Looking north from Somersham Station signal box in 1911 with the up siding to the right serving cattle pens beside the up home signal. To the left is the extensive timber goods shed with a section of the goods yard in the distance. Beyond the wagons stabled on the middle road is Somersham Junction splitting home signal with the left-hand lower arm cleared for a Ramsey High Street branch train. To the immediate right a horse box stands on the up spur.

GERS/Windwood 1505

Road access to the down side goods yard at Somersham in 1911 with the timber goods shed fronted by a brick-built goods office. Three GER open wagons devoid of cargo stand on the shed road whilst in the background is Somersham Station signal box. To the right are the wooden station buildings on the down platform and standing guardian is Somersham Station down starting signal at the north end of the down platform.   *GERS/Windwood 1513*

Somersham station and goods yard view facing south in 1911 showing to the extreme left the road access to the up side loading and cattle docks. A wagon occupies the up main line by Somersham Station signal box and beyond that can be seen the up and down platforms where Ramsey High Street branch trains departed and arrived. The extensive timber goods shed, with capacity for 1,500 quarters of grain, stands astride shed road siding whilst to the right are the coal grounds. A variety of GER open wagons occupy the busy goods yard.   *GERS/Windwood 1511*

area. Military personnel were, however, carried by the branch trains. In 1914, soon after the commencement of hostilities, the GER set up a War Relief Fund with collections being made at the branch stations. The first call resulted in collections of 14s. 1d. at Ramsey High Street, 15s. 8d. at Warboys and 7s. 4d. at Somersham for the first month of the scheme. By the first quarter of 1917 only £1 10s. 6d. was collected at Warboys, reducing to 19s. 9d. for the three months ending 30th September, 1917, £1 0s 3d for the next quarter and £1 1s. 0d. for the first quarter of 1918. No collections were made at Ramsey High Street or Somersham during the same periods.

Although goods receipts on the Ramsey High Street branch were healthy, passenger receipts were always a cause for concern to the GN&GE Committee and indeed the parent companies. Compared with other branch lines, earnings remained poor and in an attempt to reduce the operating deficit, the branch was chosen as a trial route for auto-train working. Unlike many other main line companies, the GER had never experimented with steam railcars on lightly trafficked routes but in 1914 James Holden adapted one of his 'Y65' class 2-4-2 tank locomotives No. 1311 for compressed air-operated auto-train working. Coupled to it to form the push-and-pull train were two clerestory coaches, a 48 ft 3 in. corridor composite trailer, seating nine first class and 30 third class passengers, and a driving trailer third with compartment for driver and guard and accommodation for 46 third class passengers. The auto-train commenced trial running on the Mildenhall branch on 5th October, 1914 but after several weeks was transferred to the Ramsey High Street branch. Unfortunately, the auto-train was unsuitable for both lines as it could only operate as a self-contained unit and could not work the mixed trains on the branches; it was impossible to attach tail loads especially when the locomotive was pushing the two-coach set. The train was subsequently transferred in 1915 to the temporarily restored service on the reopened Churchbury loop line between White Hart Lane and Cheshunt in north-east London.

Serving an agricultural and farming community the GER was always keen to assist with efforts to increase production and thereby engender additional traffic. To this end the railway company organised an egg and poultry demonstration train to visit many locations on the system in 1916. Although the train never visited this branch, farmers were offered cheap return fares to visit the train at St Ives.

The strain of the war taxed the resources of the railways and the country and in December 1916 the Railway Executive Committee issued an ultimatum to the effect that they would only carry on if drastic reductions were made to ordinary services. Locomotive availability was restricted because of a shortage of coal supplies. The Lloyd George Coalition thus agreed to a reduction of passenger services from 1st January, 1917 but despite this edict the Ramsey High Street branch services remained virtually unchanged as most trains ran as mixed, conveying wagons of produce in addition to the coaching stock. As local railwaymen answered the call to arms, female staff were employed to fill the resultant vacancies. After some readjustments of male staff, three women clerks were trained and then employed at Warboys with two at Somersham in the booking and goods offices, until they were transferred to other stations. One

Somersham station viewed from the south in 1911. Colne Road level crossing at 10 miles 79¾ chains is in the foreground and immediately next the station is Chatteris Road or Somersham level crossing at 11 miles 05¼ chains. The down and up GN&GE main lines bisect the level crossings and pass through the station whilst the premises of a small coal warehouse and granary to the left are served by a connection from the up main line which would form an interesting subject for a model railway layout. The points were operated from a 2-lever ground frame electrically released from the Station signal box. Note the crossing keeper's hut beside the crossing and the crossing keeper's cottage to the right.

GERS/Windwood 1514

Ramsey High Street saw the departure of many of the town's menfolk to the battlefronts during World War I. Typical of those who served their country was Sergeant Gipson who posed in front of typical GER-style platform seats bearing the station name. Recruiting bills for the Bedfordshire Yeomanry and derogatory claims against the Kaiser, have replaced railway posters on the station building.

Author's Collection

remained at Warboys until 1922. A signalwoman was also employed at Warboys during this period. After the cessation of hostilities, on Armistice Day flags were displayed at the branch stations. The festivities were short lived for from 26th September to 5th October, 1919 there was a general railway strike when services on the line were suspended.

On 5th February, 1919 an agreement was signed with the First Garden City Limited Company for the lease of a siding at Somersham to load bricks for onward transit to Letchworth. By October 1920 the agreement was terminated and the contract transferred to Fenwick Owen, the brick maker, who acted as agent for the development company.

A safety aspect of the signalling on the branch, which had apparently been overlooked when the Regulation of Railways Act 1889 was complied with, was duly rectified when authority was given on 21st April, 1921 for the distant signals guarding Heath Drove level crossing, near Warboys, to be interlocked with the crossing gates at a cost of £129.

The industrial dispute of 1919, coupled with the later General Strike of 1926 began the decline in railborne freight. Farmers and growers realized for the first time that with the improving roads, goods could be conveyed by lorry, using in some cases vehicles purchased second-hand from the army, thus allowing short haul journeys at cheaper rates than charged by the GN&GE Joint Committee. The door-to-door service was more convenient than the double handling caused by loading and unloading into and out of railway wagons. The primitive commercial road vehicles of the day were not, however, capable of continuous long hauls and the middle and long distance freight traffic remained safely in the hands of the railway company.

The monopoly enjoyed by the passenger services was rudely shattered when local bus services began operating from Ramsey and the surrounding areas of Huntingdonshire and Cambridgeshire. The GER and the Joint Committee were somewhat concerned with the loss of revenue on a service that already provided only meagre traffic and revenue returns. In order to reduce operating costs it was subsequently proposed to withdraw all booking office staff and close the ticket offices at Warboys and Ramsey High Street, and introduce conductor-guard working on all passenger trains with the guard issuing tickets. The introduction of the system required the modification of coaching stock to enable the guard to walk through the train and the estimated cost of modification to the three six-wheel coaches to be used on the Somersham to Ramsey High Street services totalled £180. The Joint Committee readily agreed the expenditure, when it was disclosed that the closure of the booking offices and withdrawal of station masters and staff would result in a net saving of £900 and the scheme was implemented in the spring of 1922. Unlike later conductor-guard schemes introduced on other GER branch lines in East Anglia later in the same year, no new halts were opened on the Ramsey High Street branch.

Ramsey East station in the late 1920s with 'F7' class 2-4-2T No. 8302 standing at the platform with the branch train formed of a three-compartment six-wheel brake third and six-compartment six-wheel composite, both converted for conductor-guard working. A covered van and goods brake van complete the complement of the mixed train. In the dock road behind the platform is a London Midland & Scottish Railway 'large' cattle wagon.   *Stations UK*

'F7' class No. 8308 standing at the buffer stops at Ramsey East in the summer of 1927. Note the fine display of roses on the fencing and the cattle wagon standing on the short cattle dock road.
Author's Collection

Chapter Four

Grouping to Closure

On 1st January, 1923 the Great Northern & Great Eastern Joint Committee amalgamated with their parent companies, the Great Central, the North Eastern and several smaller railways to form the London & North Eastern Railway (LNER). The new ownership initially made few changes except that Ramsey High Street station was renamed Ramsey East and the neighbouring Ramsey station renamed Ramsey North from 1st July, 1923. A seven-day rail strike from 20th January, 1924 brought a further decline in traffic. Passengers who had regularly patronized the railway service for short journeys turned to road transport, some never returning to make regular use of the branch again. By the summer of 1924 motor omnibus services were operating from Ramsey to St Ives on Mondays, Whittlesea on Fridays and Peterborough on Wednesdays, Saturdays and Sundays. These services, though infrequent, enjoyed instant success, providing an almost door-to-door service for townsfolk attending the local markets for shopping.

Two years later the General Strike brought additional chaos to the railways causing further decline. Despite the introduction of conductor-guard working to effect economies, the LNER management were concerned by falling receipts on many of its rural branch lines, and Ramsey East was no exception. Whilst goods traffic maintained a satisfactory level, passenger and parcels receipts were poor and fluctuated annually as figures for 1923 to 1928 show.

		Passengers	Passenger receipts	Parcel receipts	Season ticket receipts	Totals
		Nos.	£	£	£	£
1923	Ramsey East	7,878	569	213	28	810
	Warboys	4,201	273	90	12	375
	Total	12,079	842	303	40	1,185
1924	Ramsey East	6,616	451	241	–	692
	Warboys	3,800	220	57	6	283
	Total	10,416	671	298	6	975
1925	Ramsey East	6,888	577	198	–	775
	Warboys	3,928	377	51	4	432
	Total	10,816	954	249	4	1,207
1926	Ramsey East	5,463	421	195	4	620
	Warboys	2,503	262	46	2	310
	Total	7,966	683	241	6	930
1927	Ramsey East	5,392	433	212	12	657
	Warboys	2,675	268	51	4	323
	Total	8,067	701	263	16	980
1928	Ramsey East	6,158	591	169	22	782
	Warboys	2,524	251	52	3	306
	Total	8,682	842	221	25	1,088

Comparative figures for Somersham show a far healthier picture although few from that station booked to Warboys or Ramsey East.

		Passengers Nos.	Passenger receipts £	Parcel receipts £	Season ticket receipts £	Totals £
1923	Somersham	28,273	2,106	748	107	2,961
1924		28,271	2,130	1,072	119	3,321
1925		29,729	2,177	1,193	131	3,501
1926		23,100	1,671	1,631	165	3,467
1927		24,659	1,779	1,622	169	3,570
1928		22,430	1,586	1,460	130	3,176

The primitive bus services to towns and villages in the area were gradually improving in comfort and frequency, although by 1928 Ramsey still only had the same bus services as in 1924. Whilst the branch stations were not inconveniently situated, the two-coach train with its gas lighting was antiquated by comparison. The train service was adequate for most passenger traffic except on Mondays when the additional train ran for St Ives market, but fewer passengers travelled by rail. In six years the average number of passengers booking each week from the branch stations had fallen from 232 to 169 and by 1928 Ramsey East was booking an average of 20 passengers per day compared to the 75 booking at Ramsey North whilst Warboys had a mere eight!

On 23rd April, 1926 the Chief General Manager submitted a report to the Traffic Committee concerning the complaints received from farmers, traders, local councils and the National Farmers Union regarding the lack of accommodation and facilities for dealing with sugar beet and other produce from East Anglia. One of the stations where improvements were required was Somersham and on 29th April the Traffic Committee agreed to improvements costing £1,530, which would ultimately result in a net annual saving of £219.

The LNER Directors had for long been concerned with the poor returns earned from passenger traffic where competitive bus services running on roads paralleling the railway had seen further improvements. At a special Board meeting it was resolved to stem the loss of receipts by introducing 20 railway company-operated bus services with the purchase of 60 motor buses. One of the centres for the new services was St Ives, where it was envisaged routes would operate to Holme via Ramsey and Huntingdon via Godmanchester using two 20-seater vehicles and to Ely via Sutton, using four 32-seater vehicles in competition with other services. Allocations would, however, be amended in the event of the LNER coming to terms with local bus proprietors. The Engineer estimated the cost of providing garage accommodation at St Ives at £5,000 exclusive of lighting and petrol pumps. On 29th November, 1928 authority was given for the outlay on the garage at St Ives, but no further developments were made for the company was negotiating financial and operating interests in the existing local bus companies.

As the decade of recession drew to a close the LNER was suffering traffic losses, which deemed it necessary for the management at Marylebone and Liverpool Street to seek economies. Along with other branch lines, including

Mellis to Eye, Ely to St Ives and Downham to Stoke Ferry, the Ramsey East branch was closely investigated as to its viability in the future passenger railway system. The dwindling receipts of the Huntingdonshire branch and indeed its close neighbour, the Holme to Ramsey North branch, made depressing reading. After deliberating, it was decided the latter with three times the receipts of the Ramsey East line and providing the better returns, should retain its passenger service. It also had the advantage of providing a much faster service, with one change, to Huntingdon, Peterborough and London, King's Cross.

The outcome regarding the Ramsey East service was inevitable and on 3rd September, 1930 the Divisional General Manager, Southern Area, advised the Traffic Committee that as the line was working at a loss, it was proposed to withdraw the passenger services. The gross value of passenger traffic 'local to or originating and terminating on the branch' only amounted to £1,805 in 1928 and it was proposed to withdraw the passenger service on and from 22nd September, 1930. The heavy freight traffic would continue and the goods train service be adjusted to cater for the parcels and miscellaneous traffic at a cost of £393. The withdrawal of the passenger services was estimated to save £2,669 working expenses less £540 loss of receipts, bringing a net saving of £2,129. Although the Eastern National Omnibus Co., an associate of the LNER, served the area there was no regular route in the immediate district serving Ramsey, Warboys and Somersham. The LNER subsequently made arrangements with the bus company for an alternative service. Approval was given for the withdrawal of the passenger train services and notices were duly posted at local stations and in the local newspapers:

SOMERSHAM AND RAMSEY EAST
BRANCH LINE WITHDRAWAL OF PASSENGER TRAINS

The London and North Eastern Railway Company hereby give notice that on and from the 22nd September 1930 the passenger train service on the above-mentioned branch will be discontinued.

The conveyance of merchandise and live stock by goods train and of parcels, milk and fruit, and other miscellaneous traffic, including live stock charged at rates applicable to passenger train or other similar service will be continued.

Particulars of the train service for such traffic will be obtainable at stations on the branch line and from the Somersham Station Master.

Attention is drawn to the omnibus service operated in the vicinity, by the Eastern National Omnibus Company Limited and full particulars are available from the Station Masters at Somersham and St Ives.

BY ORDER

R.L .WEDGWOOD
Chief General Manager
King's Cross Station
London N1

Dated 4th September, 1930.

The final regular passenger train waiting to depart from Somersham for Ramsey East on Saturday 20th September, 1930. Standing on the front footplate of 'F7' class 2-4-2T No. 8308 are driver 'Tommy' Atkins and fireman P. Brown. On the platform are guard Sabbitt, clerk J. Grice and station master Watson. Porter H. Robinson is on the track. A number of last day travellers are looking out of the windows of the coaches.

Author's Collection

LNER notice advising the withdrawal of passenger services from the Ramsey East branch on and from 22nd September, 1930.

M. Brooks Collection

LONDON & NORTH EASTERN RAILWAY

Somersham & Ramsey East Branch Line

Withdrawal of Passenger Trains

The London and North Eastern Railway Company hereby give notice that on and from the 22nd September, 1930, the passenger train service on the above-mentioned Branch Line will be discontinued, and the following stations will be closed to passengers:

RAMSEY EAST
WARBOYS

The conveyance of merchandise and live stock by goods train, and of parcels, milk, fruit and other miscellaneous traffic, including live stock charged at rates applicable to passenger train or other similar service, will be continued. Particulars of the train service for such traffic will be obtainable at stations on the Branch Line or from the Somersham Station Master.

Attention is drawn to the omnibus services operated in the vicinity by the Eastern National Omnibus Company, Limited, full particulars of which are obtainable from the Station Masters at Somersham and St. Ives.

Compared with the railway closures of the 1950s and 1960s little opposition was made by local inhabitants to the cessation of passenger services. The LNER arranged for the Eastern National Omnibus Co. to run the replacement bus service from Monday 22nd September, 1930 from Ramsey to St Ives. As there was no Sunday service the final passenger train departed without ceremony from Somersham at 6.10 pm on Saturday 20th September with 'F7' class 2-4-2T No. 8308 hauling its two-coach train, formed of a six-wheel composite and six-wheel brake third.

The Eastern National Omnibus Co.was based at Chelmsford and served a vast area incorporating the counties of Essex, Suffolk, Hertfordshire, Bedfordshire, Northamptonshire and Huntingdonshire. The initial replacement buses were Tilling Stevens 'B10As' and these remained on the Ramsey to St Ives route for some years. The bus company was a subsidiary road service of the LNER and most buses from Ramsey and the surrounding villages maintained a connection with main line trains at St Ives and Huntingdon.

After the withdrawal of passenger services on the Ramsey East branch, the LNER authorities rearranged the freight services on the line. Milk and parcels traffic previously conveyed by passenger train were carried in the van attached to the freight train, which ran across the branch twice-daily on weekdays only. Any complacency Ramsey inhabitants had had of the future of the Ramsey North passenger services was rudely shattered a few weeks later on 22nd December, 1930 when the Divisional General Manager, Southern Area reported to the LNER Board that although the line carried an appreciable amount of goods traffic, the gross value of passenger traffic 'local to or originating or terminating on' the Holme to Ramsey North branch in 1928 only totalled £5,528, with no indication of an increase. It was not considered desirable to withdraw the passenger train service completely as the first service trip over the branch was a goods train and after arrival at Ramsey North the locomotive worked passenger services up to the 10.15 am ex-Holme. In the interests of economy it was proposed on and from 2nd February, 1931, to retain the working and then cancel all the passenger services on the line after the 10.15 am down train. The Board duly sanctioned the proposals. Thus within a few months the Huntingdonshire town enjoying the advantages of two branch lines offering passenger services was reduced to the bare offering of three trains during the early morning. A situation that was hardly conducive to attracting custom.

In February 1930 the Chief General Manager of the LNER had reported to the Traffic Committee that considerable difficulty had been experienced over a number of years on the working of freight trains between Spalding, March, Cambridge and London. The limitations imposed by the strength of certain bridges and the absence of independent running lines had been an important factor in the delays incurred by these services. Trains were restricted to a maximum of 50 wagons plus engine and brake van and as the weak bridges were being rebuilt to a completion target of December 1931, plans were formulated to install independent running lines at various locations between Spalding and Cambridge via St Ives. These would accommodate trains of 80 wagons plus engine and brake van in the up direction and 90 wagons plus engine and brake van in the down direction. The installation of the loops would obviate the necessity of shunting slower trains on to the opposite running lines for faster trains to pass and also stop pick-up goods trains blocking main lines when shunting at intermediate stations and sidings. Because of these shortcomings most traffic was being worked via Ely causing considerable congestion and delays, especially to passenger services, whilst the St Ives loop was under-utilized. As part of the scheme a new down independent loop line was to be installed immediately north of Somersham Junction at a cost of £4,071, whilst the former up side refuge siding was to be extended and converted into an up loop at a cost of £3,911, the total cost including £2,460 for signalling alterations.

The installation of additional loop lines was spread over a lengthy period and after the withdrawal of the Ramsey East passenger services, the plan for Somersham had to be revised. When the scheme was originally mooted, it was proposed to work all points and signals for the independent lines from Somersham Junction signal box. On investigation it was revealed that the Junction signal box was only open for 12 hours a day, with duties being covered by a signalman for a full shift and porter-signalman for the remainder of the time, at an annual cost of £272. In contrast Somersham Station signal box was manned daily for 24 hours by three signalmen, at an annual cost of £495. When it was realised the proposed arrangements would require the Junction signal box being manned for 24 hours at a cost of £495, an annual increase of £223, the Chief General Manager and Traffic Committee on 8th January, 1931 sanctioned the abolition of both existing signal boxes and their replacement by a single new structure. The gross cost of the new arrangement was £3,062 but the £91 value of recoverable material and the abolition of renewal costs of £310 reduced the net expenditure to £2,661. Somersham Junction and Station signal boxes were subsequently abolished and replaced by the new structure located on the up side of the main line opposite the junction on 1st November, 1931.

Lieutenant Colonel E.P. Anderson inspected the new arrangements on 24th April, 1932. He found that new up and down reception roads had been laid on either side of the main line to March and north of the junction with the Ramsey East branch. The permanent way was formed with 85 lb. per yard rails laid on stone ballast. The facing points were fully equipped and traps provided. The clearance of the check-rail opposite the nose of the crossing in the up main line was slightly slack due to difference in the size of the chairs but immediate attention was promised. The maximum clearance between the rails of the new up loop and the main line was 6 ft 1 in. and between the rails on the cess side of the loop and the signal wire stakes fixed close to the boundary fence was only 5 ft 8 in. On taking this up with the railway officers attending the inspection, Anderson was informed it was impossible to obtain more land to give a better clearance without a special Act of Parliament, as the required land consisted of smallholdings controlled by the County Council. The Lieutenant Colonel accepted that under the circumstances the best use was being made of the space available. The facing points in the up main line, situated 820 yards from the signal box, were electrically worked by a Westinghouse battery feed machine completing any movement in three seconds. The machine also bolted the trailing spring points in the up reception in the normal position, when the main line facing points were also normal. The facing points were held in the normal or reverse positions by the occupation of track circuits. As the bracketed outer home signal was located close to the points, an automatic time clearance relay was provided, holding the facing points for 1 minute and 45 seconds, sufficient time to ensure they could not be reversed under a train. Anderson noted this arrangement was in use elsewhere and the facing trap points for exit from the down loop line were similarly worked, the trailing points in the down main line being spring controlled.

The points and signals were worked from the new Somersham Junction signal box located east of the main line and north of the junction with the single line. It was equipped with a 60-lever frame, with 54 working and six spare levers. The inspector found that all signal arms were repeated in the signal box, whilst a spotlight diagram provided occupation of the various track circuits. The interlocking was correct. He noted the branch line was operated by 'One Engine in Steam' and was no longer used for passenger traffic. The level crossing at the south end of Somersham station was controlled by one lever in a two-lever ground frame, the other lever controlling movement through the trailing points in the up main line to an adjacent siding. This ground frame was controlled from the signal box, the siding points being released by Annett's key and the gate locks being electrically released from the signal box. Anderson considered the distance of the new signals was adequate for the gradients and possible speed of approaching trains. Although the loops were normally intended for goods trains there was no objection to their use by passenger trains if necessary, subject to speed limit of 15 mph

From the late 1920s sugar beet cultivation was introduced into the area served by the branch and during the winter months a considerable tonnage was conveyed to the sugar processing factories at Ely and Wissington. As the beet traffic increased during the 1930s the brickworks served by the branch also provided regular traffic, and together with the occasional fruit traffic often required the running of additional goods trains at the appropriate times of the year. By 1936 the Eastern Counties Omnibus Company, which had replaced the Eastern National Omnibus Co. were operating from Ramsey to Peterborough daily, Whittlesea on Fridays, St Ives on Mondays, Huntingdon on Saturdays and Sundays, March on Wednesdays and Saturdays, whilst the railway replacement service introduced in 1930 continued to connect the town with Somersham on weekdays only. On the branch further rationalization resulted in the abolition of Ramsey East signal box and Pidley-cum-Fenton ground frame on 30th September, 1932 and Warboys signal box on 4th May, 1936.

The occasional passenger train ventured to Ramsey East each year until the outbreak of World War II as the LNER ran excursions from Ramsey East, Warboys and Somersham to East Anglian resorts. Typical destinations included Hunstanton, Yarmouth and Clacton. On 9th July, 1939, 'J15' class 0-6-0 No. 7553 worked through from Ramsey East to Clacton and return, hauling a nine-coach train via St Ives, Cambridge, Haverhill and outward via Sudbury and Marks Tey to Clacton, returning via the Colne Valley line. Stops were made at Cambridge and Colchester on the outward trip and at Marks Tey, Haverhill and Colchester on the return run. The late Peter Proud provided the mileage and

The site of the engine shed at Ramsey East with the inspection pit filled in on 18th May, 1937. The shed was demolished the previous year. The main single branch line in the foreground and goods yard lines to the left in this view facing Somersham. Beyond the entry points to the goods yard is occupational crossing No. 28 at 6 miles 46 chains and in the distance Cattle Creep underbridge No. 2313 at 6 miles 41 chains.   *W.A. Camwell*

Somersham station from the south in the mid-1930s. The down platform to the left is host to the station master's office and booking office, whilst the more recent structure on the up platform, housed a general and ladies' waiting room. The 1931 Somersham Junction signal box can be seen in the background.   *Author's Collection*

schedule of the excursion in its marathon trip from Huntingdonshire to the Essex coast with a 3 hours 40 minute timing on the outward trip and 3 hours 55 minutes on the return. The highest point-to-point timing on the entire journey was on the return run when 40 mph was achieved between Haverhill and Bartlow. Whilst at Clacton the engine was serviced at Clacton shed.

Mileage		Schedule			
		Outward		*Return*	
		mins	mins	mins	mins
0.0	Ramsey East		00		235
3.6	Warboys	06	08	225	227
7.0	Somersham	18	20	213	215
12.5	St Ives	30	38	196	203
15.6	Swavesey	–	45	–	189
17.9	Long Stanton	–	50	–	182
20.4	Oakington	–	55	–	176
22.6	Histon	–	60	–	169
25.2	Cambridge	70	75w	154	159w
28.5	Shelford	–	82	–	147
35.4	Linton	–	94	–	135
37.4	Bartlow	–	99	–	129
43.4	Haverhill North	–	110		119w
50.5	Clare	–	123		
53.1	Cavendish	–	129		
56.9	Long Melford	–	136		
60.0	Sudbury	–	142		
64.9	Bures	–	152		
68.2	Chappel	–	160		
71.7	Marks Tey	–	168		
76.8	Colchester	178	183w		
81.3	Wivenhoe	–	191		
90.3	Thorpe-le-Soken	–	205		
92.6	Great Holland	–	215		
95.0	Clacton-on-Sea	220			
43.4	Haverhill North			114	see above
47.2	Birdbrook			–	104
51.0	Yeldham			–	94
53.5	Sible & C. Hedingham			–	88
56.8	Halstead			–	80
59.3	Earls Colne			–	74
62.9	Chappel			–	65
66.4	Marks Tey			52	57w
71.5	Colchester			–	43
76.0	Wivenhoe			–	26
85.0	Thorpe-le-Soken			–	10
87.3	Great Holland			–	05
89.7	Clacton-on-Sea			–	00

w – water stop

The approach of World War II brought an increase in materials conveyed to Somersham for Somersham airfield, Warboys for Warboys airfield and Ramsey East for Upwood airfield. Upwood to the south-west of Ramsey had been established in 1917 as a base for two night training squadrons of the Royal Flying Corps. At the cessation of hostilities the land had reverted to farming and the squadrons disbanded. The base had been rebuilt in 1937 and became the headquarters of two light bomber squadrons, once again with training as priority. Before the outbreak of hostilities the LNER merged with other major railway companies under the control of the Railway Executive Committee from 1st September, 1939. To safeguard against air raids, especially at night, station and signal box lamps remained dimmed and staff utilized shielded hand lamps to attend to train and shunting duties. As a precaution against enemy infiltration, station name boards were also removed and stored in lamp rooms and other inconspicuous places. The agricultural nature of freight handled on the line became of the utmost importance as vital provisions of homegrown food, including grain, vegetables and fruit were dispatched to markets. Rationing of petrol brought the withdrawal of many motor vans and lorries from local roads and the urgency for foodstuffs meant an increase in freight traffic leaving the branch stations for London and the major cities. It was during this period that ammunition trains served the yard at Somersham, most travelling and arriving by night before the bombs and shells were offloaded and transferred to ammunition dumps by road. After 1943 when concrete runways were laid at Upwood, and 'Mosquitos' and 'Lancasters' of 2 Pathfinder squadron established base there, armaments and stores were delivered to Warboys and lesser extent Ramsey East and increased daily from February 1944 to the end of the war when over 6,000 sorties were mounted from the base, including 36 consecutive night attacks by Lancaster bombers on Berlin. Warboys was also used as a bomber base.

Ammunition was not the only import to the area, for in addition to the usual agricultural products and coal and coke supplies to local merchants, the war years brought an influx of tinned food by rail to Ramsey East for distribution to Ministry of Food storage depots in the area. The close proximity of local airfields was no insurance against enemy air attacks and on one occasion a Luftwaffe fighter-bomber made an attack on the branch goods train in broad daylight near Pidley-cum-Fenton siding, fortunately resulting in no damage to equipment or injuries to staff. During hostilities, passenger coaches were occasionally attached to the branch goods train for the benefit of military personnel travelling to and from the local airfields, although most travelled to Ramsey using the service from Holme to Ramsey North.

After the war the railways were totally run down with shortage of rolling stock and many locomotive failures, caused by lack of maintenance, when high availability was required. Questions were asked in Parliament regarding the poor state of the transport system. The Ramsey East branch like others suffered and on several occasions the goods services were cancelled through lack of motive power or inability to provide traders with wagons. Further troubles came early in 1947 when heavy snowfalls brought delays to services, culminating in February with the line blocked for two days by drifting snow in Warboys cutting. Cambridge snowplough, initially dealing with the clearance of the more important routes, finally cleared the branch to allow services to resume.

All too frequently a locomotive failure, however trivial, played havoc with the Train Staff and Ticket system and later 'One Engine in Steam' using the Train Staff method of working. A typical example occurred in 1947 when the engine working the branch goods failed at Warboys. An urgent telephone call was made to Somersham for a relief engine to be summoned from either March or Cambridge. To enable the assisting engine to enter the branch, however, the Train Staff had to be returned to the junction. With no alternative transport available Jack Hatcher, the leading porter at Warboys, cycled 4½ miles alongside the track with the Train Staff. By the time he reached the Junction signal box, relatively unscathed, the assisting engine was waiting and a welcome ride on the footplate was made back to Warboys, with the cycle hoisted on top of the coal in the tender.

Later in the year the old coal drops and siding at Somersham were found to be in a dilapidated condition and were an operating inconvenience both for the LNER and the coal merchants. On 25th September, 1947 authority was given for the removal of the eight coal drops and the siding, which was in need of complete renewal. The facility was substituted by the installation of an additional siding with accommodation for nine wagons, together with an extension of the coal stacking ground to an area of 400 square yards, and the extension and widening of the existing sleeper crossing. The estimated cost of the work was £1,161 gross, £989 net, less the renewal cost of £863 for the coal drops, which were now unnecessary. The estimated original capital cost of the works to be displaced was £571 with an estimated saving of maintenance renewal charges of £74 per annum. The coal drop and siding together with offices and stables was let to Coote & Warren Ltd at a rent, excluding rates and taxes, of £30 per annum and when the work was completed the following year the new stacking ground rent was increased to £37 10s. 0d. per annum, inclusive of rates and taxes. The LNER in addition supplied chalk for the stacking ground free of charge.

After enjoying increased traffic in the war years, with military personnel journeying to local airfields, passenger numbers on the Ramsey North line with its limited train service decreased rapidly with only 2,665 passenger travelling in 1946. On 3rd July, 1947 the Divisional General Manager advised the intention to withdraw the loss making passenger services from the line and terminate the working arrangements with the Eastern Counties Omnibus Co.

During 1946 and 1947 Warboys airfield served as a prisoner of war camp and many stores and rations continued to be delivered by rail. When the camp closed in 1947 with the repatriation of all inmates, the traffic was lost but was more than offset when Warboys brickworks reopened as part of a national drive for the reconstruction of war-ravaged towns and cities. Once the works were up to full production it was not unusual for 40 wagons or more to be dispatched daily from the brickworks siding,

By the end of 1947 the tide was changing against the LNER as parcels and freight traffic were quickly transferring to road haulage. Petrol rationing had eased and farmers and growers took advantage to convey their produce from door to door by lorry or van avoiding the double handling into and out of railway wagons. The remaining imports of coal and coke, as well as consignments of sugar beet, were easily handled by the one freight train each way to and from Ramsey East whilst the second freight train terminated at and started from

Ramsey East station facing the buffer stops in 1947. The run-round loop is to the left. The wagons at the back of the platform are standing in the dock road.   *Author's Collection*

'J17' class 0-6-0 No. 65562 approaching Ramsey East with the Railway Correspondence & Travel Society's six coach 'Fensman' railtour train on 24th July, 1955. Note the engine is displaying the express train headcode.   *E. Sawford*

Warboys with brick traffic and any residual farm produce. On and from 6th October, 1947 the passenger train service was withdrawn from the Ramsey North branch, the last train actually running on Saturday 4th October and conveying three passengers. Latterly the timetable showed a weekday service of three trains each way in the morning and a bus substitution in the afternoon and most travellers in the final years were servicemen based at local airfields. The *Huntingdon Post* truly reported, 'Little interest was shown in the event'.

The nationalization of the railways from 1st January, 1948 brought few immediate changes to the former R&SJR which came under its fourth ownership, that of British Railways, Eastern Region. The line retained its GER/LNER atmosphere but locomotives working the services soon lost the legend NE or LNER on the tenders whilst goods rolling stock started to appear in the new corporate livery. The new owner found the task of attracting new traffic to the line increasingly difficult as road conveyance of commodities went from strength to strength in East Anglia. Soon coal merchants were receiving an increasing tonnage by road whilst larger lorries visited local farms to pick up sugar beet. The Ramsey East branch goods, long reduced to one train in each direction, was on many occasions cancelled through lack of traffic. Even when the train ran it often terminated at Warboys and conveyed few wagons. Of a minor nature Green Drove occupational crossing No. 12 at 2 miles 43 chains was widened to 15 ft in 1953, the local landowner Mr Brown paying the full cost of the scheme.

The branch received a visit from railway enthusiasts on Sunday 24th July, 1955, when the Railway Correspondence & Travel Society's 'Fensman' Railtour train formed of Gresley bogie corridor coaches and hauled by 'J17' class 0-6-0 No. 65562 traversed the line. The trip was made in fine weather and the locomotive hauled the train from Somersham to Ramsey East tender first before running round the stock and posing for photographs. The train then wended its way back to Somersham.

In 1951 Eastern National bus route 39 still operated from Ramsey to Somersham railway station as distinct from the market place where Eastern Counties buses terminated. However, where buses connected with up train services on the March to St Ives line, connections with down trains were virtually non-existent!

By the mid-1950s dwindling traffic to and from Ramsey East goods yard was of concern to the Eastern Region authorities. Deteriorating permanent way necessitating expensive renewals and the need for operating economies called for a closer examination of receipts. After investigation it was decided all Ramsey traffic could be routed via the North station and the Eastern Region management subsequently announced the closure of Ramsey East as a public goods station on and from 17th September, 1956. The station had seen only spasmodic traffic for some years and except for coal and sugar beet, loadings were light. Messrs Cordell's private siding, three-quarters of a mile to the east of Ramsey East, was retained for a further 11 months although that traffic was soon lost to road haulage and the siding finally closed on 20th August, 1957, leaving Warboys as the terminal station. The track from Warboys to Ramsey East was retained for some months and used for the storage of condemned wagons, before contractors cut up the rails, removed sleepers and other fixed assets, working from the terminus towards Warboys. The track between Warboys and the junction at Somersham received remedial maintenance and hopes were raised for a continuing service.

The Railway Correspondence & Travel Society 'Fensman' railtour train standing waiting departure at Ramsey East on 24th July, 1955. The six-coach train formed of LNER corridor stock was too long to accommodate in the short platform at the terminus, and to allow the locomotive to run-round the stock the rear of the train was aligned to the goods shed. 'J17' class 0-6-0 No. 65562, specially polished for its express passenger duties, has its safety valves lifting as passengers clamber aboard.   *E. Sawford*

'J19' class 0-6-0 No. 64640 poses with the train crew in the down platform at Warboys in 1959 before setting off for Somersham.   *Dr I.C. Allen*

'J19' class 0-6-0 No. 64640 pauses at Warboys after shunting duties and before leaving with its attendant brake van for Somersham. *Dr I.C. Allen*

'J17' class 0-6-0 No. 65528 pulls off the branch and into Somersham goods yard after working up from Warboys in 1961. *Dr I.C. Allen*

Craven two-car diesel-multiple-unit forming the 10.00 am Cambridge to Peterborough North via St Ives service departing from Somersham on 6th September, 1963. This view from Somersham signal box shows the up reception siding, with associated cattle dock and pens on the left and behind the train the down side goods yard   *R. Powell*

A Brush type '2', later class '31', diesel-electric pulls off the Ramsey East branch and past Somersham Junction signal box on 6th September, 1963. As there was no traffic from Warboys and the tail load consists of a brake van only the train has been routed directly on to the up main line to continue to St Ives instead of being routed into the goods yard. The entry points to the goods yard are on the left whilst the up side cattle dock is on the right.   *R. Powell*

The Warboys branch received the benefit of British Railways' modernization programme from 1959 when diesel-electric locomotives built by BR/Sulzer type '2', later BR class '24' and Brush type '2', later BR class '31' took over some of the working of the freight services. As the months progressed so the steam traction and the class '24' useage disappeared and the class '31s' worked all the goods trips on the line until closure.

The infamous Beeching Report on the Reshaping of British Railways was published in 1963 and although specifically referring to passenger traffic, maps were included within the document showing density of freight traffic and distribution of freight tonnage. The figures registered for the Warboys branch confirmed that the line carried under 5,000 tons per week with Somersham and Pidley-cum-Fenton dealing with under 5,000 tons per annum and Warboys under 25,000 tons per annum. These dwindling receipts, and the loss of most of the brick and sugar beet traffic from Warboys, forced British Railways to look closely at the future viability of the retention of the line between Somersham and Warboys. The Eastern Region authorities subsequently announced the closure of Warboys and Pidley-cum-Fenton public siding on and from 13th July, 1964, a date synonymous with the closure of many freight depots in East Anglia and including the neighbouring Three Horse Shoes to Benwick goods branch. Alternative freight facilities were available initially at Somersham but the freight facilities were withdrawn from the former junction station just over five months later on 28th December, 1964. With the closure of Warboys and Pidley-cum-Fenton, the erstwhile R&SJR was closed completely.

The branch was initially used for storage of condemned wagons but after a few months the contractors again arrived to remove the rails, sleepers and other infrastructure. This time the rails were cut into 20 ft lengths and loaded on to Lowmac wagons, which were shunted on to the branch each morning and removed each evening. Work commenced at Warboys working slowly back towards Somersham Junction. In less than three years Somersham station was closed when passenger services were withdrawn between St Ives and March South Junction on and from 6th March, 1967.

Returning to the replacement bus services, in the 1940s and 1950s the Eastern National Omnibus Co. and later Eastern Counties Omnibus Co. had standardized their fleets with Bristol 'L' and later 'SC' and 'MW' single-deck buses with Eastern Coach Works bodies operating the routes from Ramsey. In the early 1980s, Bristol 'LH/RELL' type single-deck vehicles operated the routes but the service offered by the Eastern Counties as part of the National Bus Organisation was spartan in the extreme; route 133 from Bluntisham to Somersham, Pidley, Warboys and Ramsey operated on Wednesdays only. The footnote to the timetable even announced that on leaving Ramsey on the return journey the bus would not follow the fixed route and on advice being given to the driver, would be driven as near as possible to passengers' front doors. In addition to Eastern Counties route 133, United Counties Omnibus Co. operated a single journey each way on Mondays only when route 216 connected Ramsey with RAF Upwood, Wistow, Warboys, Fenton, Pidley, RAF Wyton and St Ives. Eastern Counties route 229 also operated approximately six journeys each way weekdays only between Ramsey and Huntingdon via Warboys.

Somersham station from the south in June 1967 with Chatteris Road level crossing gates across the former down line. The up line had recently been lifted.   *R. Powell*

Somersham station bereft of track in June 1972 with the defunct Junction signal box in the background. A decade later the buildings were removed by the late Sir William McAlpine for preservation on his private railway in Buckinghamshire.   *R. Powell*

British Railways commenced the disposal of former railway land at Somersham when on 28th February, 1969, 3 acres 4,646 square yards of the branch was sold to D. Barlow for £30. Another 13 acres 4,317 square yards were sold to Mrs J. Dimock on 23rd September, 1971 for £50 to be followed by a further four acres to the same purchaser on 10th August, 1978 for £50.

The trackbed of the erstwhile Ramsey East branch can be easily traced and although some sections have been acquired by farmers and ploughed up, the ubiquitous railway fencing remains as evidence of the route. Somersham station remained almost complete, with awnings fronting the station buildings and old station lamps decorating the former platforms although vandals tried to set fire to one of the wooden waiting shelters. Fortunately the fire brigade doused the flames before much damage was done. In 1982 the buildings were removed by Sir William McAlpine to be erected on a new site in Buckinghamshire leaving only the platforms extant. By 1985 the station building had been restored to serve on the owner's Fawley Hill Railway. Along the branch the former Bateman's brickworks are derelict but at Heath Drove crossing the gatekeeper's cottage adjacent to the Warboys to Chatteris road remains as a private dwelling. On the approach to Warboys the Bedfordshire and Huntingdonshire Naturalists' Trust has preserved Pingle Wood cutting as a nature reserve and the area is becoming, amongst others, a habitat for the common spotted orchid. Beyond overbridge No. 2310 the former station master's house at Warboys has been demolished but beneath the brambles and undergrowth and infill of roadworks debris the western end of the platforms still stand guardian to the empty trackbed where a road has bisected the route. The goods shed and office are now the property of the London Brick Co., which has taken over the former railway yard west of the station. The Railway Hotel survives as a private house.

From Warboys to Ramsey much of the former branch has now returned to the plough and extension of existing fields. On the approach to the terminus an underbridge is retained as a connecting access between the two parts of Ramsey Golf Course. At Ramsey East only the goods shed, weighbridge and office remain as reminders of the former branch railway. The single platform station has totally disappeared under the site of a concrete production factory and the goods yard is occupied by a small industrial estate.

Pingle Wood cutting and the path of the former Ramsey East branch, east of the Warboys Road overbridge in August 1983. *Author*

The site of Warboys station from Warboys Road overbridge facing towards Ramsey East in 1983. In the foreground trees and undergrowth cover the site, whilst a road bisects the old trackbed. In the background the former goods shed and yard were used by the London Brick Co.   *Author*

The former Warboys station goods yard and goods shed being used for the storage of bricks and tiles by the London Brick Co. in August 1983.   *Author*

The derelict station buildings at Ramsey East facing towards Somersham after the track had been lifted. *Author's Collection*

The former goods shed at Ramsey East in use as a store by a local firm in August 1983. *Author*

Somersham

Key

co   Coal office
cp   Cattle pen
gdn Garden
gs   Goods shed
lc   Level crossing
ld   Loading dock
lg   Loading gauge
lr   Lamp room
pwh Permanent way hut
rc   Railway cottage
sb   Station building
smh Station master's house
sp   Signal post
wb   Weighbridge
wbo Weighbridge office

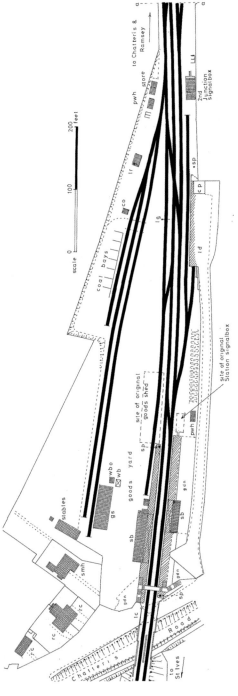

Somersham station from the north in September 1963. The goods yard and second goods shed are to the right whilst the trailing points in the up main line led to the up spur siding.
R. Powell

Chapter Five

The Route Described

Somersham station, 75 miles 73 chains from Liverpool Street via Clapton, and 11 miles 07 chains from Huntingdon East on the GN&GE Joint line was the junction for the branch to Ramsey High Street, later Ramsey East. The track layout at Somersham consisted of up and down main lines serving the platforms, located opposite each other north of the Chatteris Road level crossing and adjacent underpass. The down platform 260 ft in length was host to the main station buildings constructed of timber including ladies' waiting room, general waiting room, station master's office, booking hall and office, gentlemen's toilet and coal store, whilst the up platform, also 260 ft in length, had only a brick building which housed the ladies' and general waiting rooms. A canopy fronting the station buildings was provided on both platforms. A footbridge No. 2302 at 11 miles 06 chains connected the platforms at the south end of the station. Each platform was capable of accommodating four bogie coaches, each 63 ft 6 in. in length. It was possible to run-round eight bogie coaches by using the loop in the goods yard. The main goods yard at Somersham was on the west, or down side of the line, north of the station whilst two sidings, 170 ft and 184 ft in length respectively, on the down side of the railway, south of the Chatteris Road level crossing and immediately north of Colne Road level crossing, served a small granary and coal merchants. The station master's house and garden were located at the back of the goods yard fronting on to the access road to the station. Alongside were three railway cottages.

The main down side yard had four sidings: straight road 550 ft in length serving the original goods shed, middle road 575 ft serving the replacement goods shed, back road 510 ft and the 280 ft coal road which served Coote and Warren's coal and coke depot. The latter siding was originally equipped with coal drops but these were later removed and the siding then served coal bays. Beyond the shunting neck at the north end of the yard were located the 225 ft-long water siding and No. 1 down branch siding, 650 ft in length, which curved parallel alongside the main single branch line. On the opposite side of the branch was the 600 ft-long up branch siding. Immediately north of the up platform, trailing points from the up main line gave access to the up siding 570 ft and the up spur, 200 ft in length, which served a small loading dock.

Originally all points and signals at the station were controlled from Somersham Station signal box, located on the up side of the GN&GE main line at the north end of the up platform. This had a 29-lever frame, with 24 working and five spare levers, later enlarged to 32 levers, all working. When the Ramsey branch was constructed, a signal box called Somersham Junction equipped with a 23-lever frame, with 19 working and four spare levers, later enlarged to a 24-lever frame with 23 working and one spare lever, was installed in the fork between the branch and the main lines and parallel with the up branch siding. This signal box then assumed control of the points and signals at the junction, as well as the outlet points from the down goods yard to the branch. In 1931

The view south from Somersham station footbridge looking towards St Ives on 6th September, 1963. In the foreground is underbridge No. 2301 spanning the underpass alongside Chatteris Road level crossing and beyond that Colne Road level crossing. A wagon on the Whitemoor to Temple Mills freight train has a smoking axlebox.   *R. Powell*

Somersham station facing St Ives with the Chatteris Road level crossing at the end of the platforms.   *Author's Collection*

The down side buildings at Somersham in BR days. The structure was of brick and timber construction with a typical GER style canopy over the platform. *Author*

The up side station buildings at Somersham constructed of brick, with ornate canopy protecting the platform in the 1930s. Note the ornate array of flowers and shrubs in ornate tubs. *Author's Collection*

Somersham Junction

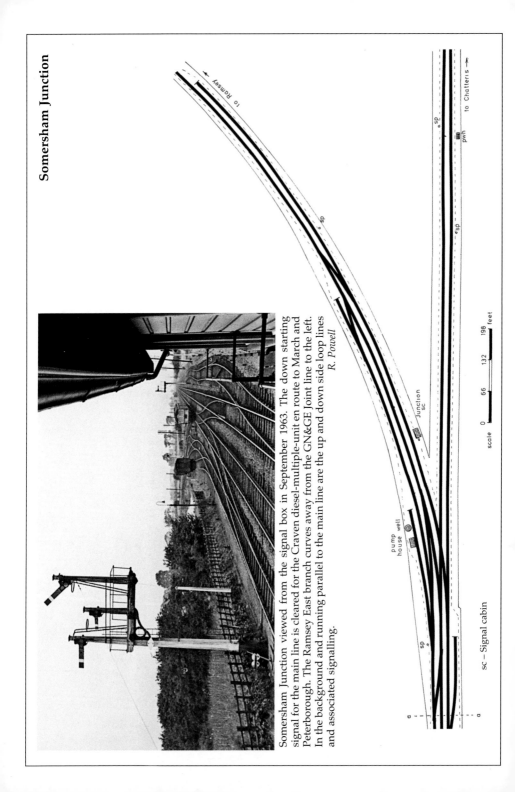

Somersham Junction viewed from the signal box in September 1963. The down starting signal for the main line is cleared for the Craven diesel-multiple-unit en route to March and Peterborough. The Ramsey East branch curves away from the GN&GE Joint line to the left. In the background and running parallel to the main line are the up and down side loop lines and associated signalling.

R. Powell

to Ramsey

to Chatteris →

Junction
sc

pump
house   well

pwh

sp

sp

sp

sp

a

a

scale

0   66   132   198   feet

sc – Signal cabin

both the Station and Junction signal boxes were abolished and a new Junction signal box, containing a 60-lever frame, with 54 working and six spare levers, later 50 working and 10 spares, was erected on the up side of the main line almost opposite the junction. The new signal box then controlled all points and signals at the station and junction and entry and exit points to the new down and up reception sidings provided in 1931 alongside the main line. These could each accommodate trains of 90 wagons in length including engine and brake van, whilst it was possible for an engine to run round 30 bogie coaches in the up loop and 35 in the down loop, if such movements were required. Both loops were worked under 'no block' regulations.

Leaving Somersham, the Ramsey branch train travelled over the down main line on a level gradient for 14 ½ chains before diverging away to the north-west on a 26 chain radius left-hand curve, passing Somersham Junction signal box and the up branch home signal and Somersham Station up branch distant signal located on the same post on the up side of the up branch siding. The gradient changed from 1 in 1100 rising to 1 in 440 rising as the curve eased to 44 chains left-hand where the single branch line and the parallel up siding bisected Mason's occupational crossing No. 1 at 0 miles 22 chains from Somersham. The Junction down branch starting signal was located on the down side of the line near the quarter-mile post where the curve eased slightly. Here the line passed the site of the old ballast pit used in the early days to supply ballast to the railway.

A closed occupational crossing bisected the branch at 0 miles 32 chains as the gradient changed from 1 in 440 rising to 1 in 880 falling for the next half mile. The GN&GE Joint Committee sold a considerable area of excess land on either side of the railway in this locality to Arthur Proud on 5th November, 1890. Park Hall Farm overbridge No. 2305 at 0 miles 39 chains spanned the railway near the half-mile post as the line followed a straight course across the open expanse of Pidley Fen. Midway between the ½ and ¾ mile posts the line passed Somersham Junction up fixed distant located on the up side of the line.

At 0 miles 70 chains from Somersham the falling 1 in 880 gradient accentuated to 1 in 396 and a few yards beyond, Lawter's footpath crossing No. 2 bisected the railway. The straight formation of the single branch continued across the rich alluvial fens bisecting Meadow's occupation crossing No. 3 at 1 mile 06 chains from Somersham. Two chains beyond the 1¼ mile post the points of Bateman's siding, later known as Owen's siding, led to Pidley Brickworks. The GN&GE Joint Committee installed the siding for the use of Alfred James Bateman, who had established the brickworks around the turn of the century, in April 1900. An agreement signed between Bateman and the railway company on 23rd June, 1900 was terminated in 1914, being subsequently transferred on 5th February, 1919 to the First Garden City Co. Ltd for the conveyance of bricks to Letchworth. On 17th November the following year an endorsed agreement was made with Joseph Fenwick Owen who had taken over the company. A supplemental agreement was then made between the LNER and Mrs Frances E. Owen on 29th November, 1927, but on 27th March the following year the brickworks became the property of the London Brick Co. and Forder's Ltd.

The points and associated signalling for the siding was operated from a five-lever ground frame located in a 9 ft by 9 ft wooden hut on the up side of the line.

Somersham Junction facing north in 1911 with the down and up GN&GE Joint main lines to and from March to the right and the Ramsey High Street branch curving away to the left. In the foreground is the water tank mounted above the brick-built tank house and beyond that on the up side of the line Somersham Junction signal box which controlled all points and signals at the junction. It was provided for the opening of the branch. As a result of modernization and rationalization both Somersham Junction signal box and Somersham Station signal box were abolished in 1931 and replaced by a new structure containing a 60-lever Westinghouse A2 frame, which controlled all points and signals at the station. *GERS/Windwood 1508*

Somersham Junction viewed from Somersham Junction signal box in 1911 with the up and down GN&GE Joint St Ives to March main lines to the left, the up and down Ramsey High Street branch lines in the centre and the branch down reception line to the right. The water tank, used to replenish branch locomotives between journeys to and from Ramsey as well as goods locomotives shunting traffic in the goods yard was served by the 225 ft-long water siding. The tall Somersham Junction splitting home signals stands gaunt against the misty skyline, the taller arm for the main line and lower arm for the Ramsey High Street branch. *GERS/Windwood 1507*

The ground frame was released by Annett's key attached to the Somersham to Warboys single line Train Staff. When there were two guards in charge of a train working the siding, the head guard was responsible for working the ground frame and checking that all trucks were placed inside the catch points. He was also responsible for checking that the points were replaced correctly for the main single line before handing the Train Staff back to the driver. The key to the locking frame hut had to be obtained initially from the Somersham station master and returned to that official when the train arrived back at the station. The siding came under the supervision of the station master at Somersham and could only be worked by a train travelling in the up direction. The railway company owned 3½ chains of siding from the tongue of the points whilst a 145 ft shunting neck was also provided on railway land. The single siding which curved away almost at right angles from the main line to terminate at a loading dock in the brickworks was 790 ft in length, of which 594 ft was on the brick company's land. In July 1891, prior to the erection of the brickworks, the GN&GE Joint Committee sold a portion of excess land to the Masters, Fellows and Scholars of St John's College, Cambridge. In Joint line days and when under LNER control it was permissible for a train not exceeding 20 wagons to be propelled between Somersham and the brickworks siding.

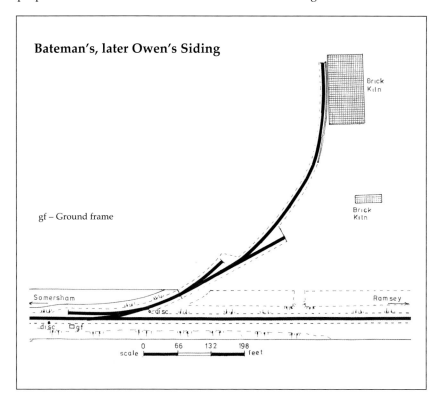

Bateman's, later Owen's Siding

Brick Kiln

Brick Kiln

gf – Ground frame

Somersham

Ramsey

disc   gf

0   66   132   198
scale   feet

Beyond Bateman's or Owen's siding the branch continued its straight course over Forder's/London Brick Co. dual occupational crossings Nos. 4 and 5. At the 1½ mile post the gradient levelled out for almost a quarter of a mile, passing Pidley-cum-Fenton down distant signal located on the west side of the line. Pickwood's occupational crossings Nos. 6 and 7 crossed the line at 1 mile 52½ chains and a few yards beyond the gradient descended at 1 in 396 across Carter's occupational crossings Nos. 8 and 9 and the flat fenland towards the first intermediate public siding at Pidley-cum-Fenton. On the approach to the siding the gradient eased from 1 in 396 falling to level track past Pidley down home signal, located on the down side of the line, and standing as a sentinel in advance of Pidley Drove public level crossing No. 10. Immediately beyond the crossing on the up side of the main single line was Pidley-cum-Fenton public siding at 2 miles 20 chains from Somersham, provided as a railhead for farmers in the scattered communities of Pidley, Fenton and Church End. The strange title of Pidley was derived from the name of the relatively unknown Saxon called Pidda, who cleared the area and built the village, which was some two miles south of the railway. Fenton, a hamlet within the parish of Pidley consisted of four cottages and a large house.

Access to the 860 ft-long single siding from the main single line was by facing connection for down trains and because of this, all shunting was performed by the up goods services. This siding was divided into 400 ft siding and 460 ft headshunt. Facilities at the siding included a loading dock and loading gauge. The points and signals were initially controlled from the small signal box containing a 9-lever frame, later enlarged to 10 levers, located on the down side of the line adjacent to the level crossing, the train being protected by fixed signals. When the signal box was later removed, the points were controlled from a ground frame, released by Annett's key attached to the Somersham-Warboys single line Train Staff. When shunting was completed at the siding, the foreman, later porter-in-charge was responsible for checking that trucks were placed inside the catch points and that the points were locked for the main single line, before handing the Train Staff back to the driver. After the points were converted to ground frame operation the signal box structure was declared redundant and was subsequently transferred in 1922 to perform the function of a waiting room at Mill Road Halt on the Elsenham to Thaxted Light Railway. At Pidley a small brick-built cottage was also provided near the crossing on the west side of the railway as accommodation for the foreman, later porter-in-charge. From 1931 a crossing keeper lived here. In LNER days after the withdrawal of passenger services, goods trains had to be brought to a stand well clear of the gates of the level

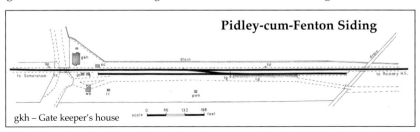

Pidley-cum-Fenton Siding

gkh – Gate keeper's house

crossing to allow trainmen to open the gates before the train passed over the crossing and again to allow the gates to be closed across the line. The siding was under the supervision of the Warboys station master.

Leaving Pidley siding, the straight course of the branch continued with the level gradient changing to 1 in 198 rising to the 2½ mile post. A short level section took the branch over Ashcroft occupational crossing No. 13 and past Pidley up distant signal located on the up side of the line. The line then climbed at 1 in 398 as the railway negotiated Heading occupational crossing No. 14 and the adjacent brick, timber and iron girder underbridge No. 2307 at 2 miles 63 chains, which carried the line over Fenton Lode or Twenty Foot Drain. Beyond the bridge the gradient stiffened to 1 in 284 as the branch cut a swathe across Warboys Heath and on towards the Fen Island known locally as Fox Hole Hills. At 3 miles 29 chains from Somersham, the railway crossed the Chatteris to Warboys road, later A141, at Heath Drove level crossing No. 17 with its adjacent crossing keeper's cottage on the up side of the line. From the crossing the straight course of the line gave way to a 45 chains radius right-hand curve with the railway climbing at 1 in 132 to gain the 50 ft contour above sea level. On the approach to Longland's occupational crossing No. 18 the gradient eased to 1 in 330 passing Wood Farm to the south of the railway and Warboys down distant signal on the down side of the line. The single branch line then altered in character as it negotiated Longland's three-arch occupational overbridge No. 2309 at 3 miles 59 chains, just beyond the entrance to Pingle Wood cutting where the railway bisected the Fox Hole Hills. Midway through the cutting the summit of the Ramsey East branch was reached as the 1 in 330 rising gradient gave way to a short level section before descending initially at 1 in 198 and then 1 in 100 past the 4 mile post and Warboys down home signal. Beyond the signal the line levelled out and passed under Warboys Road three-arch bridge No. 2310 at 4 miles 13 chains to enter Warboys station, 4 miles 31 chains from Somersham.

The station served the village, originally called Wardebusc, meaning Look Out Wood, which was located on a ridge overlooking the fens to the north and the east. By 1150 the busc had become the French bois and then the logical transformation to Wardebois and finally Warboys. The older part of the village was consolidated round the church and a mile from the station, its most notable claim to fame being the strange case of the 'Witches of Warboys', when three innocent people were put to death in 1593 on a falsified charge of witchcraft. The ramifications remained in the famous Witches sermon preached each Lady Day in All Saint's Church, Huntingdon until 1814.

The track layout at the intermediate station consisted of a crossing loop, 580 ft in length, serving both up and down side platforms. At the west end of the up loop a single trailing connection 3¾ chains in length, crossed the down loop and entered through a gate on the railway boundary fence to Warboys Brickworks siding. In the brickworks a 1½ chain connecting line from the boundary fence led to a 660 ft-long siding with a short 175 ft siding serving a loading dock at the south end of the works. Alfred Fuller established the Warboys Brickworks Company and the siding opened in 1894, but by July 1923 the undertaking was taken over by B.J. Forder & Sons Ltd and later on 31st December, 1923 by the London Brick Co. and Forder's Ltd.

Warboys station and crossing loop, 4 miles 31 chains from Somersham, view facing towards Ramsey East. On the left are the tall chimneys of the brickworks, opened by Alfred Fuller, the R&SJR Chairman, with its siding connection from the up loop line. The goods yard and goods shed are to the right with the station master's house in the foreground.

Author's Collection

Warboys

kiln

kilns & sheds

kiln

Brickworks milling shed

kiln

engine house

d r a i n

to Ramsey

p w h

fixed crane in gs

gs

gs

wb

cd

sp

rc

office

sp

sp

sp

mp. 2310

ob

to Somersham

scale

0   66   132   198 feet

cd – Cattle dock
ob – Over bridge
os – Oil store

Warboys station facing Somersham in the early 1950s. Only the down side platform was provided with buildings, so that passengers waiting for up services for Somersham, St Ives and beyond were forced to brave the elements when joining their train in inclement weather.

Stations UK

Warboys station facing towards Somersham. Beyond the tree are Warboys Road overbridge No. 2310 at the end of the platforms, then Pingle Wood cutting and in the far distance Longlands overbridge No. 2309. *Author's Collection*

Warboys station facing Ramsey East in the 1950s. The station buildings are on the down platform, whilst the station master's house is behind the tree to the right. The goods shed and goods yard are beyond the up side platform, which like the down side is heavily overgrown.
Author's Collection

Warboys station facing Ramsey East from the up side platform in 1963. Wagons are stored on the main single line beyond the station, whilst the brickworks are to the left.   *R. Powell*

Warboys down side platform with the small station buildings of similar design to those at Ramsey East. These housed the booking office and waiting rooms.　　　*J. Watling*

Another trailing connection at the west end of the up loop at Warboys gave access to the goods yard on the up side of the single branch line. The yard was served by four sidings, new road 570 ft in length, coal road 422 ft in length leading to the dock road 290 ft, which served the loading dock, and the loop shed road 400 ft in length, serving the small goods shed with capacity for the storage of 80 quarters of grain. At the east end of the shed road was the 224 ft cattle road, serving the cattle dock.

The down side platform at Warboys, 320 ft in length, was host to the main station buildings, including booking office, general waiting room, ladies' waiting room and staff room, and a separate lamp room. The up side platform of the same length was devoid of buildings. Both platforms were capable of accommodating a train of three bogie passenger coaches. Points and signals at the station were controlled from the Station signal box, initially containing a 16-lever frame, with 14 working and two spare levers, later enlarged to 17 levers, all working, located on the west side of the line at the west end of the down platform. The station master's house stood behind the up side platform with its garden backing on to the goods yard. Situated across the road from the station was the Railway Hotel, opened at the same time as the railway.

From Warboys the single branch again followed a straight course descending at 1 in 132 to the alluvial plain as the railway skirted the southern edge of Wistow Fen, with Warboys Wood a quarter of a mile away to the south of the railway. Soon after the 4½ mile post the gradient eased to 1 in 264 falling, as the private road owned by the GN&GE Joint Committee connecting Hodgson's occupational level crossing No. 20 ran parallel on the north side of the line. The straight course of the railway continued as the branch bisected Wistow Drove level crossing No. 22 at 5 miles 04 chains, with its adjacent crossing keeper's cottage on the up side and east of the road. Beyond the crossing the gradient levelled out as the line negotiated Bury Lug Fen on a shallow embankment. Shore occupational crossing No. 23 bisected the railway near the 5¼ mile post and at 5 miles 22 chains the branch was carried over Boundary Drain by girder bridge No. 2311.

Former weighbridge office in Warboys goods yard in 1983.   *Author*

The Ramsey High Street branch approach to Somersham Junction viewed from the Somersham Junction signal box in 1911 with the main down branch line in the centre, the down branch goods loop to the left and up branch line on the right. The Somersham Junction up branch home signal is located on the same post as the Somersham Station branch distant signal. Beyond the signal is Mason's occupational level crossing No. 1 at 0 miles 22 chains from Somersham.

GERS/Windwood 1506

With views of the village of Bury away to the south, the bridge heralded a change of gradient from level to 1 in 390 rising for almost a quarter of a mile. A short climb at 1 in 198 then took the railway across the Bury to Bury Fen secondary road at Jack's Corner level crossing, No. 24 at 5 miles 38 chains, before passing Ramsey distant signal on the down side of the line. Just beyond the 6 mile post a short siding, 215 ft in length was installed in the late 1920s on the up side of the line for the use of W. Cordell and others. The siding was purely for agricultural traffic with a facing connection from the main single line in the down direction. By agreement dated 12th June, 1931, the siding sited entirely on railway property, was maintained by the railway company at the expense of the trader. The line levelled out on the approach to Ramsey as the branch negotiated a 44 chain radius right-hand curve over a two-arch bridge No. 2312 across Bury stream, at 6 miles 36 chains, before passing Ramsey up advance starting signal located on the up side of the line. The down home signal on the west side of the branch heralded the approach to the terminus. The curve continued as a facing connection on the up side led to the goods yard whilst on the down side a 330 ft siding with trailing connection from the main single line led to the engine shed, which was large enough to accommodate one tender or tank locomotive. Adjacent to the shed was the coal stage and water crane.

The main single line continued past the signal box located on the down side of the line, to terminate at buffer stops 6 miles 75 chains from Somersham and just short of the Bury Road. A cattle dock stood on the down side of the line adjacent to the buffer stops served by a 106 ft-long siding. On the up side of the main single line the 410 ft-long run-round loop, later extended in 1907 to 594 feet, served the single platform, 330 ft in length at Ramsey High Street station.

Ramsey East station viewed from the buffer stops. The buildings are typical of those provided at minor stations on the Great Northern & Great Eastern Joint line. A rake of covered vans occupies the run-round loop.   *Stations UK*

Ramsey High Street

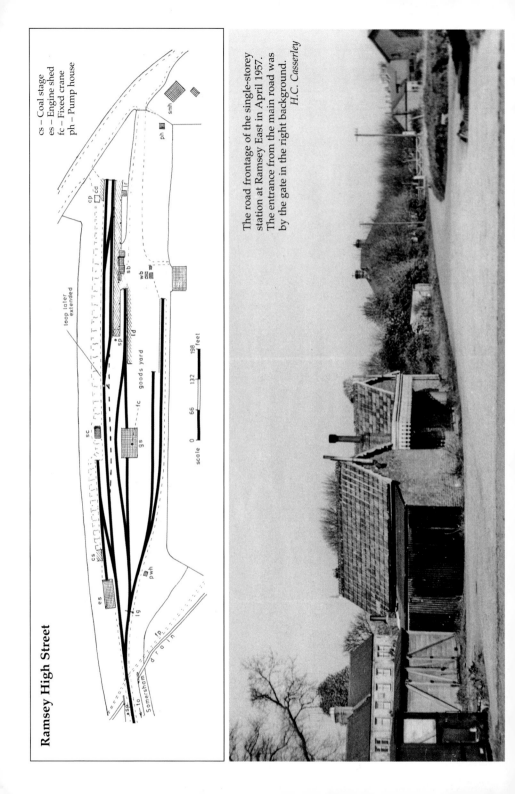

cs – Coal stage
es – Engine shed
fc – Fixed crane
ph – Pump house

loop later
extended

snh

ph

cp

cd

fr

sb

wb

ld

sp

sc

goods yard

fc

gs

cs

es

lo

pwh

lg

asp

drain

fp

Somersham

scale   0   66   132   198   feet

The road frontage of the single-storey
station at Ramsey East in April 1957.
The entrance from the main road was
by the gate in the right background.
H.C. Casserley

The platform, capable of accommodating a train of three bogie coaches, was host to a small squat building containing booking office, general waiting room, ladies' waiting room and toilet, gentlemen's toilet and staff accommodation. A newspaper account at the time of opening of the line described this quite inappropriately as having an 'imposing frontage'. A separate small structure at the west end of the platform accommodated the lamp room and oil store. Six posts with oil lamps provided platform illumination at Ramsey High Street, with two hanging oil lamps under the canopy. An engine could run-round a train of 11 bogie coaches in the extended run-round loop, if required.

Goods yard facilities included three sidings, the shed road 290 ft serving the goods shed, which had storage accommodation for 200 quarters of grain. A run-round loop, 460 ft in length, enabled locomotives using this siding to run-round wagons and this led to the 160 ft dock road. The other sidings, separated from the shed road by an access road, were the coal road and back road, 420 ft and 580 ft-long respectively. Facilities in the goods yard included a loading gauge, a 2 tons capacity fixed crane in the goods shed and a public weighbridge.

Points and signals at Ramsey High Street were controlled from the signal box located on the down side of the line opposite the goods shed and containing a 24-lever frame, initially with 21 working and three spare levers, later amended to 17 working and seven spare levers. The station master's house and garden were located on the main road adjacent to the entrance gates to the station.

The speed limit of trains on the Ramsey High Street branch was limited to 30 mph, with 10 mph on the curve at Somersham and when entering or leaving the loop at Warboys. Gradient posts were located on the up or east side of the single branch line, whilst mileage posts were sited on the down side of the line.

Ramsey East station facing the buffer stops in 1957, after the withdrawal of the goods service beyond Warboys. Before the track was lifted the former run-round loop was used for storing condemned wagons awaiting scrapping. *H.C. Casserley*

Chapter Six

Permanent Way, Signalling and Staff

Permanent Way

The initial permanent way on the Ramsey & Somersham Junction Railway was formed of steel bullhead rails weighing 70 lb. per yard, in 30 ft lengths and laid in cast-iron chairs weighing 41 lb. each. The rails were joined by wrought-iron fishplates weighing 42½ lb. per pair using four 7½ inch bolts to each pair of plates. The chairs were fixed to creosoted pine sleepers measuring 8 ft 11 in. in length by 10 in. by 5 in., using two oak trenails and two wrought-iron spikes to each chair. Eleven sleepers were placed under each section of rail and these were laid on a ballast of gravel, laid one foot in depth below the underside of the sleepers.

John Mowlem & Co., the contractors were responsible for the maintenance of the permanent way for a year after the opening of the line to traffic. During this period and for the first year of GER maintenance few improvements were made. In 1892, however, 85 lb. and 87 lb. per yard bullhead rails in 30 ft lengths were found more suitable and replaced the original track. Just before the turn of the century some second-hand 87 lb. per yard rail in 45 ft lengths was installed near Somersham.

From 1923 the LNER began replacing the 30 ft rails with lengths of 45 ft and by the mid-1930s second-hand rails originally weighing 90 and 95 lb. per yard in 45 ft lengths became standard, although a short section of 30 ft, 90 lb. per yard rail was located near Ramsey East station. Most of the sidings retained 30 ft lengths of rail. After World War II few alterations were made except that sections of second-hand British Standard 90 to 97 lb. per yard bullhead rails replaced worn-out track between Somersham and Warboys.

The original gravel ballast laid one foot in depth below the sleepers was supplied from a seam of suitable material found near Somersham station in land purchased from George Wilson. This was initially adequate for the light traffic conveyed across the branch but within two years the GER introduced ashes and clinker. The GER found ashes were ideal for the ballasting of many of their branch lines and supplies were readily available from the motive power depots on the system. Ashes and clinker were also found suitable for infilling on the sections of line which crossed fenland where track was susceptible to slight subsidence during exceptionally dry weather when the peat and silt formation tended to dry out. Once wet weather returned the formation usually returned to its normal state. When supplies of ashes were not available from locomotive sheds, wagon loads were obtained from Tate & Lyle's sugar refinery at Silvertown and after 1925 from the British Sugar Corporation factories at Wissington, Ely and Peterborough.

From 1890 the maintenance of the permanent way was covered by the GER permanent way gang based at Somersham, with a ganger and sub-ganger based at Warboys and Ramsey High Street. After the takeover of the branch in 1897 by the GN&GE Joint Committee, the GER Civil Engineer assumed responsibility for the maintenance of the permanent way, bridges and fencing on a contract basis, and was required to report on the condition of the branch to the Committee every three months. Around the turn of the century the Somersham permanent way gang took over complete maintenance and retained this authority until the early 1950s when rationalization brought the line under the control of the permanent way gang based at St Ives.

Long serving permanent way staff included G.W. Shipp, a platelayer at Bishop's Stortford who was appointed ganger at Warboys in 1894. He retired from branch duties in 1931 after serving 35 years on the line. William Mace, ganger at Somersham retired on 20th February, 1939 at the age of 65. He started his career at Chatteris in 1892 before serving at Ramsey High Street and Warboys. Station master A.W. Cook presented Mace with pipes, a tobacco pouch and tobacco on behalf of his colleagues. C.C. Cox, sub ganger at Warboys retired on 19th July, 1940. The district engineer Cambridge was responsible for maintenance of the branch with the district permanent way inspector for No. 3 district for day-to-day affairs.

In addition to tending to day-to-day maintenance, the permanent way gang was responsible for cleaning toilets where no mains sewerage existed as well as the maintenance of fencing and gates. On hot and dry sunny days they also patrolled the line acting as beaters to extinguish small fires caused by stray sparks from passing locomotives damaging crops in lineside fields.

Signalling

When Major Marindin initially inspected the Ramsey & Somersham Junction Railway on 12th September, 1888 he noted the following equipment was installed in the signal boxes:

Ramsey	24 lever frame, 21 working and 3 spare levers.
Warboys	16 lever frame, 14 working and 2 spare levers.
Pidley Siding	9 lever frame, all 9 working.
Somersham Junction	23 lever frame, 19 working and 4 spare levers.

The installations were far from satisfactory and the inspector required No. 11 facing points at Ramsey to be taken out. He also stipulated No. 7 gate lock at Pidley siding be connected up, whilst at Somersham Junction, signal levers Nos. 15 and 22 were to be interlocked. Although the inspector initially received no notification of the future mode of working the single line, the Train Staff and Ticket system was adopted in conjunction with Tyers 2-way block instruments at all signal boxes with Staff stations at Somersham Junction, Warboys and Ramsey High Street. The Train Staff utilized on the Somersham Junction to Warboys section was round in shape and coloured green whilst the Warboys to Ramsey High Street Staff was square and yellow in colour. The paper tickets for the respective sections corresponded to the colour of the Train Staff.

The original Somersham Station signal box dating from 1882 was 11 ft 0 in. wide by 24 ft in length with the operating floor 7 ft 6 in. above rail level. It was

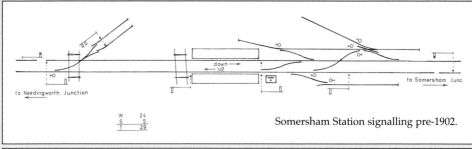

Somersham Station signalling pre-1902.

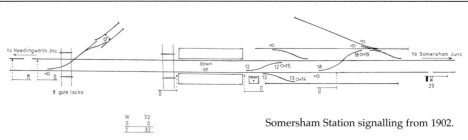

Somersham Station signalling from 1902.

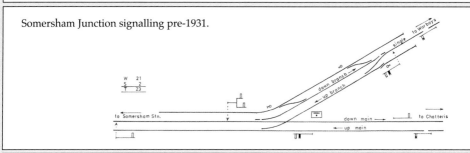

Somersham Junction signalling pre-1931.

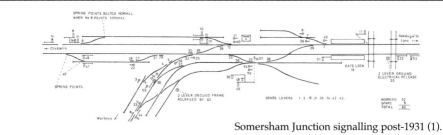

Somersham Junction signalling post-1931 (1).

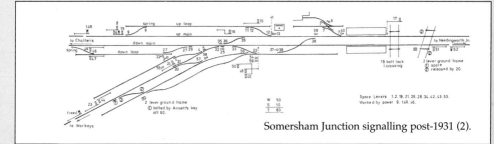

Somersham Junction signalling post-1931 (2).

The 60-lever Westinghouse A2 frame in Somersham Junction signal box on 6th September, 1963.

R. Powell

Signalman's diagram in Somersham Junction signal box, September 1963.   *R. Powell*

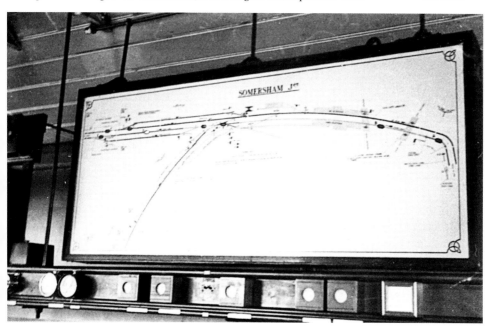

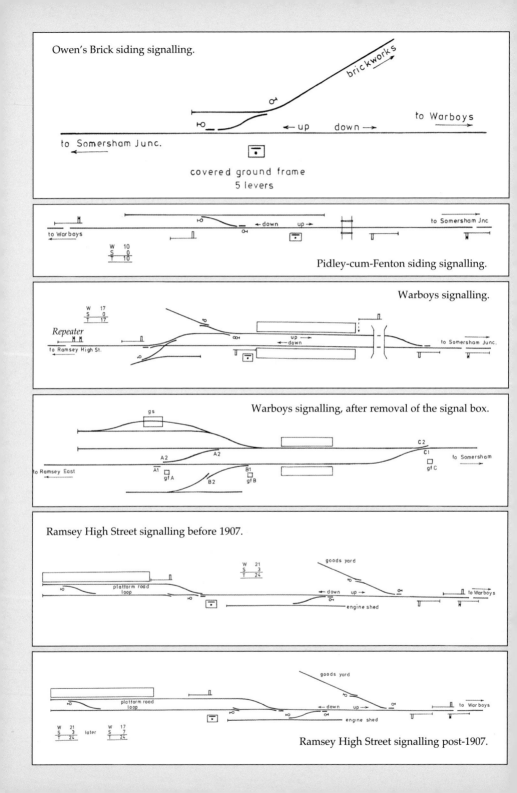

Owen's Brick siding signalling.

brickworks

← up   down →

to Warboys

to Somersham Junc.

covered ground frame
5 levers

to Warboys

← down   up →

to Somersham Jnc

W   10
S   0
T   10

Pidley-cum-Fenton siding signalling.

Warboys signalling.

W   17
S   0
T   17

Repeater

to Ramsey High St.

up →
← down

to Somersham Junc.

Warboys signalling, after removal of the signal box.

gs

to Ramsey East

A2

A2

A1

gf A

B1

B2

gf B

C2

C1

gf C

to Somersham

Ramsey High Street signalling before 1907.

goods yard

platform road
loop

W   21
S   3
T   24

← down   up →

engine shed

to Warboys

goods yard

platform road
loop

← down   up →

engine shed

to Warboys

W   21
S   3
T   24

later

W   17
S   7
T   24

Ramsey High Street signalling post-1907.

equipped with a Stevens 29-lever frame, with 24 working and five spare levers, later enlarged to a 32-lever frame with all levers working. At Somersham Junction the signal box was situated in the fork of the junction and was 11 ft 6 in. wide by 17 ft in length. The operating floor was 9 ft 6 in. above rail level and at Grouping it was equipped with a 23-lever Saxby & Farmer catch handle frame with 19 working and four spare levers, then amended to 21 working and two spare levers in 1889, and later enlarged to a 24-lever frame with 23 working and one spare lever.

Along the branch Pidley-cum-Fenton public siding was served by a small signal box containing a 9-lever McKenzie & Holland Tappett frame with 4 in. centres, all working. After World War I this was enlarged to 10 levers with all levers working but just before the Grouping a ground frame replaced the signal box, with the levers released by Annett's key on the Somersham - Warboys Train Staff. At Warboys the signal box was 11 ft 6 in. wide by 15 ft in length with the operating floor 7 ft 6 in. above rail level. The box was initially equipped with a 16-lever Saxby & Farmer 5 in. frame with 14 working and two spare levers but with the opening of the brickworks sidings it was enlarged to 17 levers, with all levers working. Ramsey High Street signal box was 11 ft 6 in. in width, 18 ft in length with the operating floor 6 ft 9 in. above rail level. Like Warboys it was equipped with a Saxby & Farmer 5 inch centred frame of 24 levers, originally with 21 working and three spare levers, which by Grouping had become 17 working and seven spare levers.

Initially Somersham Station signal box was closed after the last booked train was 'out of section' until half an hour before the first booked branch train the following morning. On Saturday nights the signal box was closed after 'train out of section' for the last booked train until 10.00am on Sunday morning. Somersham Junction signal box was closed after the 'train out of section' call was received from either Pidley-cum-Fenton or Warboys signal box for the last booked train at night, until half an hour before the first booked train was due to pass the next morning. On Saturday nights the same arrangement applied but the signal box then remained closed all Sunday and only reopened half an hour before the first train was due to pass on Monday morning. Warboys and Ramsey High Street signal boxes were closed at night and on Sundays.

GREAT NORTHERN & GREAT EASTERN JOINT LINE

STATIONS AND SIGNAL BOXES.		Miles. (Distance from Signal Box next above.)	Chains.	Down.	Up.	REFUGE SIDINGS.	OPENING AND CLOSING.
Stations.	Signal Boxes.						
Somersham	Station	..	...	...	...		See below.
,,	Junction..................	..	18	...	...		,, ,,
Warboys	Station	4	12	...	...		Closed at Night, and on Sundays.
Ramsey (High St.)	,, ...	1	36	...	...		,, ,, ,,

Opening and closing of signal boxes from GER Appendix 1910.

By 1919 Somersham Station signal box was open continuously from 5.30 am on Monday until 7.00 am the following Sunday or after the passing of the last special train. On Sunday the signal box was reopened for the running of trains from 4.15 pm until the last passenger train was signalled 'out of section'. Somersham Junction, Warboys and Ramsey High Street signal boxes were open for the running of branch trains shown in the working timetable and for trains specially advised. In 1924 Somersham Station signal box was open continuously whilst Somersham Junction signal box, 18 chains from the Station signal box was open from 6.05 am Mondays-only (MO) and 5.50am Saturdays-only (SO) until 'train out of section' for the 6.10 pm train ex-Somersham. On Tuesdays to Fridays the signal box opened at 5.50 am until the 'train out of section' call was received for the 6.25 am goods ex-Cambridge and the 11.18 am passenger train from Somersham. It then closed and was reopened at 2.58 pm until the 'train out of section' call was received for the 6.10 pm train from Somersham. Warboys and Ramsey East signal boxes were open for the running of trains shown in the working timetable and for those specially advised. As the latter signal box was then operated by a porter/signalman, the signal box phone circuit was later transferred to the station building.

After the withdrawal of passenger services from the branch, drastic alterations were made to the signalling. Somersham Station and Somersham Junction signal boxes were abolished in connection with the installation of new independent up and down loop lines on the St Ives to March section of the Joint line, and replaced by a new Somersham Junction signal box with a 60-lever Westinghouse A2 frame on 1st November, 1931. This box with 54 working and six spare levers, later amended to 52 working and 8 spares and then 50 working and 10 spare levers, controlled all points and signals at the junction and the station and was located on the up side of the main line opposite the junction at 11 miles 18 chains from Huntingdon. Ramsey East signal box and Pidley-cum-Fenton ground frame were closed on 30th September, 1932, whilst Warboys signal box was abolished on 4th May, 1936. The points leading to and from the sidings were then released and locked by Annett's key attached to the Train Staff. With the abolition of the signal boxes the Train Staff & Ticket method of working was replaced by 'One Engine in Steam', using the Train Staff only with Telephone Block.

In 1939 the Junction signal box was open continuously from 4.00am on Monday until 'train out of section' was received on the following Sunday for the last down freight train (or as ordered by Cambridge Control office) and for the passage of the 6.35 pm train ex-Peterborough North. Ten years later the signal box was open continuously from 12.15 am on Mondays until 'train out of section' was received for the last down freight train the following Sunday morning and then on Sundays for trains shown in the working timetable or those specially advised. After nationalization, in 1961 the signal box was open from 5.00 am on Mondays until after the passage of the last train on the following Sunday morning, then from 9.00 to 11.00 am and 4.00 to 11.00 pm on Sundays. Somersham Junction signal box was finally closed on 28th May, 1967.

Around the turn of the century modifications were made to the distant signals on the branch. At that time the GER distant signal arms were painted the same red as stop signals and showed the same red and green aspects to drivers at night. To avoid confusion with the home and starting signals the distant signals were fitted with a Coligny Welch lamp which showed an additional white > at night. In common with GER practice each wooden signal arm was stamped on the reverse with the name of the controlling signal box. With the coming of the LNER the distant signals were gradually repainted the familiar yellow with the black > and the Coligny Welch lamps removed or modified to serve as ordinary lamps. After closure of the line to passenger traffic and abolition of the signal boxes only Pidley, Warboys and Ramsey East distant signals remained as marker signals, unlit and with arms fixed at caution. At Somersham the lower quadrant wooden arms were replaced by LNER or BR upper quadrant arms on the same posts, although where some of the wooden posts were found to be rotting they were replaced by posts of tubular steel.

The maintenance of the signalling equipment on the branch was for many years the responsibility of the signal fitters at St Ives, an out base of the Cambridge district.

Station Masters

When the R&SJR opened to traffic the staff appointed to the line were already on the establishment of the GER but additional manpower was soon recruited locally. The station masters appointed to Ramsey High Street and Warboys in 1889 were fortunate in having houses provided adjacent to the station whilst their associate at Somersham was provided with a new house.

On the opening of the branch, the GER promoted Francis B. Perry, station master at Earith Bridge on the Ely to St Ives line to the new post of station master at Ramsey High Street. The new appointee at Warboys was A.F. Evans whilst Alfred Whiteman remained in charge at Somersham having been appointed to the junction in 1881. By 1896 Evans had moved from Warboys, his place being taken by George Ivett Marritt. Whiteman had previously been station master at Shelford on the Liverpool Street to Cambridge main line and was promoted to Somersham in 1881. He remained at the junction station until early 1899 when he was promoted to Whittlesea. William Linton, station master at Branston and Heighington on the GN&GE Joint line was appointed to the vacant position at Somersham in January 1899. His term of office at the junction was short, however, for he gained promotion to Chatteris in October 1901 and was replaced by Alfred Marjason. Francis Perry later moved from Ramsey High Street and was replaced by Arthur Thornton Fisher. Similarly at Warboys, when Marritt was promoted to Gosberton in 1905 he was succeeded by Frederick William Colam. His stay was short and in July 1907 James Henry Longmore Davies assumed charge of Warboys station. He resided in the station house and in 1914 paid an annual rent of £17, increased to £18 the following year. As a result of rationalization on the branch early in April 1922, the booking and goods offices were closed with the introduction of conductor-guard operation, and the goods accounts were handled at Somersham. The branch station master's posts were withdrawn.

The economies made by the introduction of conductor-guard working resulted in some of branch staff transferring away to other stations. In the upheaval J.H.L. Davies, station master at Warboys was transferred to Burwell on the Cambridge to Mildenhall branch in July 1922 whilst his counterpart at Ramsey High Street, A.T. Fisher, made the short move to Godmanchester on the Huntingdon to St Ives line, and then on to Ware on the Hertford branch. Davies, who began his railway career as a clerk with the GNR in February 1899, later returned to take charge of Ramsey North station. He later subsequently gained promotion to Market Rasen and retired in December 1929. As a result of these transfers Alfred Marjason, at Somersham took over the administration of the branch. After Grouping in 1923 the LNER for a short period placed the responsibility for both Ramsey North and Ramsey East stations under Herbert E. Cullen, the station master at Ramsey North, whilst Warboys remained under Somersham. At the end of 1924, however, Ramsey East was transferred back to the responsibility of the Somersham station master and the branch remained so until closure. In the meantime Frederick Tebb had replaced Marjason at Somersham but in August 1927 he gained promotion to Cromer. Station master S.A. Watson was promoted from Firsby to replace Tebb in October 1927 and retired from the post on 30th September, 1931. In November 1931 A.W. Weald, a relief clerk from Cambridge, took over as station master. Marjason died on 25th April, 1934 whilst Watson passed away on 20th December, 1945. Weald was later promoted to Chelmsford in April 1935. A.W. Cook, promoted in May 1935 from Drighlington and Adwalton, on the ex-GNR Wakefield to Bradford line, took over at the junction station. In February 1941 Cook gained promotion to take charge of Braintree including Cressing and the following month W. Lungley, station master at Dunmow was transferred to take charge of Somersham and the branch stations. He retired from the post on 30th July, 1949 and was succeeded by G.S.H. Robertson from November 1949 until January 1953; W.W. Lord served from February 1953 until November 1955; G.P. Brown January 1956 until his retirement on 30th July, 1960; R.D. Ellis from August 1960 until December 1963 when G.L. Hlubeck took over. J. Holmes was the last serving station master at Somersham.

Traffic staff

Of the traffic staff, special mention must be made of George Willimont who started his railway career in 1882 and served as signalman at Takeley on the Bishop's Stortford to Braintree branch before transferring to Ramsey High Street where he served as signalman for another 32 years. To his credit he was the twenty-third person to join the membership of the GER Pension Fund. Frederick Pendle was porter/signalman for many years at Ramsey High Street together with George Harwood who was porter at the terminus. W.E. Hawkes, a grade 1 porter at Ramsey East died suddenly on 14th March, 1931, at the relatively young age of 28 years. He had entered the service in December 1916 and had served at the terminus as porter/signalman, district relief porter and then grade 1 porter. One of the guards based at Ramsey High Street, Charles

Blake, died on 23rd November, 1930 shortly after the passenger services ceased. One of the earliest porter/signalmen to serve at Warboys was Sidney Bird, who was appointed to the position in 1892. After a few years he was promoted to signalman at Smeeth Road before moving on to Emneth and finally Kings Dyke where he remained for 37 years before retiring on 5th September, 1936. W G. Manser was porter/signalman at Warboys and when he married in 1912 at Huntingdon, his colleagues presented him with a breadboard and knife. Similarly on 3rd November, 1914, goods porter G. Swannell of Warboys was presented with a table lamp as a wedding present from station master Davies, subscribed by all the branch personnel.

A. Baker, who was appointed clerk at Ramsey High Street in November 1898, was promoted to station master at Guyhirne. A.E. Clarke was senior clerk at Warboys from 1915 until the closure of the booking office in 1922 whilst this station also boasted a woman porter/signalman in the early 1920s. J. Whitsey foreman at Warboys for many years retired on 24th March, 1931.

Mrs Hatcher, the resident crossing keeper at Heath Road crossing was the wife of Jack Hatcher, leading porter at Warboys. Another crossing keeper in the area was J. Hinder, who in 1897 lost a leg in an accident during shunting operations at Whitemoor. The GER management arranged for him to be appointed as crossing keeper and he served at Whittlesea, Heath Road, Warboys and Somersham before retiring from Short's Drove crossing, Somersham on 12th October, 1928 after 46 years' service. A. Hindes was another crossing keeper at Heath Drove.

John Whitsey served for almost a quarter of a century at Pidley-cum-Fenton siding, initially transferring from Postland in 1907 before retiring on 28th July, 1931 after 38 years' service. He lived in the cottage by the crossing rent-free, in return for operating the gates.

Long-serving members of staff at Somersham included clerk E. Grice and signalman J.E. Robinson, who retired on 18th August, 1940. Another porter Harold Robinson joined the GER at Somersham as a gate lad on 19th March, 1917 before being promoted to a porter's position. He subsequently died at the age of 45 on 23rd December, 1945. In 1914 three station staff living in the station cottages were G. Smith and W. Manser who paid an annual rent of £6 10s. 0d. and F. Marrows who paid £5 4s. 0d. per annum.

The establishment of staff at the branch stations in the halcyon days before the 1922 rationalization was:

Pidley-cum-Fenton	1 goods foreman
Warboys	Station master
	2 booking clerks
	2 porters
	1 porter/signalman
	1 signalman
	1 goods porter

Ramsey High Street	Station master
	2 booking clerks
	2 porters
	1 porter/signalman
	1 signalman
	2 guards (after 1922 conductor-guards)
	1 goods porter
	1 goods clerk

By 1943 the establishment at the branch stations was:

| Somersham | Station master class 2 |

Goods Office	Chief clerk class 4
	1 clerk class 5
	2 female clerks class 5
	1 junior clerk

Passenger Office	1 clerk class 5
	1 junior clerk
	2 porters
	1 checker
	3 signalmen
	1 signalman: rest day relief
	1 relief porter

| Heath Road Level Crossing | 1 female crossing keeper |

| Warboys | 1 leading porter |
| | 1 porter |

| Ramsey East | 1 leading porter |

The subsequent reduction in traffic after World War II brought the following alterations in staff numbers in 1950:

Somersham	Chief clerk class 4
	2 goods clerks class 5
	2 passenger clerks class 5
	1 additional passenger porter in place of checker

| Warboys | 1 leading porter |

Chapter Seven

Timetables and Traffic

The Ramsey High Street branch was a relative latecomer to the Huntingdonshire railway scene. As mentioned earlier, many abortive attempts were made to link Ramsey with the main line railway network, initially as a through route and then after the opening of the Ramsey Railway from Holme by continuing the line through to the GER system. Although Ramsey was a relatively large town for the locality, the area to the east was flat fenland, a landscape broken only by the low fen hills. The failure of the railway from Somersham to connect with the Holme branch at Ramsey virtually sealed the Ramsey High Street branch to a domiciled fate. Ramsey was only 75 miles from King's Cross, with usually only one change of train, at Holme. Via the GN&GE route and thence the GER to Liverpool Street, the traveller had to make at least two changes in the 85-mile journey. The population of the villages served by the branch was small and the surrounding countryside concentrated on arable farming. As most of the population worked on the land, little use was made of the branch for daily travel to work; most journeys tended to be concentrated on Mondays for St Ives market, augmented generally by longer more infrequent journeys to destinations in East Anglia. Brickyards and later sugar beet became the salvation for goods traffic on the branch, but the railway company did little to encourage the growth in the community. It was of no surprise therefore that this seven-mile branch, supporting a service of between four and eight passenger trains on weekdays only, became an early victim of line closures after Grouping. Passenger services were withdrawn after only 41 years, whilst the population of the catchment area served remained almost constant with a total of around 9,000 souls.

Year	1861	1871	1881	1891	1901	1911	1921	1931	1951	1961
Somersham	1,621	1,562	1,409	1,351	1,229	1,404	1,466	1,417	1,317	1,401
Pidley-cum-Fenton	569	587	448	388	363	366	426	555	399	376
Warboys	1,911	1,880	1,676	1,661	17,58	1,790	1,720	1,593	1,909	1,950
Wistow	532	485	391	401	352	370	294	345	353	348
Bury	362	332	349	417	406	416	331	303	1,064	1,165
Ramsey	4,500	4,734	4,617	4,684	4,823	5,328	5,135	5,180	5,770	5,697
Total incl. Somersham	*9,495*	*9,580*	*8,890*	*8,902*	*8,931*	*9,674*	*9,372*	*9,393*	*10,812*	*10,937*
Total excl. Somersham	*7,874*	*8,018*	*7,481*	*7,551*	*7,702*	*8,270*	*7,906*	*7,976*	*9,495*	*9,536*

The initial passenger train service offered by the GER and the R&SJR in September 1889 consisted of seven trains in each direction, Tuesdays to Saturdays with eight each way on Mondays, St Ives market day. No Sunday services were offered.

Down			MO						
		am	am	am	pm	pm	pm	pm	pm
Somersham	dep.	7.17	10.42	11.41	12.36	2.25	3.55	5.01	7.33
Warboys	dep.	7.27	10.52	11.51	12.46	2.35	4.05	5.11	7.43
Ramsey HS	arr.	7.33	10.58	11.57	12.52	2.41	4.11	5.17	7.48

Up			MO						
		am	am	am	pm	pm	pm	pm	pm
Ramsey HS	dep.	8.10	10.00	11.05	12.04	1.51	3.19	4.20	6.54
Warboys	dep.	8.16	10.06	11.11	12.10	1.57	3.25	4.26	7.00
Somersham	arr.	8.26	10.16	11.21	12.20	2.07	3.35	4.36	7.10

MO – Mondays only

The working timetable for 1890 continued to offer a total of eight passenger trains Mondays only and seven passenger trains Mondays excepted, and two goods trains in each direction. The first down goods of the day, 7.15 am ex-Somersham, conveyed traffic for Pidley-cum-Fenton siding through to Warboys, to enable the 8.29 am up goods train ex-Ramsey High Street to take the wagons back to the siding, as the points lay in a trailing connection for up services. The afternoon down goods train, which served the branch line, was a through train from St Ives departing at 2.20 pm. The first and last down passenger services, 10.42 am MO, 11.41 am MX, and 7.33 pm ex-Somersham, were permitted to convey not exceeding four trucks of important goods or cattle. In the up direction the first freight train departed Ramsey High Street at 5.45 am on Mondays only, conveying goods for St Ives market and called at Warboys to attach and detach traffic. On other weekdays this service departed at the later time of 8.29 am and shunted Pidley-cum-Fenton siding as required. The last up passenger train of the day at 6.54 pm was allowed to convey not exceeding four trucks of important goods or cattle.

Prior to the rationalization of operating expenses in March 1895, the GER continued to operate the basic eight passenger trains MO and seven Mondays excepted (MX) in each direction, the additional trains on Mondays running for St Ives market day. Journey times from London to Ramsey varied from 2 hours 42 minutes on the 7.41 pm ex-Somersham due at Ramsey High Street at 7.57 pm, which had a connection off the 5.15 pm from Liverpool Street, whilst passengers catching the 2.30 pm from Liverpool Street took 3 hours 41 minutes to reach the Huntingdonshire town on the 5.55 pm from Somersham. In the up direction passengers fared no better for the 12.04 pm ex-Ramsey High Street offered only a 2 hours 46 minutes service to the capital, with changes to connecting services at Somersham and Cambridge. The slowest journey was on the connection off the 5.23 pm from Ramsey High Street, which arrived at Liverpool Street 3 hours and 2 minutes later.

In contrast to the extensive service offered for the first six years of the branch, the cuts of 1895 almost halved the services and introduced for the first time mixed trains. The working timetable for 1897 showed the much reduced train plan in which four passenger trains and one mixed train ran in each direction on weekdays only. These were supplemented by two goods trains daily, one of which ran through to Ramsey High Street, whilst the other was a short trip working between Somersham and Warboys and return, essentially to clear brick traffic from the recently opened Warboys brickworks. In the down direction the 9.12 am mixed train from Somersham was authorized to attach or detach wagons at Warboys, for which five minutes additional time was allowed. The last down passenger train of the day was a through train from St Ives, departing at 6.23 pm to Ramsey High Street and was permitted to convey cattle from Somersham to the terminus if the trucks were fitted with the Westinghouse brake. Of the two goods workings, the 12.30 pm ex-Somersham was worked by the branch engine and ran to Warboys only calling at Pidley-cum-Fenton siding if required, whilst the second was a through train from Ely departing at 10.45 am and running via Sutton and St Ives, which ultimately arrived at Ramsey High Street at 3.00 pm. This train was permitted to work trucks between Somersham and the terminus if required.

In the up direction the mid-morning passenger train departed at 10.00 am on Mondays to provide connection at Somersham for St Ives market, but ran 65 minutes later on Tuesdays to Saturdays. The return goods working from Warboys to Somersham departed at 1.35 pm and called at Pidley siding to pick up or put down traffic. After arrival at the junction the branch locomotive ran light to St Ives for water and this operation continued until the water tank was provided at Somersham in July 1899. Freight traffic from Ramsey High Street departed on the 4.00 pm goods train, which returned to Ely via St Ives and Sutton, and any residue of traffic not taken by this train was cleared by the 5.27 pm mixed train from Ramsey High Street. The branch locomotive then hauled the empty stock from Somersham to St Ives to form the 6.33 pm down passenger train back to Ramsey.

By 1907 the passenger service provided on the branch totalled seven each way MO and six in each direction MX. One mixed train continued to run each way, whilst the two freight services in each direction ran to and from Ramsey High Street. The first down goods train 7.00 am ex-Somersham called at Pidley-cum-Fenton siding, if required, whilst any additional goods traffic for Ramsey was forwarded attached to the 8.56 am mixed train from Somersham, provided the load did not exceed three trucks. The second down goods train to serve the line continued to run as a through service from Ely departing at 10.30 am via Sutton and St Ives, and was permitted to collect wagons at Somersham for Ramsey only. The last passenger train of the day, the 7.52 pm ex-Somersham, was also allowed to convey cattle provided the trucks were fitted with the Westinghouse brake. Returning visitors to St Ives market also benefited by the provision of the 3.55 pm MO departure from the junction.

St Ives market traffic was the reason for the altered working in the up direction on Mondays. The first up goods train departed later at 6.00 am to allow drovers and farmers additional loading time for livestock, whilst on Tuesdays to Saturdays the train departed at 5.52 am. The mid-morning passenger train departed Ramsey High Street at 10.00 am MO, affording visitors additional time at the market as on other days it departed 65 minutes later. The afternoon freight service departed Ramsey at 3.25 pm and ran through to Ely via St Ives and the Sutton branch. This train served the recently opened Bateman's siding and shunted on Mondays only at Warboys for the 3.55 pm MO Somersham to Ramsey High Street passenger train to pass. Wagons were to be collected from Warboys in any order and sorted during shunting operations at Somersham. The last up passenger train, the 7.00 pm ex-

SOMERSHAM AND RAMSEY BRANCH.

SINGLE LINE.

NO SUNDAY TRAINS.

. The Trains on this Single Line are worked by Train Staff and Train Staff Ticket, according to " Train Staff Regulations."

No Engine or Train is to be run on this Branch without a Train Staff or Train Staff Ticket. The Train Staff Stations are Somersham, Warboys and Ramsey.

The figures under which a Bar, thus ——— is placed, shew where Trains from opposite directions are appointed to cross each other.

Miles from Somersham	DOWN TRAINS. Week Days.		1	2	3	4	5	6	7	8	9	10	11	12
			A		B							C		
			Gds.	Mxd.	Pass.	Pass.	Gds.	Pass.	Pass.	Pass.	Pasr.	Pass.		
			a.m.	a.m.	a.m.	p.m.	p.m.	p.m.	p.m.	p.m.	p.m.	p.m.		
... SOMERSHAM		arr.	...	...	...	...	...	...	...	...	...	...	...	...
		dep	7 5	9 0	11 42	12 38	2 0	2 35	3 55	4 58	6 0	7 48	...	...
2¼ Pidley-cum-Fenton Siding		,,	×	...	...	...	×	...	...	...	...	...	...	...
4½ Warboys		arr.	7 25	9 11	11 51	12 47	2 10	2 44	4 4	5 7	6 10	7 57	...	...
		dep	7 45	9 12	11 52	12 48	2 55	2 45	4 5	5 8	6 11	7 58	...	...
7 RAMSEY (High Street)		arr.	7 53	9 18	11 58	12 54	3 1	2 51	4 11	5 14	6 17	8 4	...	...

A To convey 3 wagons for Ramsey only if absolutely necessary.

B No. 5. May work Trucks from Somersham to Ramsey if required. From Ely at 10.45 a.m., via Sutton. To shunt at Warboys for No. 6 Passenger Train.

C No. 10. Carriages from St. Ives to Somersham. May work Cattle from Somersham to Ramsey if Trucks are fitted with Brake pipes.

Miles from Ramsey	UP TRAINS. Week Days.		1	2	3	4	5	6	7	8	9	10	11	12
										D			E	
			Gds.	Pass.	Pass.	Pass.	Pass.	Pass.	Pass.	Gds.	Pass.	Pass.	Mxd.	
			a.m.	a.m.	a.m.	a.m.	p.m.	p.m.	p.m.	p.m.	p.m.	p.m.	p.m.	
... RAMSEY (High Street)		dep.	6 0	8 10	10 0	11 5	12 5	1 40	3 19	3 30	4 16	5 25	6 40	...
2¼ Warboys		arr.	6 10	8 15	10 5	11 10	12 10	1 45	3 24	3 40	4 22	5 30	6 46	...
		dep	6 25	8 16	10 6	11 11	12 11	1 46	3 25	4 40	4 23	5 31	6 47	...
4¾ Pidley-cum-Fenton Siding		,,	...	...	...	...	...	...	...	*	...	...	...	...
7 SOMERSHAM		arr.	6 35	8 26	10 16	11 21	12 21	1 56	3 35	4 50	4 33	5 41	6 58	...
		dep	On Mons runs 15 min. earlier	...	Mons Not only. Mons	...	...	...	...	...	5 30	...	7 0 ToSt. Ives.	...

D No. 8. Runs to Ely, via Sutton.   E To work 3 wagons from Ramsey only.

Ramsey High Street, was permitted to work not exceeding three loaded wagons to Somersham to clear the branch of important or perishable goods. The summer timetable for 1908 showed up departures from Ramsey High Street at 5.50 am goods MX, 6.00 goods MO, 10.00 MO, 11.05 am MX, 12.07, 1.40, 3.19, 3.25 goods, 4.16 MO, 5.24 and 7.00 pm. The 3.25 pm goods train ran through to Ely via St Ives and Sutton, and called at Bateman's siding when required, and cleared Warboys of all loaded wagons. On Mondays only it also shunted at Warboys for the 3.55 pm down passenger train to pass. The last up passenger train, the 7.00 pm ex-Ramsey High Street was also allowed to convey eight loaded trucks and if so ran as a mixed train. In the down direction the branch trains departed Somersham at 7.00 am goods, 8.55 mixed, 11.44, 12.38, 2.00 goods ex-Ely via Sutton and St Ives, 2.28, 3.55 MO, 5.00, 6.00 and 7.52 pm. The 8.55 am mixed train was permitted to work three loaded trucks through to Ramsey High Street whilst the 7.52 pm passenger train could work cattle trucks between Somersham and Ramsey if the vehicles were fitted with the Westinghouse brake.

The GER passenger timetable for 1914 offered the following service on the branch:

Down		M							
		am	*am*	*pm*	*pm*	*pm*	*pm*	*pm*	*pm*
Somersham	*dep.*	9.08	11.48	1.34	2.38	3.55	5.14	6.05	7.50
Warboys	*dep.*	9.20	11.58	1.44	2.48	4.05	5.20	6.15	7.59
Ramsey HS	*arr.*	9.26	12.04	1.50	2.54	4.11	5.30	6.21	8.06

Up						M		M	
		am	*am*	*pm*	*pm*	*pm*	*pm*	*pm*	*pm*
Ramsey H S	*dep.*	7.42	10.29	1.04	2.08	3.10	4.46	5.36	7.20
Warboys	*dep.*	7.48	10.35	1.14	2.15	3.20	4.52	5.40	7.27
Somersham	*arr.*	7.58	10.45	1.20	2.25	3.32	5.02	5.52	7.36

M – Mixed train

The fastest journey times from London was 2 hours 14 minutes by the 5.52 pm train from Liverpool Street which connected with the 7.50 pm ex-Somersham, whilst in the reverse direction connections off the 7.42 am ex-Ramsey High Street enabled passengers to arrive at Liverpool Street 2 hours and 33 minutes later at 10.15 am.

The restrictions imposed by World War I were not as severe as on some other branch lines, and the timetable only showed a reduction of one train in each direction. The timetable for 1917 showed up departures from Ramsey High Street at 6.00 am goods, 7.38, 8.40 goods ex-Warboys, 10.00 am MO, 10.26 am MX, 1.12, 3.05 mixed, 4.20 goods MX ex-Warboys to Ely via St Ives and Sutton, 4.36 MO goods ex-Warboys to Ely via St Ives and Sutton, 5.28 mixed and 7.35 pm. The 4.20 pm MX, 4.36 pm MO goods called at Pidley-cum-Fenton and Bateman's sidings as required and were permitted to convey 26 loaded mineral and 37 loaded goods wagons Warboys to Pidley-cum-Fenton and 35 loaded mineral and 50 loaded wagons respectively Pidley to Somersham. In addition the 5.28 pm mixed train was permitted to work not exceeding eight loaded trucks from Ramsey High

SOMERSHAM AND RAMSEY BRANCH.

See page 50

WEEK DAYS.

		morn		morn		noon		even.		even.	
LONDON { L'pool St.	dep.	5 53	—	8 35	—	12 0	—	2 35	—	—	—
{ St. Pancras	„										
Cambridge — — — —	„	8 20	...	10 25	—	1 31	—	4 8	...	...	—
St. Ives	„	8 53	...	10 57	—	2 8	—	4 43	...	...	—
Somersham — —	arr.	9 4	—	11 8	—	2 14	—	4 54	...	—	—

				morn		noon		even.		even.	
King's Lynn	dep.	...	...	8 47	...	11 50	...	2 6	...	4 33	...
Wisbech— — — —	„	6 27	...	9 22	—	12 25	—	2 44	...	5 8	...
March	„	7 37	...	10 27	...	1 0	—	3 14	...	5 31	...
Somersham — —	arr.	8 2	—	10 52	—	1 26	—	3 39	—	5 56	—

		Mxd morn						even.		even.	
SOMERSHAM	dep.	9 14	...	11 18	...	2 19	...	5 2	...	6 5	
Warboys — — — — —	„	9 26	—	11 28	—	2 29	—	5 12	...	6 15	
RAMSEY (High Street)	arr.	9 33	...	11 34	...	2 35	...	5 19	...	6 22	

MO Mondays only.

See page 50

WEEK DAYS.

		Mxd morn		MO morn		NM morn		even.		Mxd even.		Mxd even.	
RAMSEY (High Street)	dep.	7 33	...	10 0	...	10 26	...	1 0	...	3 5	...	5 28	...
Warboys — — — — —	„	7 45	...	10 6	—	10 32	...	1 6	...	3 15	...	5 35	—
SOMERSHAM	arr.	7 57	...	10 16	—	10 42	...	1 16	...	3 27	—	5 47	—

									MO		Mxd		Mxd	
Somersham	dep.	9 4	...	11 8	...	11 8	...	2 14	3 51	4 54	—	8 3	—
March — — — —	arr.	9 29	...	11 33	...	11 33	...	2 39	4 16	5 23	—	8 28	—
Wisbech	„	10 21	...	12 33	...	12 33	...	3 0		5 45		...	
King's Lynn — — —	„	11 1	—	1 9	—	1 9	—	3 57	—	6 32	—	—	—

Somersham	dep.	8 2	...	10 25	...	10 52	...	1 26	...	3 39	...	5 56	—
St. Ives — —	arr.	8 12	...	10 36	—	11 2	...	1 36	...	3 49	...	6 6	—
Cambridge	„	8 50	...	11 38	...	11 38	...	2 13	...	4 25	...	6 45	—
LONDON { St. Pancras	„												
{ L'pool St.	„	10 23	...	2 7	...	2 7	...	5 2	...	6 10	...	8 20	...

NM Not Mondays.

GER passenger timetable 1919.

Street. Down departures from Somersham were 7.00 am goods, 8.10 goods to Warboys, 9.14 mixed, 11.18 am, 2.00 goods to Warboys ex-Ely via Sutton and St Ives, 2.19, 3.55 MO, 5.10, 6.05 and 8.08 pm. The last two passenger trains were permitted to convey cattle traffic from Somersham to Ramsey High Street if the wagons were fitted with Westinghouse brakes. The 7.00 am goods train called at Pidley-cum-Fenton siding when required, whilst the 2.19 pm passenger train was permitted to haul two trucks of cattle to Ramsey if the wagons were Westinghouse fitted.

By 1920 services had again been reduced and up workings from Ramsey High Street departed at 5.50 am goods, 7.38, 10.00 MO, 10.26 am MX, 1.00, 3.05, 4.15 goods ex-Warboys, 5.30 and 6.55 pm goods. The early morning goods train was required to clear Fuller's Brick Co. siding of traffic and place empty wagons whilst the engine hauling the 7.38 am ex-Ramsey High Street also performed yard shunting at Somersham. The last up passenger train departed at the unbelievably early hour of 5.30 pm, a full two hours earlier than previous years and hardly conducive to attracting potential traffic even from this rural fenland community. The 4.15 pm goods ex-Warboys worked Bishopsgate, Spitalfields and down line traffic only and called at Pidley-cum-Fenton and Bateman's sidings as required, leaving the 6.55 pm goods to clear all the remaining traffic from Warboys yard. Down services departed Somersham at 6.45 am goods, 9.14 mixed, 11.18 am, 2.19, 3.35 engine and brake van to Warboys, 5.04, 6.05 and 7.35 pm goods. The 2.19 pm passenger train was permitted to convey two cattle wagons en route from St Ives to Ramsey High Street on Mondays only if the wagons were fitted with the Westinghouse brake. The engine and brake van booked to run from Somersham to Warboys was the locomotive off the 3.05 pm up working and was also permitted to work cattle wagons to Warboys on Mondays if required. During this period both up and down trains were allowed the following times for the 6 miles 75 chains journey across the branch: passenger 18 minutes, mixed 19 minutes and goods 35 minutes.

The final GER working timetable for 1922 showed the basis of the service, which remained almost unchanged until the withdrawal of passenger services from the line in 1930. In the up direction the service consisted of four MO and three MX passenger trains supplemented by one mixed train, whilst two freight trains ran daily, one starting from Warboys on Saturdays excepted. The MO passenger train departure for patrons of St Ives market continued to run but the corresponding train MX departed Ramsey High Street at 10.26 am. An additional MO passenger train ran from the terminus at 1.00 pm, whilst the 3.05 pm mixed train was permitted to clear the stations of all important traffic but was not to attach traffic at Warboys. The morning up goods train, 5.50 am ex-Ramsey, cleared Fuller's Brick Company siding of loaded wagons and placed empty wagons as required whilst Warboys and Pidley-cum-Fenton sidings were cleared by the 4.15 pm afternoon trip from Warboys to Somersham. In the down direction the branch was served by three MO and two MX passenger trains whilst the goods service consisted of two trains SX, one terminating at Warboys and one train SO. The branch engine with brake van returned light ex-Somersham at 2.30 pm SO after working the 12.45 pm SO up freight, although if traffic was available it ran as a freight train. By now the

SOMERSHAM AND RAMSEY BRANCH.

See page		morn		morn		MO morn		even.		even.					
62	LIVERPOOL STREET ... dep.	5 50	...	8 30	...	11 50	...	2 34	...	even.	...	...	...	...	...
	Cambridge — — — — "	8 20	...	10 25	—	1 31	—	4 10	—	—	—	—	—	—	—
	St. Ives ... "	8 53	...	10 57	...	2 3	—	4 43	—	—	—	—	—	—	—
	Somersham — — — arr.	9 4	—	11 8	—	2 14	—	4 54	—	—	—	—	—	—	—

See page				morn		MO morn		even.		even.			
62	King's Lynn ... dep.	...	...	9 46	...	11 50	...	1 52	...	4 15	...	...	...
	Wisbech — — — — — "	6 19	—	10 13	...	12 27	—	2 28	—	5 7	—	—	—
	March "	7 34	—	10 28	—	12 53	—	3 5	—	5 33	—	—	—
	Somersham — — — arr.	7 59	—	10 53	—	1 18	—	3 34	—	6 1	—	—	—

		Mxd				MO				Mxd	
	SOMERSHAM ... dep.	9 14	...	11 18	...	2 19	...	5 4	...	6 10	—
	Warboys — — — — — "	9 26	—	11 28	—	2 29	—	5 14	—	6 22	—
	RAMSEY (High Street) ... arr.	9 33	...	11 34	...	2 35	...	5 20	...	6 29	...

WEEK DAYS.

See page		morn		MO morn		NM morn		MO even.		even.		even. Mxd		even.	
	RAMSEY (High Street) ... dep.	7 36	...	10 0	...	10 26	...	12 54	...	3 5	...	5 35			
	Warboys — — — — — "	7 42	...	10 6	—	10 32	—	1 0	...	3 12	—	5 41			
	SOMERSHAM ... arr.	7 52	...	10 16	...	10 42	...	1 10	...	3 24	—	5 51	...		

See page		morn		MO morn		NM morn		MO even.		MO even.		even.		even.	
62	Somersham ... dep.	9 4	...	11 8	...	11 8	...	2 14	...	3 51	4 54	...	8 7	...
	March — — — — arr.	9 29	—	11 33	—	11 33	—	2 39	—	4 16	5 20	—	8 34	—
	Wisbech ... "	10 15	—	11 51	—	11 51	—	3 0	...	—	5 47	—	8 55	—
	King's Lynn — — — "	10 52	—	12 39	—	12 39	—	3 53	...	—	6 34	—	—	—

See page		morn		MO morn		NM morn		MO even.		even.		even.		even.	
62	Somersham ... dep.	7 59	...	10 26	...	10 53	...	1 18	...	3 34	...	6 1			
	St. Ives — — — arr.	8 12	...	10 36	—	11 3	—	1 28	—	3 46	—	6 11	—		
	Cambridge ... "	8 50	...	11 39	...	11 39	...	2 4	...	4 27	—	6 55	—		
	LIVERPOOL STREET — "	10 23	—	2 7	—	2 7	—	5 9	—	6 10	—	8 33	—		

MO Mondays only.
NM Not Mondays.

X From 23rd July to 10th September inclusive passengers can arrive St. Pancras station 4.2 p.m.
Z Commencing 17th September arrives King's Lynn 1.9 p.m.

Tickets from Warboys and Ramsey are issued on the train.

The LNER public timetable 1923 still shows the station name as Ramsey (High Street).

MO passenger train for returning visitors to St Ives market departed at the earlier time of 2.24 pm from Somersham and was permitted to work not exceeding two wagons of cattle. The last down mixed train the 6.05 pm ex-Somersham was also permitted to work cattle traffic to Ramsey High Street, leaving brake goods* for the branch stations to be worked by freight train only.

After Grouping the LNER renamed Ramsey High Street to Ramsey East, on and from 1st July, 1923. The 1924 branch timetable was slightly adjusted with three MO and two MX passenger trains supplemented by two mixed trains in the down direction. Of these the 2.19 pm MO ex-Somersham was allowed to work not exceeding two wagons of cattle as before. The last down passenger train the 6.10 pm from Somersham was also allowed to work cattle traffic to Ramsey East only. Freight services showed the main alterations, for the 6.45 am ex-Somersham ran MX whilst the MO train departed at the later time of 8.05 am and ran only as far as Warboys. The 2.15 pm SO goods train was permitted to work traffic to Warboys and Ramsey East if required, and was allowed 15 minutes for shunting at the intermediate station. The final down goods of the day was a through working from Cambridge SX, departing at 1.35 pm and terminating at Warboys. The up workings remained essentially as in earlier years with four MO and three MX passenger trains and one mixed train, supplemented by two goods services MO ex-Warboys, two goods MX, one starting from Ramsey East and the other from Warboys and one goods train on Saturdays. The importance of the brick traffic to the railway company from both Warboys and Fuller's siding meant that the 4.15 pm ex-Warboys, which conveyed most of the traffic, was extended as a through working to Park Yard near Tottenham. Similarly the early morning goods MX departed Ramsey East at 5.50 am clearing Fuller's siding of traffic and placing empty wagons for the afternoon loadings. The branch engine, after working the 7.36 am passenger train from Ramsey East, performed shunting duties at Somersham and on Mondays this train was permitted to work not exceeding two trucks from Ramsey East for St Ives provided the wagons were Westinghouse brake fitted. The afternoon mixed train, 3.05 pm from Ramsey East, cleared the terminal station of all important parcels traffic. The fastest down journey from London to Ramsey East was 2 hours 56 minutes available by the 2.34 pm from Liverpool Street connecting with the 5.04 pm from Somersham whilst in the up direction passengers catching the 7.35 am from Ramsey East were in Liverpool Street in 2 hours 48 minutes arriving at 10.23 am.

The miners' strike of 1926 forced the LNER to make economies to conserve fuel supplies and as with many other lines the passenger service on the Ramsey East branch was reduced. Two trains ran in each direction with an additional train each way on Mondays only, for St Ives market. From 31st May, 1926 departures from Ramsey East were 7.30 am, 1.00 pm MO and 3.05 pm returning from Somersham at 11.18 am, 2.10 pm MO and 6.10 pm. After several weeks the normal timetable was reintroduced.

The 1927 working timetable for the branch showed a weekdays-only service of four passenger trains MO, three passenger trains MX, one mixed, two goods trains MO and one goods train MX in the up direction. By this date the 5.50 am MX goods train ex-Ramsey East was suspended. The branch engine working

---

* Small consignments of freight capable of being loaded in a brake van as opposed to conveyance in an open wagon or a covered van.

the 7.36 am passenger train ex-Ramsey East performed shunting duties on arrival at Somersham before hauling the 8.05 am MO goods train to Warboys and the 8.40 am MO return goods to Somersham. Because of the suspension of the 5.50 am goods train ex-Ramsey East the 7.36 am was permitted on MO to convey to Somersham not exceeding two Westinghouse-fitted trucks with traffic for St Ives. The afternoon up mixed train, 3.05 pm departure from Ramsey East, was required to clear the terminal of important goods traffic, but was not to attach traffic at Warboys. On SX the engine and guard were to work a trip to Billup's siding between Somersham and Chatteris, departing Somersham at 4.00 pm, to perform shunting duties before returning to the junction for the next branch working. The 12.30 pm SO goods train ex-Ramsey East called at Pidley siding, if required, to clear traffic.

In the down direction the weekdays-only service consisted of three passenger trains MO, two passenger trains MX, two mixed trains, two goods trains MO and one goods working MX. The 6.45 am MX goods train ex-Somersham, the return working of the 5.50 am up train, was also suspended. The 2.19 pm MO passenger train ex-Somersham was permitted to work two wagons of cattle en route from St Ives to Ramsey East if the vehicles were fitted with Westinghouse brake pipes. The 6.10 pm mixed train ex-Somersham,the final train of the day, was permitted to work cattle from Somersham to Ramsey East, however brake goods to Warboys and Ramsey East was to worked by goods train only. Finally the 1.35 pm SX goods train ex-Cambridge,arriving at Somersham at 3.12 pm and departing at 3.25 pm ran only as far as Warboys arriving at 3.35 pm. This train returned at 4.15 pm ex-Warboys as a through train to Park Yard, Tottenham, clearing Warboys of all traffic and serving Pidley siding and Owen's siding if required, and shunting Somersham from 5.00 pm to 6.15 pm before continuing its journey.

By 1928 the working timetable showed a total of three MX and four MO passenger trains, one mixed and one goods MX and two goods MO trains in the up direction with departures from Ramsey East at 7.36 am, 8.40 MO goods ex-Warboys, 10.00 MO, 10.20 am MX, 12.30 SO goods, 1.00 MO, 3.00 mixed, 4.15 SX goods ex-Warboys and 5.35 pm. On Mondays the branch locomotive shunted Somersham yard after working the 7.36 am, whilst in the absence of any goods services the mixed trains were required to clear Ramsey East goods yard of any traffic, the 3.00 pm in consequence was not required to collect any traffic from Warboys. After working this service the locomotive ran light to shunt Billup's siding. Park Yard was no longer the destination of the 4.15 pm goods train from Warboys, which terminated at Cambridge and shunted Pidley-cum-Fenton and Owen's brickyard sidings. In the down direction the service provided two MX and three MO passenger trains, two mixed and two goods SX and three goods SO trains on weekdays. Trains departed Somersham at 8.05 am goods to Warboys, 9.11 mixed, 11.18 am, 2.15 goods SO, 2.19 MO, 3.25 goods to Warboys, 5.04 and 6.10 pm mixed. Of these the 2.19 pm MO passenger train was permitted a tail load of two Westinghouse brake fitted cattle wagons, whilst the 5.04 pm was also permitted to work cattle but to Ramsey East only. The 3.25 pm goods train worked through from Cambridge.

The working timetable for 8th July to 22nd September, 1929 was:

Down		Gds MO	Mxd	Pass	Gds SO	Pass MOA	Gds B	Pass	Mxd C
		am	*am*	*am*	*pm*	*pm*	*pm*	*pm*	*pm*
Somersham	a.						3.12		
	d.	8.05	9.11	11.18	2.15	2.19	3.25	5.04	6.10
Pidley-c-Fenton	d.								
Warboys	a.	8.15	9.22	11.27	2.25	2.28	3.35	5.13	6.21
	d.		9.23	11.28	2.40	2.29		5.14	6.22
Ramsey East	a.		9.30	11.34	2.50	2.35		5.20	6.29

Up		Pass D	Gds MO	Pass MO	Pass MX	Gds SO	Pass MO	Mxd E	Gds F	Pass
		am	*am*	*am*	*am*	*pm*	*pm*	*pm*	*pm*	*pm*
Ramsey East	d.	7.36		10.00	10.20	12.30	1.00	3.00		5.35
Warboys	a.	7.41		10.05	10.25	12.40	1.05	3.06		5.40
	d.	7.42	8.40	10.06	10.26	1.10	1.06	3.07	4.15	5.41
Pidley-c-Fenton	d.					*			*	
Somersham	a.	7.52	8.50	10.16	10.36	1.45	1.16	3.19	5.00	5.51
	d.								6.15	

A   May work not exceeding two wagons of cattle from St Ives to Ramsey East, if the wagons are fitted with Westinghouse brake pipes.

B   1.35 pm ex-Cambridge.

C   May work cattle from Somersham to Ramsey East. Somersham to work brake goods to Warboys and Ramsey East by goods train only.

D   Engine to perform station work at Somersham. On Mondays may convey from Ramsey East to Somersham not exceeding two Westinghouse fitted trucks for St Ives.

E   To clear Ramsey East of important traffic. Not to attach at Warboys. Except Saturdays engine and guard to make a trip to Billup's siding at 4.00pm.

F   To Cambridge. To clear all traffic from Warboys and call at Pidley-cum-Fenton and Owen's sidings.

*   Calls if required

The final working timetable to include passenger services from July 1930 was very similar to that of 1929 (*overleaf*). Compared with the GE section the GN section offered seven passenger trains in each direction between Ramsey North and Holme, although this was reduced in February 1931 to a morning-only service.

After the withdrawal of passenger services from the branch the LNER provided a service of two goods trains in each direction, although only one ran through to and from Ramsey East. The timetable from 18th July to 11th September, 1932 showed the following services:

Down		Gds A	Gds B	Up		Gds C	Gds D
		am	*pm*			*am*	*pm*
Somersham	arr.	7.45	3.12	Ramsey East	dep.	10.45	
	dep.	9.10	3.25	Warboys	arr.	10.55	
Pidley-c-F	dep.				dep.	11.15	4.15
Warboys	arr.	9.25	3.35	Pidley-c-F	dep.	11.40	*
	dep.	9.45		Somersham	arr.	11.50	5.00
Ramsey East	arr.	9.55			dep.	12.55	6.15

SOMERSHAM, WARBOYS AND RAMSEY EAST (Single Line).

DOWN WEEK DAYS.

Miles from S'mersh'm			1	2	3	4	5	6	7	8	9	10	11
				Gds. MO	Mxd.	Pass.	Gds. SO	Pass. MO	-	Gds.	Pass.	Mxd.	
				a.m.	a.m.	a.m.	p.m.	p.m.		p.m.	p.m.	p.m.	
	Somersham	arr.	—	—	—	—	—	—	—	3 12	—	—	—
		dep.	.....	8 5	9 11	11 18	2 15	2 19	.....	3 25	5 4	6 10	.....
2 20	Pidley-cum-Fenton Sd. „		—	—	—	—	—	—	—	—	—	—	
4 31	Warboys	arr.	.....	8 15	9 22	11 27	2 25	2 28	.....	3 35	5 13	6 21	.....
		dep.	—	—	9 23	11 28	2 40	2 29	—	—	5 14	6 22	.....
6 75	Ramsey East	arr.	.....	.....	9 30	11 34	2 50	2 35	.....	.....	5 20	6 29	.....

UP WEEK DAYS.

		1	2	3	4	5	6	7	8	9	10	11	12	13
			Pass. MO	Gds. MO	Pass. NM	Pass.		Gds. SO	Pass. MO	Mxd.	Gds.		Pass.	
			a.m.	a.m.	a.m.	a.m.		p.m.	p.m.	p.m.	p.m.		p.m.	
Ramsey East	dep.	.....	7 36	.....	10 0	10 20	.....	12 30	1 0	3 0	.....	.....	5 35	.....
Warboys	arr.	—	7 41	—	10 5	10 25	—	12 40	1 5	3 6	—	—	5 40	—
	dep.	.....	7 42	8 40	10 6	10 26	.....	1 10	1 6	3 7	4 15	.....	5 41	.....
Pidley-cum-Fenton Sg. „		—	—	—	—	—	—	*	—	*	—	—	—	—
Somersham	arr.	.....	7 52	8 50	10 16	10 36	.....	1 45	1 16	3 19	5 0	.....	5 51	.....
	dep.	—	—	—	—	—	—	—	—	—	6 15	—	—	—

—6 May work not exceeding two wagons of cattle from St. Ives for Ramsey East if the wagons are fitted with Westinghouse brake pipes.   8 1.35 p.m. ex Cambridge.
—10 May work cattle from Somersham to Ramsey East. Somersham to work brake goods to Warboys & Ramsey East by goods train only.

—2 Engine to perform station work at Somersham. On Mondays may convey from Ramsey E. to Somersham not exceeding two Westinghouse fitted trucks for St. Ives.
=9 To clear Ramsey E. of important traffic. Not to attach at Warboys. Engine to run light to Billups Siding. See page 15.   10 To Cambridge. To clear all traffic from Warboys and call at Pidley-cum-Fenton and Owen's sidings.

Passenger trains are worked on the "Conductor Guard" principle.

LNER working timetable 1930, the last to show passenger services.

A   5.25 am MO, 6.00 am MX ex-Whitemoor. On Mondays arrive Somersham 7.15 am. On Mondays if any cattle at Warboys or Ramsey East for St Ives market, the engine and brake to run down for the same and work to St Ives. Engine and brake returning from St Ives to Somersham to work 9.10 am goods to Warboys. If this trip is not required and there is St Ives cattle from Wimblington, Chatteris or Somersham, the engine and brake of the 5.25 am is to leave Somersham for St Ives at 7.30 am, due St Ives at 7.50 am, engine and brake returning from St Ives to Somersham at 8.10 am for 9.10 am to Warboys.

B   2.50 pm ex-St Ives extended to Ramsey East when required.

C   To March.

D   To Cambridge. Starts from Ramsey East when required. To clear all traffic from Warboys and call at Pidley-cum-Fenton and Owen's sidings. At Pidley-cum-Fenton siding the guard to obtain the Train Staff from the driver and work the ground frame as necessary.

*   Calls if required.

From 1st May, 1933 the 10.45 am ex-Ramsey East ran to Whitemoor whilst the afternoon down train departed Somersham at the earlier time of 2.30 pm. This terminated at Warboys at 2.40 pm but was extended if required to Ramsey East. On the return working it departed Warboys at 4.15 pm and ran in the same timings as 1932. After arrival at Somersham the engine and brake van went to Chatteris for yard shunting SX but on Saturdays the train continued through to Cambridge. These timings continued until April 1935 (*see page 122*). Then from the 8th July, 1935 further minor alterations were made. Two trains ran in each direction with the following amended timings:

Down		Gds A	Gds B	Up		Gds C	Gds D
		am	*pm*			*am*	*pm*
Somersham	*arr.*	7.45	3.12	Ramsey East	*dep.*	11.10	
	dep.	9.10	3.25	Warboys	*arr.*	11.20	
Pidley-c-F	*dep.*				*dep.*	11.35	4.15
Warboys	*arr.*	9.30	3.35	Pidley-c-F	*dep.*	11.55	*
	dep.	10.15		Somersham	*arr.*	12.05	5.00
Ramsey East	*arr.*	10.25			*dep.*	12.55	6.15

A   5.25 am SO, 6.00 am SX ex-Whitemoor. On SO arrives Somersham at 7.15 am. Allowed 5 minutes extra for opening and closing the gates at Pidley-cum- Fenton.

B   Extended to Ramsey East when required.

C   To Whitemoor. On SO after arrival at Somersham engine may work special trip between Somersham and Warboys and then run light from Somersham to St Ives to work the 4.30 pm St Ives to Ely.

D   Engine and brake run to Chatteris. Starts from Ramsey East when required.

*   Calls if required.

These timings were operative until 6th July, 1936 when the working timetable showed the 11.10 am departure from Ramsey East on Saturdays departing at the later time of 12.00 noon, calling at Warboys from 12.10 to 12.45 pm, Pidley-cum-Fenton siding departing 1.05 pm, Somersham arriving 1.15 pm, departing 2.15 pm for Whitemoor.

The 1937 working timetable continued to show two freight trains serving the branch, one running through to Ramsey East each weekday and the other terminating and starting back from Warboys SX. The first down working was

Left: Notice in the LNER public timetable 1934.

Below: LNER working timetable April 1935.

Bottom: LNER working timetable 1944.

Table 56. SOMERSHAM AND RAMSEY (East).

THE PASSENGER TRAIN SERVICE HAS BEEN WITHDRAWN FROM WARBOYS AND RAMSEY (EAST), BUT PARCELS AND MISCELLANEOUS TRAIN TRAFFIC PREVIOUSLY DEALT WITH AT THESE STATIONS WILL CONTINUE TO BE ACCEPTED.

Omnibus services operated by the Eastern National Omnibus Co., Ltd., serving these places are available. For particulars of these services apply to the Station Masters or to the Eastern National Omnibus Co., Ltd., Stukeley Road, Huntingdon (telephone—Huntingdon 159).

For train service to and from Somersham see Table 53.

SOMERSHAM, WARBOYS AND RAMSEY EAST (Single Line).

Worked by train staff without tickets and by only one engine in steam (or two or more engines coupled together). For regulations for working see Appendix. Parcels and Miscellaneous traffic and Live Stock at passenger train rates will also be conveyed by Goods Service.

DOWN WEEK DAYS.

Miles from Somersham M.C.		1	2	3	4	5	6
		Gds.			Gds.		
		SX			SX		
		a.m.			p.m.		
—	Somersham ⑤ {dep	7 45	—	—	—	—	—
2 20	Pidley-cum-Fenton Sd. {arr / dep	9 10	—	—	2 30	—	—
4 31	Warboys {arr / dep	9 30	—	—	2 40	—	—
6 75	Ramsey East ⑤ {arr	10 25	—	—	—	—	—

UP WEEK DAYS.

Miles from Somersham		7	8	9	10	11	12
			Gds.			Gds.	Gds.
			a.m.			SX p.m.	
	Ramsey East ⑤ {dep	—	11 10	—	—	4 15	—
	Warboys {arr / dep	—	11 35	—	—	—	—
	Pidley-cum-Fenton Sg. {arr / dep	—	11 55	—	—	—	5 0
	Somersham ⑤ {arr	—	12 5	—	—	—	12 50

1. 5.25 a.m. SO 6.0 a.m. SX ex Whitemoor on Sats. arr. Somersham 7.15 a.m. See side note for Mons. Allowed 5 mins. between Somersham and Warboys for the opening and closing of gates at Pidley-cum-Fenton Sdge. 4 Extended to Ramsey E. when reqd. 8 To Whitemoor.

6.0 A.M. SX WHITEMOOR TO RAMSEY.

On Mondays if any cattle at Warboys or Ramsey for St. Ives Market the engine and brake to run down for same and work to St. Ives.

Engine and brake returning from St. Ives to Somersham to work 9.10 a.m. goods to Warboys.

... and Warboys and then run light Somersham to St. Ives to work 4.30 p.m. St. Ives to Ely. SO Eng. and brake runs to Chatteris see page A 53. Starts from Owen's sidings. At Pidley-cum-Fenton Sd., clear all traffic from Owen's Sd., Guard to obtain train staff from Driver ...

SOMERSHAM, WARBOYS AND RAMSEY EAST

SINGLE LINE.

Worked by train staff without tickets and by only one engine in steam (or two or more engines coupled together). For regulations for working see "Appendix." Parcels and Miscellaneous traffic and Live stock at passenger train rates will also be conveyed by Goods Service.

DOWN WEEK DAYS.

Miles from Somersham M.C.		1 & 2	3	4	5	6
		Gds.	Gds.	Gds.		
		SX	SO			
		a.m.	a.m.	p.m.		
—	Somersham ⑤ {arr / dep	8 20 / 8 20	9 30	—	—	—
2 20	Pidley-cum-Fenton Sd. {arr / dep	9 10 / 9 30	—	2 30	—	—
4 31	Warboys {arr / dep	9 30 / 10 15	10 30	2 40	—	—
6 75	Ramsey East ⑤ {arr	10 25 / 10 40	—	—	—	—

UP WEEK DAYS.

Miles from Somersham		7	8	9	10	11	12
			Gds.	Gds.			Gds.	Gds.
			SX	SO			SX	
			a.m.	noon.			p.m.	
	Ramsey East ⑤ {dep	—	11 0	12 0	—	—	—	—
	Warboys {arr / dep	—	11 10	12 10	—	—	4 15	—
	Pidley-cum-Fenton Sd. {arr / dep	—	11 25	12 45	—	—	—	—
	Somersham ⑤ {arr	—	11 55	1 15	—	—	5 0	—

1 & 2 6.40 a.m. ex Whitemoor (See page 42). See side note for Mondays. Allowed 5 mins. between Somersham and Warboys for the opening and closing of gates at Pidley-cum-Fenton Siding. 4 Extended to Ramsey East when required.

6.40 A.M. (S X) WHITEMOOR TO RAMSEY.

On Mondays if any cattle at Warboys or Ramsey for St. Ives Market the engine and brake to run down for same and work to St. Ives.

Engine and brake returning from St. Ives to Somersham to work 9.10 a.m. goods to Ramsey.

11 Engine and brake runs to Chatteris. Starts from Ramsey East when required. To clear all traffic from Warboys and call at Pidley-cum-Fenton and Owen's sidings. At Pidley-cum-Fenton Siding, Guard to obtain train staff from Driver and work ground frame as necessary.

the 5.25 am SO, 6.00 am SX from Whitemoor yard which, after shunting at Somersham entered the branch at 9.10am returning from Ramsey East at 11.10 am SX and 12.00 noon SO. On Mondays if any cattle traffic was awaiting at Warboys or Ramsey East for St Ives market, the engine and brake van on this trip was authorized to collect the traffic and work a special through to St Ives returning to Somersham to work the 9.10 am train. The afternoon goods 2.30 pm SX ex-Somersham to Warboys returning at 4.15 pm was extended to Ramsey East if any traffic required movement. On the return journey the train cleared Warboys, Pidley-cum-Fenton and Owen's sidings before continuing to Somersham. After completion of shunting duties at the junction the engine and brake van then ran to Chatteris.

From 4th July, 1938 the morning service was retimed to leave Whitemoor at 6.40 am, arriving at Somersham at 7.50 am. On SX the train departed the junction at 9.10 am and ran as before, but SO the train departed Somersham at 9.30 am, calling at Warboys from 9.50 to 10.30 am arriving at Ramsey East at 10.40 am. The return train departed Ramsey East at 11.10 am SO and 12.00 noon SX. The afternoon services were unchanged.

By 1939 the branch was served by one freight train in each direction augmented by a short working from Somersham to Warboys and back SX, although this latter working could be extended to and from Ramsey East when traffic warranted. Down trains departed Somersham at 9.10 am SX and 9.30 am SO returning from Ramsey East at 11.00 am SX and 12.00 noon SO. The afternoon SX trip to Warboys departed Somersham at 2.30 pm and returned at 4.15 pm. The SX morning down service was the 6.40 am from Whitemoor yard. On MO if cattle traffic was on hand at either of the branch stations for St Ives market, the usual arrangements applied (*see above*). The engine and brake van then worked the 9.10 am from Somersham to Ramsey East.

The working timetable operative from 1st January, 1940 showed two goods trains in each direction SX and one train SO and these timings continued throughout World War II and until 1947.

Down		Gds SX am	Gds SO am	Gds SX pm	Up		Gds SX am	Gds SO pm	Gds SX pm
Whitemoor	d.	6.40	6.40		Ramsey East	d.	11.00	12.00	
Somersham	a.	7.50	7.50		Warboys	a.	11.10	12.10	
	d.	9.10	9.30	2.30		d.	11.25	12.45	4.15
Pidley-c-F	d.				Pidley-c-F	d.	11.45	1.05	*
Warboys	a.	9.30	9.50	2.40	Somersham	a.	11.55	1.15	5.00
	d.	10.15	10.30	R					
Ramsey East	a.	10.25	10.40						

6.40 am ex-Whitemoor allowed 5 minutes between Somersham and Warboys for the opening of the crossing gates at Pidley-cum-Fenton.

6.40 am SX ex-Whitemoor. On Mondays if any cattle at Warboys or Ramsey East for St Ives market the engine and brake to run down for the same and work to St Ives, engine and brake returning to work the 9.10am goods to Ramsey East.

2.30 pm ex-Somersham extended to Ramsey East when required.

4.15 pm ex-Warboys starts from Ramsey East when required. To clear all traffic from Warboys and call at Pidley-cum-Fenton and Owen's sidings.

* Calls if required

From 3rd March, 1947 only one train served the branch in each direction. On Saturdays only, the 6.20 am ex-Whitemoor departed Somersham at 9.30 am and after shunting at Warboys for 40 minutes arrived at Ramsey East at 10.40 am. The return working departed at 12.00 noon calling at Warboys and Pidley siding and arrived back at Somersham at 1.15 pm. The SX working ran later, the branch being served by the 10.50 am train from March Up Yard, which eventually departed Somersham at 12.45 pm. With 55 minutes allowed for shunting at Warboys, the train arrived at the terminus at 2.10 pm. The return working departed at 2.50 pm and as well as shunting at Warboys cleared all traffic from Pidley-cum-Fenton and Owen's siding. Arrival at Somersham was at 5.00 pm. On Mondays if there was any cattle traffic at Warboys or Ramsey East for St Ives market the usual arrangements applied. The engine and brake then returned to Somersham to work the 12.45 pm down goods.

The timetable remained unaltered until after nationalization and from 27th September, 1948 the 12.00 noon SO ex-Ramsey East was retimed to depart at 11.15 am, calling at Warboys from 11.25 am to 12.15 pm and continuing to Somersham arriving at 12.45 pm. Further alterations were made in the timetable commencing on 7th February, 1949 when the 2.50 pm SX Ramsey East to Somersham departed from Warboys at the earlier time of 4.00 pm and calling at Pidley-cum-Fenton siding if required, arrived at Somersham at 4.45 pm. These timings remained in operation until 10th September, 1951 when the timetable was totally recast.

Down		SX	SO	Up		SO	SX
		am	am			pm	pm
Whitemoor	dep.	10.45	10.45	Ramsey East	dep.	2.10	2.50
Somersham	arr.	11.58	11.58	Warboys	arr.	2.20	3.00
	dep.	12.45	12.30		dep.	3.00	4.00
Pidley-c-F	dep.			Pidley-c-F	dep.		*
Warboys	arr.	1.05	12.50	Somersham	arr.	3.30	4.45
	dep.	2.00	1.15			A	B
Ramsey East	arr.	2.10	1.25				

A   To perform shunting as required at Somersham
B   To clear all traffic from Ramsey East and Warboys and to call at Pidley-cum-Fenton. On Mondays if there is any cattle at Warboys or Ramsey East for St Ives market the engine and brake van to run down for same and work to St Ives. Engine and brake then to return from St Ives to Somersham to work the 12.45 pm goods to Ramsey East.

The 12.30 pm SO Somersham to Ramsey East and 2.10 pm return working was withdrawn in the timetable operative from 30th June to 14th September, 1952, but were reinstated with effect from 15th September. Evidently the reduction in traffic did not warrant the running of the Saturday services and when the working timetable was reissued from 3rd November, 1952 the trains were again withdrawn. Until closure the branch was thereafter, only served by trains running Mondays to Fridays. From 21st September, 1953 further minor changes were made to the timings.

Down		SX	Up		SX
		am			*pm*
Whitemoor	*dep.*	10.45	Ramsey East	*dep.*	2.40
Somersham	*arr.*	11.58	Warboys	*arr.*	2.50
	dep.	12.40		*dep.*	3.50
Pidley-c-F	*dep.*		Pidley-c-F	*dep.*	R
Warboys	*arr.*	1.00	Somersham	*arr.*	4.35
	dep.	1.50			
Ramsey East	*arr.*	2.00			

R – Calls if required

From 13th June, 1955 the 2.40 pm ex-Ramsey East was retimed to depart Warboys at 3.40 pm and serving Pidley-cum-Fenton siding if required, arrived at Somersham at 4.25 pm. These timings remained in force until the freight service was withdrawn from Ramsey East on and from 17th September, 1956.

With the publication of the new working timetable the truncated branch was served by the 11.55 am ex-Whitemoor class 'K' goods service.

Down		SX	Up		SX
		pm			*pm*
Somersham	*arr.*	2.05	Warboys	*dep.*	3.25
	dep.	2.45	Pidley-c-F	*dep.*	R
Pidley-c-F	*dep.*		Somersham	*arr.*	4.05
Warboys	*arr.*	3.05		*dep.*	4.30
					To March
					down yard

R – Calls if required

For the short period Cordwell's private siding was in use until 20th August, 1957 wagons were propelled from Warboys and hauled back.

From 6th May, 1957 the timetable was altered yet again with the train leaving Whitemoor an hour earlier at 10.55 am and consequently running an hour earlier across the branch.

Down		SX	Up		SX
		pm			*pm*
Somersham	*arr.*	12.47	Warboys	*dep.*	2.35
	dep.	1.40	Pidley-c-F	*dep.*	*
Pidley-c-F	*dep.*		Somersham	*arr.*	3.05
Warboys	*arr.*	2.00		*dep.*	3.30
					To March
					down yard

* Calls if required

These revised timings were further amended in the timetable effective from 15th June, 1957 when the 2.35 pm ex-Warboys was booked to run an hour later throughout after the brick company complained that the earlier timing did not allow enough time to load the wagons. From 15th September, 1958 the train departed Warboys at 3.35 pm and arrived at Somersham at 4.08 pm, leaving for March Down Yard at 4.34 pm. The next alteration to the branch freight was made on and from 2nd November, 1959 with the following timings.

SOMERSHAM, WARBOYS AND RAMSEY EAST

SINGLE LINE

Worked by train staff without tickets and by only one engine in steam (or two or more engines coupled together). For regulations for working see "Appendix"

DOWN — WEEKDAYS

	No.	1	2	3	4
	Class		K	K	
	Description				
Miles from Somersham	Departs from		Whitemoor 6.30 a.m.	Whitemoor 10.45 a.m.	
	Previous Times on Page		J 68	J 71	

			SO	SX	
			am	am	
	Somersham ....(S)	....	8 25	11 48	....
	Somersham	..	9 30	12 45	..
2 20	Pidley-cum-Fenton Siding	......	....	....	....
4 31	Warboys	..	9 50	1 5	..
	Warboys..............	..	10 30	2 0	....
6 75	Ramsey East .. .. (S)	..	10 40	2 10	..

2nd 3   Allowed 5 minutes between Somersham and Warboys for the opening and closing of gates at Pidley-cum-Fenton Siding.

UP — WEEKDAYS

Miles from Ramsey E.		No.	5	6	7	8
		Class		K		K
		Description				
M. C.				SO		SX
				am		PM
2 44		Ramsey East ....(S)	.....	11 15	.....	2 50
		Warboys	..	11 25	..	3 0
		Warboys................	..	12 15	.....	4 0
4 55		Pidley-cum-Fenton Siding	.. ..	.. ..	..	✳
6 75		Somersham ....(S)	.....	12 45	.....	4 45

6   To perform shunting as required at Somersham.

8   To clear all traffic from Ramsey E. and Warboys and call at Pidley-cum-Fenton. At Pidley-cum-Fenton Siding, Guard to obtain train staff from Driver and work ground frame as necessary.

10.45 a.m. SX WHITEMOOR TO RAMSEY

On Mondays if any cattle at Warboys or Ramsey for St. Ives Market the engine and brake to run down for same and work to St. Ives.

Engine and brake returning from St. Ives to Somersham to work 12.45 p.m. goods to Ramsey.

Miscellaneous traffic and live stock at passenger train rates will also be conveyed by Goods Service.

BR (ER) working timetable 1950.

BR (ER) working timetable 1961.

WEEKDAYS   SOMERSHAM AND WARBOYS

			K					F
DOWN			11.55 am from Whitemoor		**UP**			To Whitemoor
Mileage					Mileage			
M C					M C			
			SX					SX
			PM					PM
0 0	SOMERSHAM .... arr	....	1 29	..	0 0	Warboys .... dep	....	2 55
	.. .. dep	..	1 55	..	2 11	Pidley-cum-Fenton Siding	..	R
2 20	Pidley-cum-Fenton Siding	....	....	..	4 31	SOMERSHAM .... arr	....	3 28
4 31	Warboys.. .. .. arr	....	2 15	..		.. .. dep	..	3 55

Down		SX	Up		SX
		pm			*pm*
Whitemoor	*dep.*	12.00	Warboys	*dep.*	3.35
Somersham	*arr.*	1.43	Pidley-c-F	*dep.*	R
	dep.	2.15	Somersham	*arr.*	4.08
Pidley-c-F	*dep.*			*dep.*	4.55
Warboys	*arr.*	2.35			*To*
					Whitemoor

R – Calls if required

This timetable lasted barely two months for from 4th January, 1960, the 3.35 pm SX ex-Warboys was retimed to leave Warboys at the earlier time of 2.50 pm. After calling at Pidley-cum-Fenton, if required, the train arrived at Somersham at 3.23 pm and after shunting the yard departed for Whitemoor at 4.00 pm. Later in the year from 21st November, 1960 the train was again retimed as under:

Down	Class	K	Up	Class	F
		SX			SX
		am			*pm*
Whitemoor	*dep.*	11.55	Warboys	*dep.*	2.55
Somersham	*arr.*	1.26	Pidley-c-F	*dep.*	R
	dep.	1.55	Somersham	*arr.*	3.28
Pidley-c-F	*dep.*			*dep.*	3.55
Warboys	*arr.*	2.15			*To*
					Whitemoor

R – calls if required

This timetable remained in operation until the withdrawal of freight services from the branch on and from 13th July, 1964, although by then trains were running as class 8.

Fares

During the early years first, second and third class fares were offered on the branch services but in 1893 the second class fares were abolished. With the opening of the new line, the GNR reduced its fares from Ramsey to London King's Cross to the same rate as the GER charged from Ramsey High Street to London Liverpool Street via St Ives.

Fares charged in 1914 to the branch stations from Liverpool Street were:

	First Class				*Third Class*			
	Single		*Return*		*Single*		*Return*	
	£	*s.*	*d.*	£	*s.*	*d.*	£	*s.*	*d.*
Somersham	9	8	19	1	5	4	10	8
Warboys	10	6	1	0	4	5	8½	11	5
Ramsey High Street	11	0	1	1	1	5	11	11	10

'J15' class 0-6-0 No. 7553 approaching Stanway, near Colchester, with a Ramsey East to Clacton excursion train in July 1939.   *P. Proud*

A pair of handbills advertising excursion trains in 1937.

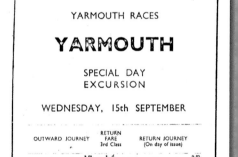

Local fares from Somersham were:

Warboys		10	1	3	4½		9
Ramsey High Street	1	2	2	0	7	1	2

from Warboys to Ramsey High Street

4	7	2½	5

Excursions

For the 41 years the Ramsey High Street branch was open for passenger traffic, excursion facilities were offered to various seaside resorts and places of interest in East Anglia, as well as to London and the cities of Cambridge, Ely and Norwich. The programmes offered were not, however, as extensive as that enjoyed by other GER branches.

The GER quickly took advantage of possible traffic and ran its first excursion to Hunstanton on Wednesday 25th September, 1889, departing Ramsey High Street at 8.01 am and returning from Hunstanton at 7.20 pm. Fares charged were 3s. 6d. second class and 3s. 0d. third class, with children aged 3 to 14 years half price and under 3 years free of charge. Despite being a weekday, 43 passengers joined at Ramsey High Street and 30 at Warboys. By October both the GNR and GER were offering cheap excursion fares to London on the same day each week, an action, which brought outright criticism from the travelling public who wished the facilities on separate days. The complaints were fully justified for on 17th October, 1889, 27 passengers travelled from Ramsey on the 7.15 am departure via the GNR route to London with facilities to return on the 4.20 pm or 12.00 midnight trains from King's Cross. In contrast only seven passengers booked via the GER on the 8.10 am from Ramsey High Street but these excursionists were only permitted to return on the 5.15 pm train from Liverpool Street.

Queen Victoria's Diamond Jubilee in 1897 was a time of great celebration and a general holiday was granted. In order to permit as many people to visit the capital the railway companies issued return tickets to London. For the event the GER issued tickets from Somersham, Warboys and Ramsey High Street available on 22nd June or by the last local branch train the previous evening, enabling passengers to wait at the junction for the early morning up mail train, thus providing an earlier arrival at Liverpool Street. Tickets were available for return on 22nd June or up to 8.00 am on the 23rd and many took advantage of the offer.

Excursions throughout the years were not solely aimed at pleasure-seekers but also local businessmen. Such an excursion was nurtured by the desire of the GER to attract further agricultural traffic in East Anglia. On Wednesday 2nd November, 1921 local fruit growers were invited to take advantage of a special cheap day outing to a fruit growers exhibition in London. The railway company arranged for their 'Apple Show Express' routed from King's Lynn via Wisbech, March, St Ives and Cambridge to Liverpool Street to call additionally at Somersham. Several local growers took advantage of the offer with excursion fares from Ramsey High Street and Warboys.

The LNER maintained the programme of excursions and cheap day facilities after Grouping. Even after passenger services were withdrawn in September 1930 residents of Ramsey, Warboys and Somersham were able to enjoy days out at the seaside as excursions continued during the summer months.

Arrangements for working excursion trains were quite complex and involved much non-revenue earning mileage. A special to Yarmouth races on Wednesday 20th September, 1933 required the empty coaching and locomotive to depart from Cambridge at 4.20 am to form the 6.10 am departure from Ramsey East calling at Warboys and Somersham. After reversal the train continued to March (reverse) and then non-stop via Ely avoiding curve to Brandon where the locomotive took water. The train continued avoiding Norwich via the Wensum curve which gave arrival at Yarmouth Vauxhall at 10.18 am. Only part of the train came from Ramsey East with the remainder being added at Somersham. The formation consisted of six bogie coaches and six 6-wheel saloons, the latter for private parties, and the return was made by the same route.

Examples of excursions offered included a cheap evening excursion to Hunstanton on Sunday 4th July, 1937 for a return fare of 2s. 0d. and a day excursion to Yarmouth Races on Wednesday 15th September, 1937 at a return fare of 8s. 6d. In July 1939 one of the destinations was Clacton. Excursion facilities on a regular basis ceased on the outbreak of World War II, although after hostilities in the late 1940s and early 1950s occasional excursions still ran from the branch stations to Hunstanton and Yarmouth.

Goods traffic

In the years prior to the opening of the Ramsey & Somersham Junction Railway a number of carriers served this area of Huntingdonshire, travelling with their waggons over the poorly-maintained roads and cart tracks. From Ramsey, Stacey operated a van to Huntingdon on Saturdays and St Ives on Mondays, whilst from Warboys, William Ashley ran a service to Huntingdon on Saturdays and Mrs Ellen Noble operated a van to St Ives on Mondays and Fridays, and Huntingdon on Saturdays. Philip Newman served the village of Pidley and operated to St Ives on Mondays and Huntingdon on Saturdays. Much of the freight traffic to London and the North was already being handled by the GNR via Holme, and with the added competitive service offered by the GER much of the carrier trade initially disappeared from the roads. By 1906 Warboys had no regular carrier service by road but Ramsey continued to enjoy a van to Peterborough and by 1914 Storey was operating to St Ives on Mondays and Fridays and Peterborough on Wednesdays and Saturdays. Local carriers also provided a useful integrated collection and delivery service from farms to the goods yards at Pidley, Warboys and Ramsey High Street.

The R&SJR served an area of some 50,000 acres of good agricultural soil, suitable for the growing of root crops and although hay, straw and barley formed the initial commodities conveyed by rail, these items were soon augmented by vegetables including potatoes, swedes, turnips, mangold wurzels and other root crops which were forwarded to the markets at St Ives, March, Wisbech, Cambridge and Huntingdon. Vegetables were later forwarded to the London markets at Spitalfields and Covent Garden whilst barley was sent further afield to the maltings at Bury St Edmunds and Godmanchester.

J.H.L. Davies the station master at Warboys wrote to the *GER Magazine* on 20th January, 1921:

A somewhat remarkable coincidence has come under notice here this month in connection with the use of trucks. GER wagon No. 01991 was despatched from here to Bishopsgate on 3rd January with a load of carrots from a farmer consigned to several merchants at Bishopsgate. On 7th January the same wagon came back here among the supply of empties and was loaded and consignees being the same - in one week. This is remarkable in two ways, first that the coincidence was not noticed until afterwards and therefore was spontaneous, and secondly in the fact of the open truck coming back here, although not labelled 'Warboys'.

Milk was regularly dispatched from both stations on the branch to Somersham for connection with the St Ives and Cambridge train in the familiar 17 gallon churns. Two loads were normally sent during the summer months with only one consignment in winter, usually by the mid-morning train. The area served by the branch was not noted for its dairy farming and the relatively light amounts of traffic conveyed by train were lost to the railway when the passenger services were withdrawn in 1930. From then road carriers collected the churns direct from farms and conveyed the product direct to dairies at St Ives or Peterborough.

Livestock handled at the branch stations was two-way traffic with young calves being imported from all parts of the country including Ireland and Scotland. The fattened cattle were later exported to St Ives, Cambridge, March, Wisbech and other East Anglian markets. At one time cattle were also forwarded to Tufnell Park en route to Smithfield Market. Until the closing of the line to passenger traffic it was permissible to attach cattle wagons fitted with Westinghouse brakes to the branch passenger services. The busiest day for the transhipment of cattle was on Mondays when beasts were loaded at Ramsey High Street, Warboys, Pidley and Somersham for conveyance to St Ives market. The return working brought imports of sheep and pigs as well as cattle purchased by local farmers. Ramsey also held a market every Wednesday although it was a mere shadow of the larger market at St Ives. The busiest time for movement of livestock on the branch coincided with the annual cattle fair held at Ramsey each year on 22nd July, Sundays excepted, when additional cattle trains were operated across the branch before and after the event. Cattle wagons were regularly conveyed on the branch until after World War II.

A small amount of horse traffic was also conveyed, and although not on the same scale as cattle traffic, the local gentry often made use of horseboxes to convey their mounts to local shows or bloodstock sales. By the end of World War I this traffic declined and horseboxes were then a rarity on the line.

Coal and coke traffic was handled at all stations and sidings from the opening of the railway, initially in privately-owned wagons from Sherwood, Newstead, Kirkby, Stanton, Shirebrook and Clipstone collieries. The wagons travelled via

'J17' class 0-6-0 No. 65521 leaves Somersham Junction with the branch goods to Warboys. The signal in the clear position is Somersham up home signal on the March to St Ives line. The points leading to Somersham goods yard are in the foreground.   *Dr I.C. Allen*

Former LMS '4F' class 0-6-0 No. 44219 shunts wagons in the new road at Warboys in 1959. To the right is the small cattle dock whilst behind the locomotive is the goods shed. To the left is the connection to the brickworks, whilst wagons occupy the former main line to Ramsey East.
Dr I.C. Allen

Peterborough, where the Stanground sidings acted as a clearing-house for empty wagons being returned to the collieries as well as loaded vehicles en route to the branch stations. Other wagons were routed via the GN&GE Joint line and later Whitemoor yard. From the early 1920s coke was conveyed in increasing quantities for horticultural purposes but after World War II this commodity was mostly conveyed by road.

From the mid-1920s sugar beet was cultivated on an increasing scale in the fertile fenland around Pidley, Warboys and Ramsey. The months from October to January were busy times at these goods yards as farmers' carts and tumbrils brought the beet to be loaded into wagons for onward conveyance to the sugar processing factories at Wissington, Spalding, Ely and to a lesser extent Peterborough. For the price of a 'pint' the station staff often manipulated wagon labels to ensure that certain farmer's consignments were given priority to the sugar beet factory. After World War II much of the sugar beet traffic was transferred to road haulage as the British Sugar Corporation changed the delivery point from Ely or Wissington to Peterborough for beet grown in the area around Ramsey. Other traffic was transferred to the Ramsey North branch but even this finally succumbed to road transport.

By far the largest tonnage of goods conveyed by the branch freight trains were bricks, which were loaded at Warboys and Owen's siding. Once R&SJR Director Alfred Fuller had established his brick and tile works alongside the railway at Warboys in 1893, and the sidings were connected to the main single branch line in 1894, considerable traffic was forwarded by rail. For many years the three large chimneys above the kilns, which dominated the skyline, belched smoke over the surrounding landscape as many millions of white bricks were manufactured. Workers initially excavated the clay by picks and shovels from the locally known, 'Key Hole', but later mechanical excavation was introduced. The clay was then conveyed in trucks on a narrow 2 ft gauge railway system up to the works and finally the kilns. The clay pit was to the west of the works and the wagons were initially rope hauled but later the line extended for over half a mile. There were also traversers working on a gauge of 2 ft 11 in. and also a 4 ft 3 in. gauge in the kilns, augmented at a later stage by 6 ft 4 in. gauge traversers.

Alfred Fuller later sold the works to Forder's Ltd and by 1923 the brickworks were taken over by the London Brick Co. and Forder's Ltd, and later totally by the London Brick Co. By the 1930s the 60 men employed within the works were producing 300,000 'Warboys Whites' weekly, with an annual output of 15,000,000 bricks and demand was almost exceeding supply. Most bricks were dispatched by rail but by the late 1920s some that were required locally were sent by road. The railway company, however, continued to handle the greater tonnage of 'Warboys Whites', the bricks being sent to Letchworth for the creation of houses in the First Garden City and later Cambridge for the new estates being developed on the outskirts of the University City. Warboys brickworks closed soon after the outbreak of World War II but then reopened after hostilities. Six diesel-mechanical four-wheel and one petrol-mechanical four-wheel, 2 ft gauge locomotives were transferred from various brickworks between 1948 and 1952 to assist with the transporting of wagons of clay to the kilns and bricks to the standard gauge interchange siding for onward transit. A seventh diesel-mechanical locomotive was added in 1959 and five others in 1966 to 1972 after the closure of the branch to Warboys. The brickworks closed in 1984 and the tramway was lifted the following year.

The brickyard siding between Somersham and Pidley-cum-Fenton was opened in 1900 to serve the Somersham Brick Co. owned by Alfred James Bateman, but in 1919 the GN&GE Joint Committee signed an agreement with the new owner the First Garden City Co. Ltd. In November of the following year the works changed hands again and came under the ownership of Joseph Fenwick Owen and from then the siding was known locally as Owen's siding. The name persisted even after the brickworks came under the ownership of London Brick Co. and Forder's Ltd and later the London Brick Co. A narrow gauge tramway at one time ran to the claypit to the north-west of the works but the whole site was abandoned in 1941.

During World War II meat and other foodstuff was conveyed across the branch for storage in the various Ministry of Food cold storage depots in the area. Armaments and bombs for airfields in the locality were also offloaded at Warboys. The ammunition was usually conveyed under cover of darkness for transit by road to ammunition dumps located at well-camouflaged sites away from the airfields in the neighbourhood. The ammunition was usually conveyed in open wagons, sheeted over to conceal their deadly cargo, although the prominent red flashed labels advised 'Shunt With Great Care' and 'Place As Far As Possible From The Engine, Brake Van and Wagons Labelled Inflammable'.

Over the years a considerable tonnage of 'smalls' traffic destined for local shops and traders was conveyed across the branch but, to effect economies, on 4th February, 1947 a railhead was established at Ely for such merchandise. Thereafter a road collection and delivery service was established connecting Ely with stations on the Ely to St Ives line and the Ramsey East branch and parcels delivery was withdrawn from local station control. To 30th November, 1947 14,424 tons of merchandise was conveyed.

The following facilities were available for handling goods and livestock traffic at the branch stations:

Somersham	Loading dock
	Loading gauge
	Fixed crane 1 ton capacity
	Cart weighbridge 10 ton capacity
	Weighing machine 1 ton 2 cwt capacity
	Goods shed with storage for 1,500 quarters of grain
	Water supply for animals in transit
Pidley-cum-Fenton	Loading dock
	Loading gauge
	Cart weighbridge 7 tons capacity
	Weighing machine 5 cwt capacity
Warboys	Loading dock
	Loading gauge
	Fixed crane 2 tons capacity in goods shed

Cart weighbridge 8 tons capacity
Weighing machine 1 ton 12 cwt capacity
Goods shed with storage capacity for 80 quarters of grain
Water supply for animals in transit

Ramsey High Street   Loading dock
Loading gauge
Fixed crane 2 tons capacity in goods shed
Cart weighbridge 7 tons capacity
Weighing machine 1 ton 12 cwt capacity
Goods shed with storage capacity for 200 quarters of grain
Water supply for animals in transit

Somersham and Ramsey High Street could also handle furniture vans on wheels, whilst Warboys and Ramsey High Street had the necessary lifting tackle to lift round timber, road vans and containers into and out of wagons. All stations except Pidley also had lock-up premises for small packages. In GER days the latest time for receipt of animals or goods for forwarding the same day was as follows: Ramsey High Street 4.30 pm, Warboys 3.45 pm, Pidley siding 3.45 pm and Somersham 4.00 pm.

The GN&GE Joint Committee employed independent carriers to convey cartage to and from stations on the branch and on 8th April, 1897 the agreement for collection and delivery was made with Mr Mutton at Ramsey High Street and Mr Cawcute at Warboys, but by 1920 the GER was providing the cartage at Somersham and Warboys.

The timing allowance for freight trains between Somersham and Ramsey East in LNER and BR days was as follows for class 'F', 'H', 'J' and 'K' trains.

	Starting allowance minutes	Stopping allowance minutes	Passing allowance minutes
Somersham to Warboys*	3	2	15
Warboys to Ramsey East	2	2	6
Ramsey East to Warboys	2	2	6
Warboys to Pidley-cum-Fenton*	2	2	7
Pidley-cum-Fenton to Somersham*	2	2	7

* Allowed five minutes extra between Somersham and Warboys for operating crossing gates at Pidley-cum-Fenton siding.

These timings were later amended to:

Somersham to Warboys	20 minutes
Warboys to Ramsey East	10 minutes
Ramsey East to Warboys	10 minutes
Warboys to Pidley-cum-Fenton	11 minutes
Pidley-cum-Fenton to Somersham	9 minutes

The load limits of freight, authorized to be hauled by locomotives between Somersham and Ramsey High Street in GER days, were as follows:

	Number of wagons			
	Goods		*Coal*	
	Down	*Up*	*Down*	*Up*
First Class Engines	40	40	35	35
Second Class Engines	35	35	30	30
Third Class Engines	28	28	24	24

The 'E22' class 0-6-0Ts and 'Little Sharpie' 2-4-0s were classified as third class engines, whilst the 'T26' class 2-4-0s were allowed a second class load.

Around the turn of the century the loads for goods engines were revised as under:

	Down		*Up*	
Class of locomotive	*Minerals*	*Goods*	*Minerals*	*Goods*
A	50	50	50	50
B	34	48	25	35
C	30	42	22	31
D	26	37	20	28
E	23	33	18	26
F	23	33	17	24
G	20	28	15	21
H	19	27	14	20

The loads of up goods trains worked by a class 'C' locomotive could be increased to 35 wagons of minerals and 50 wagons of goods from Pidley-cum-Fenton siding to Somersham.

The locomotive classes regularly allocated for branch duties were classified as follows:

GER class	*LNER class*	*Type*	*Classification*
Little Sharpie	–	2-4-0	H
Y65	F7	2-4-2T	E
E22	J65	0-6-0T	H
M15	F4	2-4-2T	D
Y14	J15	0-6-0	C
T26	E4	2-4-0	B

By 1935 the wagon limits of trains on the Ramsey East branch was 75 vehicles although loads of this size were never handled. The full list of authorized loads then permitted was:

	Somersham-Ramsey East		
Class of locomotive	*Minerals*	*Goods*	*Empties*
1	32	48	62
2	36	54	69
3	40	59	75
4	44	64	75
5	49	70	75
6	54	75	75

Class of locomotive	Ramsey East-Pidley Minerals	Goods	Empties	Pidley-Somersham Minerals	Goods	Empties
1	24	36	48	36	54	69
2	26	39	52	40	59	75
3	29	43	58	45	65	75
4	32	48	62	50	71	75
5	36	54	69	55	75	75
6	40	59	75	60	75	75

After World War II the load limit for locomotives hauling class 'J' and 'K' freight trains across the branch were:

	Somersham-Ramsey East		
Class of locomotive	Heavies	Goods	Empties
1	24	42	48
2	31	55	62
3	34	60	68
4	38	67	75
5	40	71	75

Class of locomotive	Ramsey East-Pidley Heavies	Goods	Empties	Pidley-Somersham Heavies	Goods	Empties
1	22	39	44	34	60	68
2	23	41	46	34	60	68
3	26	46	52	39	69	75
4	29	51	58	44	75	75
5	32	57	64	46	75	75

A class '3' goods engine was a 'J15', class '4' a 'J17' and class '5' a 'J19'. The use of tow-ropes for shunting vehicles in adjacent sidings from the main single line was not permitted at Somersham or the branch stations. In the last years of operation it was permitted to propel 12 wagons from Warboys to Ramsey East. The *Freight Train Loads Book* effective from 6th April, 1964 permitted trains of 100 wagons between Somersham and Warboys but the Brush type '2' diesel-electric locomotives working the branch at that time were in fact limited to a tail load of 68 wagons on a class '8' train. Of course loads of this length were never conveyed as the branch was heavily in decline and closed three months later.

GER 'Y' class 2-4-0 as rebuilt in the latter years of its life. The 'U13' class, which hauled the initial services on the Ramsey High Street branch, closely resembled these 'Y' class rebuilds.

Samuel Johnson's 'Little Sharpie' 2-4-0s saw service on the Ramsey High Street branch in the early years. No. 107 was one of those allocated to Cambridge for service on cross-country and branch line duties and is here shown at King's Lynn shed on 1st April, 1902.   *LCGB/Ken Nunn*

Chapter Eight

Locomotives and Rolling Stock

The relatively light formation of the permanent way on the Ramsey East branch precluded the use of the heaviest GER locomotive classes from working the services. The rural area served and the small loads conveyed were capable of being handled by the lighter classes of tank and tender engines, which with their low axle loading were ideal for the route. The GER was fortunate in having locomotives of unrestricted route availability and these classes handled all passenger and freight services on the only branch of the GN&GE Joint Railway.

Initially the LNER only permitted the following classes of locomotive on the line: tender 'D16' for occasional excursion trains, 'E4', 'J15' and 'J17'; tank 'F4', 'F7', 'J65' to' J70' inclusive, 'Y1', 'Y3', 'Y5', 'Y6' and 'Y10'. Later the Ramsey East branch was classified as route availability RA3 with classes 'D16' and 'J19' of higher route availability '5', and 'J17' of route availability '4' permitted. Double-heading of trains was, however, prohibited. British Railways continued to classify the branch RA3 and also permitted the 'D16', 'J17' and 'J19' classes of higher route availability. After closure of the railway beyond Warboys and cessation of steam working on the GE line, the following diesel locomotives were allowed between Somersham and Warboys: '8/4', '8/5' later class '15', '10/4' later class '24', '11/4' later class '25', '12/2', '13/2' and '16/2' all later class '31'.

The locomotive allocated to work the branch trains on the opening day was 'U13' class 2-4-0 No. 382. She was one of a class of 10 introduced into service between September and December 1882, during the period when T.W. Worsdell had been appointed as locomotive superintendent at Stratford in succession to Matthew Bromley but had not taken up his position because of an engagement with the Pennsylvania Railroad in the USA. During the interregnum there was a shortage of locomotive power and M. Gillies, who was temporarily in charge took the safe option of introducing the 10 'U13' class, which were identical to the latest rebuilds of Sinclair's 'Y' class and in fact took the running numbers of withdrawn locomotives. No. 341 and 376 were also allocated to the Cambridge district and probably worked on the Ramsey High Street line alongside the 'Little Sharpies'. With other members of the class, the trio were later transferred to the duplicate list by having a '0' prefix added to the running number and after a relatively short life were withdrawn as follows. No. 0376 in 1892 and 0341 and 0382 in 1894. The leading dimensions of the 'U13' class were:

Cylinders		18 in. x 24 in.
Motion		Stephenson with slide valves
Boiler		
	Max. diameter	4 ft 2 in.
	Barrel	10 ft 9 in.
	Firebox	5 ft 5 in.
Heating surface		
	Tubes 203 x 1¾ in.	1,027.2 sq. ft
	Firebox	94.9 sq. ft
	Total	1,122.1 sq. ft

Grate area		15.27 sq. ft
Boiler pressure		140 psi
Leading wheels		3 ft 9 in.
Coupled wheels		6 ft 3 in.
Tender wheels		3 ft 8½ in.
Wheelbase		
	Engine	15 ft 2 in.
	Tender	11 ft 5 in.
Weight in working order		
	Engine	35 tons 9 cwt
	Tender	25 tons 14 cwt
	Total	61 tons 3 cwt
Max. axle loading		12 tons 12 cwt
Water capacity		2,000 gallons

In the initial years a motley collection of engines were used on the branch. At some time representatives of Samuel Johnson's 'No. 1' class were outbased at Ramsey High Street. They were nicknamed 'Little Sharpies', as 30 of the 40 2-4-0s were built by Sharp, Stewart & Co. between October 1867 and August 1872. During the years 1889 to 1895 the whole class was rebuilt and most were then allocated to cross-country and branch line duties. Cambridge depot had a small allocation and although their booked diagrams included regular workings between Cambridge and March, Ipswich and Colchester, they were also used on the Ely to St Ives line and the Ramsey High Street branch. They proved unpopular with the Ramsey crews who were forced to run the locomotives tender first in one direction because of the lack of an engine turntable on the branch. Several were placed on the duplicate list before withdrawal by having a '0' prefix added to their running number. Engines known to have worked on the line included:

GER No.	GER duplicate No.	Date duplicated	Withdrawn
1	01	1911	1913
3			1904
27			1910
32			1901
33			1913
36			1901
47			1908
48			1911
104	0104	1905	1911
106			1903
107	0107	1905	1911
118			1903
160	0160	1901	1902
161	0161	1901	1901

The leading dimensions of the class were:

Cylinders		16 in. x 22 in.
Motion		Stephenson with slide valves
Boiler	*Max. diameter*	4 ft 2 in.
	Length	9 ft 1 in.

Firebox		4 ft 6 in.
Heating surface		
	Tubes 223 x 1⁵/₈ in.	881.24 sq. ft
	Firebox	78.00 sq. ft
	Total	959.24 sq. ft
Grate area		12.4 sq. ft
Boiler pressure		140 psi
Leading wheels		3 ft 8 in.
Coupled wheels		5 ft 8 in.
Tender wheels		3 ft 8 in.
Weight in working order		
	Engine	30 tons 15 cwt
	Tender	18 tons 6 cwt
	Total	49 tons 1 cwt
Max. axle loading		10 tons 10 cwt
Water capacity		1,184 gallons

Between 1875 and 1878 William Adams introduced into service fifty 0-4-4Ts for local passenger services, with construction being shared between Neilson & Co., Robert Stephenson & Co. and Kitson & Co. Many of these '61' class were allocated for use in the London area and some had cut down mountings for use on the North Woolwich branch, whilst several were outbased at country depots. Cambridge district had a few and at least two were allocated to work the Ramsey High Street branch. By the time they were associated with the Huntingdonshire branch the class had been rebuilt with new boilers. The two locomotives known to have worked the line were

GER No.	*Withdrawn*
62	1906
64	1907

The leading dimensions of the '61' class were:

Cylinders		17 in. x 24 in.
Motion		Stephenson with slide valves
Boiler	*Outside diameter*	4 ft 2 in.
	Length	10 ft 0 in.
	Firebox	4 ft 8 ¹⁵/₁₆ in.
Heating surface		
	Tubes 223 x 1⁵/₈ in.	980.0 sq. ft
	Firebox	94.9 sq. ft
	Total	1,074.9 sq. ft
Grate area		15.27 sq. ft
Boiler pressure		140 psi
Driving wheels		4 ft 10 in.
Trailing wheels		2 ft 10 in.
Wheelbase		21 ft 7 in.
Weight in working order		46 tons 17 cwt
Max. axle loading		16 tons 14 cwt
Water capacity		1,000 gallons

Samuel Johnson's 'No. 1' class 'Little Sharpie' No 33, with others allocated to the Cambridge district regularly worked the Ramsey High Street branch in the early years. They were unpopular with footplate staff because, in the absence of a turntable, they ran tender first in one direction exposing the crews to the elements. Tank locomotives soon displaced these engines on the branch.

Adams GER '61' class 0-4-4T.

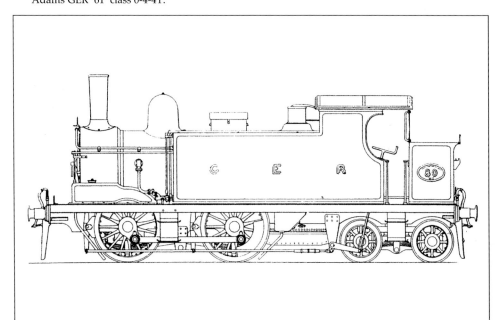

Two classes of small tank locomotives were also sent to work the Ramsey High Street services in the initial years. Totalling 10 in number, William Adams-designed 'K9' class 0-4-2Ts were built between 1877 and 1878. Ironically they were the only locomotives built at Stratford Works while Adams was in office. At first only a hand brake was fitted but the class was later fitted with the Westinghouse brake. A half-cab was originally provided when the locomotives were built but after a few years back weather plates were fitted and later a roof was extended to completely cover the footplate. No. 9 and two others were outbased at the Huntingdonshire shed working the branch in the early years at one time or another, but because of their small size they were considered inadequate when mixed trains were introduced and were transferred elsewhere. The class was withdrawn from service between 1903 and 1907, No. 9 being condemned in 1903.

The principal dimensions of the class were:

Cylinders		15 in. x 22 in.
Motion		Stephenson with slide valves
Boiler		
	Max. diameter	4 ft 2 in.
	Barrel length	9 ft 1 in.
	Firebox	4 ft 5³/₈ in.
Heating surface		
	Tubes 203 x 1¾ in.	874.87 sq. ft
	Firebox	75.43 sq. ft
	Total	950.30 sq. ft
Grate area		12.30 sq. ft
Boiler pressure		140 psi
Driving wheels		4 ft 10 in.
Trailing wheels		3 ft 8 in.
Wheelbase		14 ft 0 in.
Weight in working order		38 tons 11 cwt
Water capacity		850 gallons
Coal capacity		15 cwt

During the early years the other class allocated to work the line was Massey Bromley-designed '140' class 0-4-4Ts. R. & W. Hawthorn & Co., Newcastle-upon-Tyne built the 10 locomotives, Nos. 140 to 149 in 1880 and 1881 (Works Nos. 1822-1831). In 1890 No. 144 had its bogie removed and a single pair of trailing wheels, 3 ft 9 in. in diameter, substituted and placed 10 ft 6 in. behind the driving wheels giving a total wheelbase of 17 ft 4 in. Members of this class ran on the Ramsey High Street branch in both original and rebuilt form as conversion took place between 1891 and 1897. Withdrawal of the class was completed with the scrapping of No. 147 in 1906, after a few had been transferred to the duplicate list by having an '0' prefix added to the running number. The leading dimensions of the class as built were:

Cylinders	16 in. x 22 in.
Motion	Stephenson with slide valves
Firebox	4 ft 11½ in.

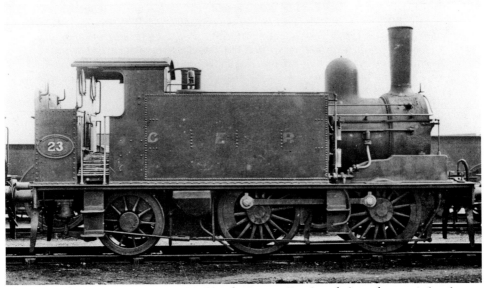

Adams 'K9' class 0-4-2Ts were utilized on the Ramsey East branch for a short period and a representative, No. 23, is shown at Stratford in 1905. *LCGB/Ken Nunn*

GER Bromley '140' class tank locomotives as rebuilt to 0-4-2T.

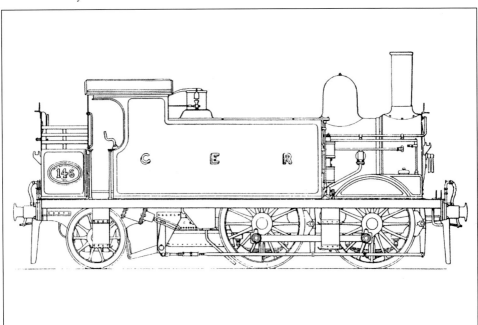

Heating surface

	Tubes 199 x 1¾ in.	857.2 sq. ft
	Firebox	84.6 sq. ft
	Total	941.8 sq. ft
Grate area		13.9 sq. ft
Boiler pressure		140 psi
Coupled wheels		5 ft 4 in.
Trailing wheels		2 ft 10 in.
Wheelbase		19 ft 1 in.
Weight in working order		42 tons 7 cwt
Max. axle loading		14 tons 19 cwt
Water capacity		977 gallons

Detailed difference when rebuilt as 0-4-2Ts were:

Trailing wheels	3 ft 9 in.
Wheelbase	17 ft 4 in.
Weight in working order	40 tons 19 cwt
Max. axle loading	13 tons 15 cwt

In 1889 James Holden introduced 10 six-coupled tank engines for light branch duties and classified them 'E22'. Four years later a further 10 locomotives were built with detailed differences. Initially many of the locomotives were sent to work on the Fenchurch Street to Blackwall services in East London with the result they were soon nicknamed the 'Blackwall Tanks'. After 1893 the Cambridge district was allocated three of the class with one usually outbased at Saffron Walden. One of the others was often allocated to Ramsey High Street and the little tank locomotives easily handled the two- or three-coach branch trains and were popular with the footplate staff. No. 150 the first of the class and No. 152 were initially used on the Huntingdonshire line to be later replaced by No. 151, 158 and for a short while No. 247. Their stay on the Ramsey High Street line was interspersed with the transfer to King's Lynn for use on the Stoke Ferry branch but by 1910 their association with the Ramsey High Street branch was at an end. They were later classified 'J65' by the LNER and had '7000' added to their numbers. Subsequent disposals were:

GER No.	LNER 1924 No.	LNER 1946 No.	BR No.	Withdrawn
150	7150	–	–	June 1937
151	7151	–	–	July 1937
152	7152	–	–	October 1935
158	7158	–	–	March 1932
247	7247	8213	–	February 1948

The leading dimensions of the 'J65' class were:

Cylinders	*2 inside*	14 in. x 20 in.
Motion		Stephenson with slide valves
Boiler	*Max. diameter*	4 ft 2 in.
	Barrel length	9 ft 1 in.
	Firebox	4 ft 6 in.

During the early years on the Ramsey High Street branch, the services were worked by Massey Bromley's '140' class 0-4-2Ts, although individual numbers of locomotive working the line are unknown. A representative of the class No. 145 is shown shunting at Yarmouth in March 1902.
LCGB/Ken Nunn

Holden's 'E22' class 0-6-0Ts worked the branch for some years before the advent of the 'Y65' class 2-4-2Ts. A regular engine to be outbased at Ramsey High Street shed was No 151, here shown at Stratford with the front coupling rods removed.   *Author's Collection*

Heating surface

	Tubes 227 x 1⁵/₈ in.	909.4 sq. ft
	Firebox	78.0 sq. ft
	Total	987.4 sq. ft
Grate area		12.4 sq. ft
Boiler pressure		160 psi
Coupled wheels		4 ft 0 in.
Tractive effort		11,106 lb.
Length over buffers		27 ft 2 in.
Wheelbase		13 ft 4 in.
Weight in working order		36 tons 11 cwt
Max. axle loading		13 tons 3 cwt
Water capacity		650 gallons
Coal capacity		2 tons 10 cwt

The locomotive class longest associated with the Ramsey High Street branch, was the 'Y65' designed by S.D. Holden and introduced into service in 1909 and 1910. Built for light branch passenger work to replace the 'E22' class 0-6-0Ts, they were the least successful of Holden's 2-4-2Ts. Twelve locomotives Nos. 1300 to 1311 were constructed at Stratford Works and their small boiler and enormous cabs soon earned them the nickname of 'Crystal Palaces'. Because of their inability to haul loads of any length, the GER authorities obviously thought the Ramsey High Street branch, with its relatively easy gradients and moderate loadings was eminently suited to their limited capabilities. The 'Y65s' then became the regularly-allocated class, a long-standing connection, which continued until the withdrawal of passenger services in 1930. No. 1306, initially allocated to Stoke Ferry was soon transferred to the Cambridge district and outbased at Ramsey High Street. Others subsequently sub-shedded at Ramsey included No. 1302, which had seen earlier service at Buntingford and Southend, Nos. 1307, 1308 and 1310. In 1914 No. 1311 was equipped with an additional Westinghouse pump on the end of the left-hand side tank for compressed air auto-train working. Trials with a two-coach auto-train were conducted on the Cambridge to Mildenhall branch for several weeks before the train was transferred to work for a short period on the Somersham to Ramsey High Street line. It then took up regular duties in 1915 on the temporarily-reopened Churchbury loop line operating a shuttle service between White Hart Lane and Cheshunt, essentially for munitions workers employed at establishments in the Lea Valley. After Grouping the LNER reclassified the 'Y65s' to 'F7' and renumbered the locomotives 8300 to 8311 inclusive. In the years prior to the withdrawal of the passenger services Nos. 8308 and 8310 invariably shared the duties week and week about at Ramsey East and the haulage of the final train on Saturday 20th September, 1930 fell to No. 8308. Nos. 8308 and 8310 later found fresh fields of operation being transferred to Scotland in June and October 1932 to work the Gifford, Lauder and Selkirk branches and the Galashiels to Peebles line. The subsequent disposal of the 'F7' class known to have worked on the Ramsey High Street branch was as follows:

In 1914 the GER commenced auto-train trials and converted two bogie coaches to form a set with the driving controls on the brake third vehicle. To work the train 'Y65' class 2-4-2T No. 1311 was equipped with an additional compressed air pump and ancillary items. The train commenced trials on the Cambridge to Mildenhall branch before working for a short period between Somersham and Ramsey High Street. The set then operated the temporary service on the Churchbury loop where No. 1311 is shown with her two-coach train on the 3.20 pm Cheshunt to Lower Edmonton service at Theobalds Grove on 20th March, 1915.   *LCGB/Ken Nunn*

'Y65' class 2-4-2Ts were the mainstay of the Ramsey High Street branch services in the last two decades of passenger workings. No. 1310 was regularly out-based at the Huntingdonshire shed and is shown still bearing her original number at Stratford on 12th February, 1925. The class was reclassified by the LNER to 'F7' and No. 1310 was renumbered 8310.   *LCGB/Ken Nunn*

GER No.	LNER 1924 No.	LNER 1946. No.	BR No.	Withdrawn
1302	8302	–	–	May 1931
1306	8306	–	–	April 1931
1307	8307	7596	–	June 1943
1308	8308	7597	7093	November 1948
1310	8310	7598	7094	November 1948
1311	8311	–	–	September 1931

The principal dimensions of the 'F7' class were:

Cylinders	2 inside	15 in. x 22 in.
Motion		Stephenson with slide valves
Boiler	Max. diameter	3 ft 11½ in.
	Length	9 ft 1 in.
	Firebox	4 ft 6 in.
Heating surface		
	Tubes 199 x 1⅝ in.	797.2 sq. ft
	Firebox	75.7 sq. ft
	Total	872.9 sq. ft
Grate area		12.2 sq. ft
Boiler pressure		160 psi
Leading wheels		3 ft 6 in.
Coupled wheels		4 ft 10 in.
Trailing wheels		3 ft 6 in.
Tractive effort		11,607 lb.
Length over buffers		30 ft 11 in.
Wheelbase		19 ft 6 in.
Weight in working order		45 tons 14 cwt
Max. axle load		14 tons 3 cwt
Water capacity		1,000 gallons
Coal capacity		2 tons

In the rare event of the non-availability of a 'Y65' class 2-4-2T for the branch services, Cambridge usually sub-shedded an 'M15' class or later 'M15R' rebuilt class 2-4-2T at Ramsey High Street. Initially designed by T.W. Worsdell, the first locomotives entered service in 1884. Three years later 40 of the class were at work but proved troublesome and their excessive fuel consumption, partly caused by the incorrect setting of the Joy's valve gear, led to their being nicknamed 'Gobblers'. When James Holden was appointed mechanical engineer of the GER he removed the Joy's valve gear and fitted the more conventional Stephenson valve gear. Between 1903 and 1909 a further 120 locomotives were built and put to work on the London suburban services. From 1911 to 1923 the GER rebuilt 30 engines with boilers pressed to 180 psi and brass rimmed parallel chimneys and classified them 'M15R'. Withdrawal of the 1884 to 1887 locomotives commenced in 1913 and the remainder were condemned by the LNER, the final batch going in 1929. Some of Holden's 1903 to 1909 batch, were withdrawn in the same year although it was 1956 before the 'M15', classified 'F4' by the LNER, was extinct. The 'M15Rs' were classified 'F5' at the same time and both classes made spasmodic appearances on the Ramsey High

'F4' class 2-4-2T No. 7799 at Stratford in April 1926 after being withdrawn from traffic the previous month. No. 7799 was occasionally outbased at Ramsey High Street shed in GER days and was also used on the Saffron Walden branch.   *LCGB/Ken Nunn*

The GER 'T26' class, later LNER 'E4' class 2-4-0s were regularly used on excursion trains, officers 'specials and other out of course workings on the Somersham to Ramsey High Street line. No. 62788 waits on the spur before leaving Cambridge shed on 15th October, 1949. This locomotive was provided with an improved cab with larger side sheets and a single window in 1936, after being transferred to the North East area by the LNER the previous year to work the Darlington to Tebay and Penrith services.   *LCGB/Ken Nunn*

Street branch before and after World War I. The few that were allocated to Cambridge were far more valuable to the GER and later LNER motive power foreman at Cambridge or on the Saffron Walden branch and as soon as a 'Y65'/'F7' class 2-4-2T was again available it was dispatched 'post haste' to Ramsey to release the 'F4' or 'F5' for more onerous duties. Locomotives known to have worked from Ramsey High Street shed included:

GER No.	LNER 1924 No.	LNER 1946 No.	BR No.	Withdrawn
174	7174	7170	–	April 1948
790	7790	7219	67219*	November 1956
799	7799	–	–	March 1926

* Reclassified to 'F5' in 1948

The principal dimensions of the 'F4' and 'F5' classes were:

		M15 (F4)	M15R (F5)
Cylinders		17½ in. x 24 in.	
Motion		Stephenson with slide valves	
Boiler	Max. diameter	4 ft 2 in.	
	Barrel length	10 ft 2 ½ in.	
	Firebox	5 ft 5 in.	
Heating surface			
	Tubes	227 x 1⁵/₈ in.	
	Surface	1,018.0 sq. ft	1,018.0 sq. ft
	Firebox	98.4 sq. ft	96.7 sq. ft
	Total	1,116.4 sq. ft	1,114.7 sq. ft
Grate area		15.3 sq. ft	15.2 sq. ft
Boiler pressure		160 psi	180 psi
Leading wheels		3 ft 9 in.	
Driving wheels		5 ft 4 in.	
Trailing wheels		3 ft 9 in.	
Tractive effort		15,618 lb.	17,571 lb.
Length over buffers		34 ft 10 in.	
Wheelbase		23 ft 0 in.	
Weight in working order		51 tons 11 cwt	53 tons 19 cwt
Max. axle loading		14 tons 18 cwt	16 tons 0 cwt
Water capacity		1,200 gallons	
Coal capacity		3 tons 10 cwt	

From time to time the GER 'T26' class 2-4-0s nicknamed 'Intermediates' visited the branch. The class of 100 was built to the design of James Holden at Stratford Works between 1891 and 1902. Most were assigned for mixed traffic duties, long cross-country routes and slower traffic on the main line. From about the turn of the century the 'T26s' often worked excursion trains, special freight services and officers' specials across the Ramsey High Street branch. The LNER classified the class 'E4' but in the late 1920s and early 1930s many were scrapped. By 1936 Cambridge only had an allocation of two of the class and their visits to the branch were rare. From 1942 the class was reduced to 18 locomotives of which 11 were allocated to Cambridge. Despite the increase in allocation the Ramsey East branch saw few sightings of the class before their final demise. The last locomotive to be withdrawn No. 62785, condemned in December 1959, was restored to its former glory in GER livery as No. 490 and is now part of the National Railway Collection. The 'T26s'/'E4s' known to have worked across the branch included:

GER No.	LNER 1924 No.	LNER 1946 No.	BR No.	Withdrawn
460	7460	–	–	April 1929
463	7463	2781	62781	January 1956
473	7473	–	–	December 1935
474	7474	–	–	April 1929
477	7477	2783	62783	December 1954
490	7490	2785	62785	December 1959
496	7496	2788	62788	March 1958
506	7506	2791	62791	April 1955
1252	7409	2794	62794	August 1955
1253	7410	–	–	January 1935

The leading dimensions of the 'E4' class were:

Cylinders	2 inside		17½ in. x 24 in.
Motion			Stephenson with slide valves
Boiler	Max. diameter outside		4 ft 4 in.
	Barrel length		10 ft 0 in.
	Firebox		6 ft 0 in.
Heating surface			
	Tubes 242 x 1⅝ in.		1,063.8 sq. ft
	Firebox		100.9 sq. ft
	Total		1,164.7 sq. ft
Grate area			18.0 sq. ft
Boiler pressure			160 psi
Leading wheels			4 ft 0 in.
Coupled wheels			5 ft 8 in.
Tractive effort			14,700 lb.
Length over buffers			48 ft 2 in.*
Wheelbase			16 ft 6 in.
Weight in working order			40 tons 6 cwt
Max. axle loading			14 tons 3 cwt
Tender			
	Wheelbase		12 ft 0 in.
	Wheel diameter		4 ft 1 in.
	Weight in working order		30 tons 13 cwt
	Water capacity		2,640 gallons
	Coal capacity		5 tons

* Engine and tender

Members of the '477' class 0-6-0s allocated to Cambridge and March depots hauled the initial through freight services on the branch in the final years of their life. Originally introduced between 1871 and 1873 and numbered in the series 477 to 526 the engines came from a number of builders, Beyer, Peacock,

Robert Stephenson, Dübs, Nasmyth Wilson and the Yorkshire Engine Co. All were withdrawn from service between 1897 and 1902. The principal dimensions of the class were:

Cylinders	*2 inside*	17 in. x 24 in.
Motion		Stephenson with slide valves
Boiler	*Max. diameter outside*	4 ft 2 in.
	Barrel length	10 ft 0 in.
	Firebox outside length	5 ft 5 in.
Heating surface		
	Tubes 223 x 1⅝ in.	980.0 sq. ft
	Firebox	94.9 sq. ft
	Total	1,074.9 sq. ft
Grate area		15.27 sq. ft
Boiler pressure		140 psi
Coupled wheels		5 ft 2 in.
Tender wheels		3 ft 8 in.
Wheelbase		
	Engine	15 ft 6 in.
	Tender	12 ft 0 in.
Weight in working order		
	Engine	32 tons 13 cwt
	Tender	26 tons 5 cwt
	Total	58 tons 18 cwt
Max. axle loading		12 tons 6 cwt
Water capacity		2,038 gallons

From the outset GER 'Y14' class 0-6-0 tender locomotives hauled special freight, ballast and through goods trains from March, Ely or Cambridge, across the branch. Designed by T.W. Worsdell and introduced in 1883, such was their success that building continued until 1913. All except 19 of the 289 members of the class were built at Stratford Works with the remainder constructed by Sharp, Stewart & Co. Members of this ubiquitous class equipped with the Westinghouse and later vacuum brakes were also sent to Ramsey East to work through excursion trains to seaside resorts. On one occasion in July 1939, 'J15' No. 7553 worked a through train from the branch to Clacton-on-Sea via Cambridge and Haverhill on a round trip of 185 miles. They also worked special trains through to Hunstanton via March, Wisbech and King's Lynn. Members of the class known to have worked on the Ramsey East branch included:

GER No.	LNER 1924 No.	LNER 1946 No.	BR No.	Withdrawn
508	7508	5428	–	August 1949
509	7509	5429	–	November 1950
510	7510	5430	65430	January 1956
511	7511	5431	65431	March 1951
512	7512	5432	65432	March 1958
518	7518	–	–	April 1937
520	7520	5437	–	September 1950
521	7521	–	–	June 1939
522	7522	–	–	March 1936

GER No.	LNER 1924 No.	LNER 1946 No.	BR No.	Withdrawn
523	7523	5438	65438	June 1958
524	7524	–	–	March 1936
526	7526	5439	–	November 1951
527	7527	5354	–	February 1951
529	7529	–	–	December 1931
530	7530	5355	–	April 1951
531	7531	–	–	August 1928
532	7532	5356	65356	April 1957
533	7533	–	–	May 1928
535	7535	–	–	March 1936
536	–	–	–	August 1923
546	7546	5474	65474	February 1960
547	7547	5475	65475	September 1959
548	7548	5476	65476	September 1962
549	7549	5477	65477	February 1960
555	7555	5453	65453	August 1962
559	7559	5457	65457	February 1962
563	7563	5461	65461	April 1960
564	7564	5462	65462*	September 1962
570	7570	5468	65468	September 1959
571	7571	5469	65469	August 1962
627	7627	–	–	November 1933
628	7628	–	–	December 1931
642	7642	5442	65442	May 1958
646	7646	5446	65446	December 1960
680	7680	–	–	June 1932
681	7681	–	–	October 1932
682	7682	–	–	January 1932
683	7683	–	–	November 1931
685	7685	–	–	October 1929
689	7689	–	–	June 1936
803	7803	–	–	December 1935
805	7805	–	–	April 1928
806	7806	–	–	October 1939
825	7825	5352	–	May 1948
826	7826	–	–	September 1929
831	7831	–	–	November 1936
832	–	–	–	August 1923
840	7840	5363	–	August 1949
842	7842	–	–	November 1934
843	7843	5364	–	June 1949
845	7845	–	–	December 1938
846	7846	5365	–	July 1950
847	7847	5366	65366	June 1952
848	7848	5367	–	January 1950
849	7849	5368	–	May 1948
851	7851	–	–	October 1936
856	7856	–	–	October 1936
857	7857	5374	–	November 1950
887	7887	5390	65390	December 1958
890	7890	–	–	February 1935

GER No.	LNER 1924 No.	LNER 1946 No.	BR No.	Withdrawn
897	7897	5396	–	March 1951
908	7908	5403	–	August 1947
920	7920	5410	–	February 1948
921	7921	5411	–	April 1948
928	7928	5417	65417	August 1956
929	7929	5418	–	March 1948

* No 65462 is preserved

The leading dimensions of the 'J15' class were:

Cylinders	2 inside	17½ in. x 24 in.
Motion		Stephenson with slide valves
Boiler	Max. diameter	4 ft 4 in.
	Barrel length	10 ft 0 in.
	Firebox outside length	6 ft 0 in.
Heating surface		
	Tubes 242 x 1⅝ in.	1,063.8 sq. ft
	Firebox	105.5 sq. ft
	Total	1,169.3 sq. ft
Grate area		17.9 sq. ft
Boiler pressure		160 psi
Coupled wheels		4 ft 11 in.
Tender wheels		4 ft 1 in.
Tractive effort		16,942 lb.
Length over buffers		47 ft 3 in.*
Wheelbase		
	Engine	16 ft 1 in.
	Tender	12 ft 0 in.
	Total	35 ft 2 in.
Weight in working order		
	Engine	37 tons 2 cwt
	Tender	30 tons 13 cwt
	Total	67 tons 15 cwt
Max. axle loading		13 tons 0 cwt
Water capacity		2,640 gallons
Coal capacity		5 tons

* Engine and tender

The advent of eight-coupled heavy goods locomotives on the Whitemoor to Temple Mills and other ex-GER main lines freight workings from the 1930s gradually released two ex-GER tender locomotive classes for cross-country and branch line freight services. The monopoly of the 'J15s' was broken when the LNER 'J17' and 'J19' 0-6-0s began working the freight services on the Ramsey East branch. The 'J17s' built to the design of J. Holden were initially introduced from 1900 as GER class 'F48' with round-topped fireboxes. Another batch of 30 were built with Belpaire fireboxes as class 'G58' from 1905 to 1911. Thereafter some of the earlier locomotives were rebuilt with Belpaire fireboxes and reclassified. After Grouping the 'F48s' became LNER class 'J16' and the 'G58s' LNER class 'J17', but by 1932 all the round-topped firebox locomotives had been rebuilt with a Belpaire firebox as class 'J17', and class 'J16' became extinct. Their superior tractive effort was much appreciated by the footplate crews working sugar beet trains from Ramsey East and Warboys or brick traffic from Warboys and Owen's siding. Usually March depot provided the 'J17' locomotive on through freights after the withdrawal of the passenger services. Locomotives known to have worked the branch included:

GER No.	LNER 1924 No.	LNER 1946 No.	BR No.	Withdrawn
1153	8153	5503	65503	August 1960
1165	8165	5515	65515	September 1958
1167	8167	5517	65517	May 1955
1168	8168	5518	65518	September 1958
1170	8170	5520	65520	February 1961
1171	8171	5521	65521	February 1962
1172	8172	5522	65522	September 1958
1173	8173	5523	65523	May 1957
1174	8174	5524	65524	March 1955
1175	8175	5525	65525	April 1959
1176	8176	5526	65526	August 1959
1177	8177	5527	65527	April 1959
1178	8178	5528	65528	November 1961
1179	8179	5529	65529	May 1958
1180	8180	5530	65530	January 1960
1181	8181	5531	65531	April 1959
1182	8182	5532	65532	February 1962
1183	8183	5533	65533	January 1960
1185	8185	5535	65535	May 1958
1187	8187	5537	65537	January 1957
1188	8188	5538	65538	April 1959
1189	8189	5539	65539	August 1960
1190	8190	5540	65540	April 1959
1191	8191	5541	65541	September 1962
1193	8193	5543	65543	May 1955
1196	8196	5546	65546	January 1960
1197	8197	5547	65547	September 1954
1198	8198	5548	65548	December 1960
1204	8204	5554	65554	September 1961
1205	8205	5555	65555	March 1960
1206	8206	5556	65556	March 1961
1211	8211	5561	65561	December 1959
1212	8212	5562	65562	August 1958
1213	8213	5563	65563	January 1960
1214	8214	5564	65564	August 1960
1216	8216	5566	65566	July 1960
1220	8220	5570	65570	April 1960
1221	8221	5571	65571	February 1958
1223	8223	5573	65573	October 1958
1225	8225	5575	65575	February 1958

GER No.	LNER 1924 No.	LNER 1946 No.	BR No.	Withdrawn
1226	8226	5576	65576	September 1962
1227	8227	5577	65577	February 1962
1228	8228	5578	65578	March 1962
1229	8229	5579	65579	November 1954
1230	8230	5580	65580	November 1959
1231	8231	5581	65581	April 1962
1232	8232	5582	65582	September 1962
1233	8233	5583	65583	February 1962
1234	8234	5584	65584	February 1960
1235	8235	5585	65585	November 1954
1236	8236	5586	65586	April 1962
1237	8237	5587	65587	December 1958
1238	8238	5588	65588	May 1961
1239	8239	5589	65589	January 1961

The leading dimensions of the 'J17' class were:

Cylinders	2 inside		19 in. x 26 in.
Motion			Stephenson with slide valves
Boiler	Max. diameter outside		4 ft 9 in.
	Barrel length		11 ft 9 in.
	Firebox outside length		7 ft 0 in.
Heating surface			
	Firebox		117.7 sq. ft
	Tubes		863.5 sq. ft
	Flues		282.7 sq. ft
	Total evaporative		1,263.9 sq. ft
	Superheater		154.8 sq. ft
	Total		1,418.7 sq. ft
Tubes			156 x 1¾ in.
Flues			18 x 5 in.
Elements			18 x $1^3/_{32}$ in.
Grate area			21.24 sq. ft
Boiler pressure			180 psi
Coupled wheels			4 ft 11 in.
Tender wheels			4 ft 1 in.
Tractive effort			24,340 lb.
Length over buffers			50 ft 6 in.*
Wheelbase	Engine		17 ft 8 in.
	Tender		12 ft 0 in.
	Total		38 ft 0 in.
Weight in working order			
	Engine		45 tons 8 cwt
	Tender		38 tons 5 cwt
	Total		83 tons 13 cwt
Max. axle loading			16 tons 11 cwt
Water capacity			3,500 gallons
Coal capacity			5 tons

* Engine and tender

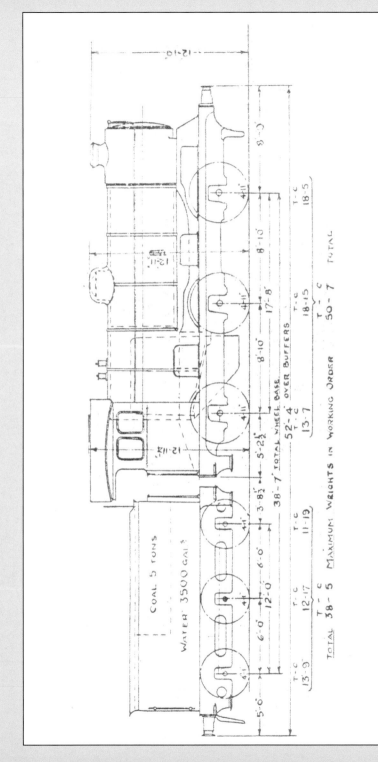

A.J. Hill's GER 'T77' class 0-6-0 as rebuilt with larger boiler and round-top firebox and classified 'J19' by the LNER.

The second goods class to oust the 'J15s' was A.J. Hill's designed 'E72' and 'T77' 0-6-0s, which became LNER class 'J19'. A total of 10 'E72s' were introduced in 1912 and were the first of the company's goods engines to carry superheated boilers as the 'F48'/'G48' classes were still saturated. The twenty-five 'T77s', with several modifications, were built between 1916 and 1920. At Grouping the LNER classified the initial build as class 'J18' and the final batch as class 'J19'. Between 1934 and 1939 all 35 were rebuilt with larger boilers and round-topped fireboxes. They were known in the rebuilt form as class 'J19/2' but the suffix '/2', was usually ignored. March and Cambridge depots provided the locomotives for the through freight workings to the branch and the following are known to have visited the line.

GER No.	LNER 1924 No.	LNER 1946 No.	BR No.	Withdrawn
1240	8240	4640	64640	November 1959
1241	8241	4641	64641	January 1960
1242	8242	4642	64642	March 1960
1243	8243	4643	64643	November 1961
1245	8245	4645	64645	December 1958
1246	8246	4646	64646	October 1961
1247	8247	4647	64647	March 1960
1248	8248	4648	64648	August 1959
1143	8143	4653	64653	January 1961
1144	8144	4654	64654	January 1960
1145	8145	4655	64655	August 1961
1146	8146	4656	64656	May 1960
1149	8149	4659	64659	April 1960
1261	8261	4661	64661	August 1959
1266	8266	4666	64666	January 1961
1267	8267	4667	64667	September 1961
1268	8268	4668	64668	December 1959
1269	8269	4669	64669	December 1961
1251	8251	4671	64671	February 1962
1252	8252	4672	64672	January 1959
1253	8253	4673	64673	August 1962

The leading dimensions of the 'J19' class were:

Cylinders	2 inside	20 in. x 28 in.
Motion		Stephenson with 10 in. piston valves
Boiler	Max. diameter outside	5 ft 1½ in.
	Barrel length	11 ft 9 in.
	Firebox length outside	7 ft 0 in.
Heating surface		
	Firebox	126.0 sq. ft
	Tubes	957.1 sq. ft
	Flues	346.3 sq. ft
	Superheater	302.5 sq. ft
	Total	1,731.9 sq. ft
Tubes		172 x 1¾ in.
Flues		21 x 5¼ in.
Elements		21 x 1¼ in.
Grate area		21.4 sq. ft

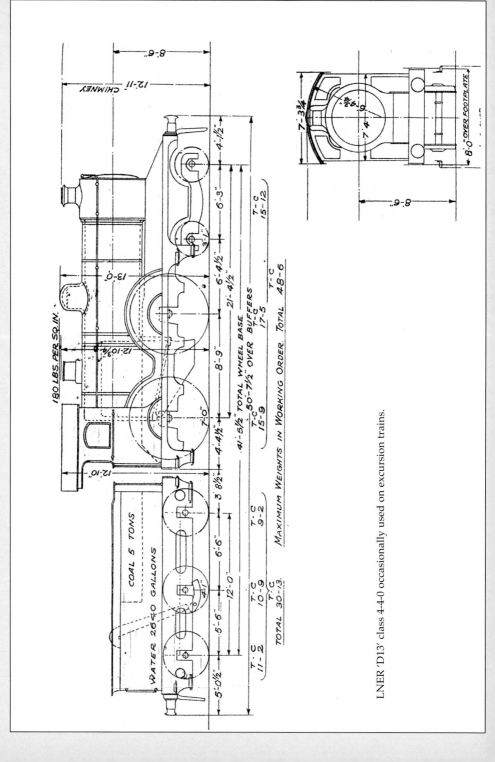

LNER 'D13' class 4-4-0 occasionally used on excursion trains.

Boiler pressure		160 psi
Coupled wheels		4 ft 11 in.
Tender wheels		4 ft 1 in.
Tractive effort		25,817 lb.
Length over buffers		52 ft 4 in.*
Wheelbase	Engine	17 ft 8 in.
	Tender	12 ft 0 in.
	Total	38 ft 7 in.
Weight in working order		
	Engine	50 tons 7 cwt
	Tender	38 tons 5 cwt
	Total	88 tons 12 cwt
Max. axle loading		18 tons 15 cwt
Water capacity		3,500 gallons
Coal capacity		5 tons 0 cwt

* Engine and tender

Other locomotives, which occasionally traversed the branch included the LNER 'D13' class 4-4-0s on excursion trains. Originally built as GER class 'T19' 2-4-0s, 101 were constructed between 1886 and 1897. Sixty were rebuilt as 4-4-0s between 1905 and 1908 and 50 of these entered service with the LNER. Cambridge had a small allocation and the following appeared on branch excursion trains.

GER No.	LNER 1924 No.	Withdrawn
713	7713	May 1933
717	7717	March 1930
732	7732	May 1933
742	7742	November 1935
779	7779	April 1935
1012	8012	December 1935
1016	8016	May 1938
1020	8020	April 1936
1021	8021	August 1936
1023	8023	January 1944
1028	8028	January 1938
1035	8035	May 1943
1037	8037	December 1934

The LNER 'D14', 'D15' and 'D16' class 4-4-0s also made sporadic visits to the Ramsey East branch on excursion trains. The 111 GER 'S46' and 'D46' classes, later LNER 'D14' and 'D15' class locomotives dated from 1900, with the final 10 emerging as class 'D16' in 1923. Throughout the years they were rebuilt and the majority that survived into British Railways ownership formed the 'D16/3' sub-class. Locomotives allocated to Cambridge usually worked the trains but March occasionally sent a locomotive to work the excursion. Those known to have worked across the branch included:

GER No.	LNER 1924 No.	LNER 1946 No.	BR No.	Withdrawn
1790	8790	2601	62601	January 1957
1823	8823	2574	62574	December 1955
1840	8840	2551	62551	July 1956
1876	8876	2527	62527	July 1952

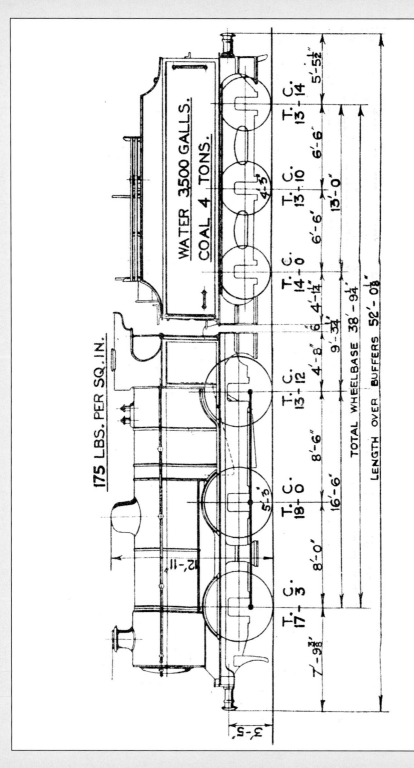

Former LMS '4F' class 0-6-0.

Occasional use was made in the latter years of ex-London Midland & Scottish Railway (LMS) 0-6-0s designed by Fowler and introduced into service. Nos. 44219 and 44391 allocated to Northampton were known visitors but there were several others in the last years of steam operation.

Another class associated with the branch to Warboys during the final years of steam was the ex-LMS '4MT' 2-6-0s designed by H.G. Ivatt, grandson of the former GNR locomotive engineer H.A. Ivatt. After the closure of the former Midland & Great Northern Railway route from Peterborough to Yarmouth and Norwich in 1959 many of the engines formerly allocated to Yarmouth Beach, Melton Constable and South Lynn sheds were dispersed throughout the Eastern Region, and March received a small allocation. The LMS '4MT' 2-6-0s quickly displaced the former ex-GER locomotives and the additional power proved popular with local enginemen, as did the enclosed cab and tender cab, which gave crews greater protection in inclement weather. Locomotives known to have worked across the branch on the pick-up goods working were Nos. 43061 and 43084.

Stranger on the Ramsey East branch. Former LMS '4F' class 0-6-0 No. 44219 departs from Warboys for Somersham with a brake van. The change in gradient under the Warboys road overbridge leading to the station is noticeable. The locomotive allocated to Northampton was borrowed by March depot to work the branch freight but was extremely unpopular with the enginemen. *Dr I.C. Allen*

With the withdrawal of steam traction in East Anglia March depot occasionally utilized one of Ipswich's allocation of BR Sulzer type '2' diesel electric locomotives Nos. D5036 to D5049, later designated class '24', on the freight trip to Warboys. The principal dimensions of these Bo-Bo locomotives were:

Type	Bo-Bo
Weight in working order	75 tons
Tractive effort - maximum	40,000 lb.
Wheelbase	36 ft 6 in.
Wheel diameter	3 ft 9 in.
Bogie wheelbase	8 ft 6 in.
Bogie pivot centres	28 ft 0 in.
Width overall	9 ft $1^3/_8$ in.
Length overall	50 ft 6 in.
Height overall	12 ft 8 in.
Minimum curve negotiable	4½ chains
Max. permitted speed	75 mph
Fuel tank capacity	630 gallons
Brakes	Oerlikon type, compressed air and hand brakes on the locomotive. Vacuum brake equipment giving proportional air braking on the locomotive.
Power equipment	6-cylinder diesel engine, Sulzer 4-stroke type 6 LDA28 1,160 hp at 750 rpm.
Traction motors (4)	BTH type 137BY 4 pole force ventilated.

The use of class '24s' was sporadic and usually Brush type '2' diesel-electric locomotives, classes '31/0' and '31/1', were used on the branch goods and they remained the staple motive power until freight services were withdrawn between Somersham and Warboys on and from 13th July, 1964. Locomotives

A Brush type '2' class '31' diesel-electric trundles a Whitemoor to Temple Mills freight train through Somersham on 6th September, 1963. Locomotives of this type handled the Warboys branch goods train in the last years before closure.   *R. Powell*

known to have worked across the branch included D5569, D5578, D5579, D5580, D5581, D5582, D5599, D5619, D5621, D5629, D5634, D5635, D5636, D5662, D5667, D5670, D5696, D5698 and D5804. The leading dimensions of the Brush type '2' locomotives were:

Type	A1A-A1A
Weight in working order	104 tons*, 106 tons†
Tractive effort – maximum	42,000 lb.
Wheelbase	42 ft 10 in.
Wheel diameter	3 ft 7 in.
Bogie wheelbase	14 ft 0 in.
Bogie centres	28 ft 10 in.
Width overall	8 ft 9 in.
Length overall	56 ft 9 in.
Height overall	12 ft 7½ in.
Minimum curve negotiable	4½ chains
Maximum permitted speed	80 mph – D5520-D5534
	90 mph – D5535-D5699, D5800-on
Fuel tank capacity	550 gallons
Brakes	Compressed air and handbrakes on the locomotive. Vacuum brake equipment giving proportional air braking on the locomotive
Power equipment	*Mirlees 12-cyl* *English Electric diesel* diesel engine JVs engine 12SVT 1,470hp 12T 1,250hp at at 850 rpm 900 rpm
Traction motors (4)	Brush DC type TM 73-68 4-pole force ventilated

* Mirlees engine. † English Electric engine.

The details quoted are those extant at the time the '13/2' class (late class '31') operated on the Warboys branch. Many alterations were subsequently made.

Facilities and staff

Ramsey High Street, later Ramsey East, shed was a sub-shed of Cambridge motive power depot, which supplied locomotives to operate the services on the branch. From the opening of the line two sets of footplate staff were stationed at Ramsey together with a cleaner who was usually booked on night duty to coal and water the engine for the following day's duty. The two sets of footplate staff alternated between early and late turns. The first set signed on at 4.50 am to work the goods and two passenger trains to Somersham and back whilst the second set relieved the first set at 12.30 pm to work three round trips to Somersham. The locomotive foreman or as he was later called driver-in-charge at Ramsey High Street received a half-day's extra pay for administrative duties, which included the submission of drivers' tickets and coal and oil returns to the district motive power office at Cambridge. The majority of drivers at Ramsey only signed the route knowledge sheets for the branch and on to St Ives, March and Huntingdon, although occasionally an individual signed through to

Cambridge. Later the men also signed to Billup's siding between Somersham and Chatteris. Cambridge, March, St Ives and Ely footplate staff also signed the road to Ramsey High Street, the first two especially after 1930 when all freight services were worked by either Cambridge or March engine and men.

The drivers in GER and LNER days were strict with firemen and cleaners, especially if the Ramsey branch engine was not spotlessly clean. The senior driver would inspect the engine every morning if he was on early turn, and woe betide the cleaner if he found any part not cleaned to high standards. A common test was to wipe a clean rag along the footplate or on the inside of the frame and wheels to make sure cleaning had not been skimped.

In addition to his normal duties the cleaner emptied and refilled footwarmers for carriages and hand-coaled the locomotive from the small coal stage adjacent to the engine shed. The coal had first to be offloaded from a wagon and because of the absence of a coalman at the depot the cleaner was paid an additional 6½d. per ton for this duty. The shed pit had also to be scraped clean of oil, grease and ashes and sanded every morning. Shed windows were cleaned each week whilst the shed floor and yard adjacent to the engine shed was swept and tidied daily. Charlie Lambert, who was the last cleaner at Ramsey East depot before closure, well remembers what a lonely place the engine shed was at night, located quite a distance from any houses. The only noises were from horses and

RAMSEY DEPOT.

No. 1.

arr. a.m.		dep. a.m.
	On Duty	4 50
	Loco'	5 35 L
	Ramsey	5 50 G M X
6 20	Somersham	6 45 G M X
7 20	Ramsey	7 36
7 52	Somersham	8 5 G M O
8 15	Warboys	8 40 G M O
8 50	Somersham	9 11
9 30	Ramsey	{ 10 0 M O / 10 20 M X
M O 10 16 } M X 10 36 }	Somersham	11 18
		p.m.
11 34	Ramsey	{ 12 30 G S O / 1 0 M O-
p.m.		
S O 1 43 } M O 1 16 }	Somersham	{ 2 19 M O / 2 15 G S O
M O 2 35 } S O 2 50 }	Ramsey	3 5
3 24	Somersham	5 4
5 20	Ramsey	5 35
5 51	Somersham	6 10
6 29	Ramsey	1
	Loco'	

Men change at Ramsey 12.30 p.m.

Locomotive and enginemen's diagrams Ramsey East depot, July 1925.

cattle in the surrounding fields and the occasional owl, augmented by the loud bangs and groans from the 'F7' class tank engine as she stood making steam. To break the solitude the local policeman used to pay a visit for a chat and, especially in winter, for a warm on the footplate and a cup of tea. Another aspect of this rural depot in the early years was tube cleaning, the senior fireman performed the task and was paid four hours Sunday rate for the work. The practice ceased when the branch locomotive was changed over each week and returned to Cambridge. Boiler washing appears never to have been attempted at Ramsey East depot and all such work and remedial repairs and maintenance was performed at Cambridge.

Motive power staff based at Ramsey High Street, were characters in their own right and, as with many small depots on the GER system, the two drivers never spoke to each other unless they had comments to make on the performance of the locomotive. This rather strange, independent and odd attitude was not prevalent among the firemen and cleaner who appeared to get on well together. In the early years mixed or goods trains on the branch often made unscheduled stops between sidings and stations when a pheasant or other game bird in full flight had been hit by the locomotive. With a speed of only 20 to 30 mph, the train was quickly halted and the crew were to be seen descending from the footplate to retrieve the trophy from the lineside. The locomotive crew never stopped if the train was a passenger working. One of the first drivers to be stationed at Ramsey was Charles Steel, who entered the service of the GER as an engine cleaner at Peterborough in October 1865. He was promoted to fireman in August 1868 and transferred to March as driver in July 1873. On the opening of the Ramsey High Street branch he transferred to the new Ramsey depot and worked on the branch until retirement in August 1910 and subsequently passed away on 25th November, 1917 aged 74 years. At the time of the withdrawal of passenger services on 20th September, 1930, Herbert Atkins, known to everyone as 'Tommy' but never to his face, was driver-in-charge at Ramsey East shed. The remaining footplate staff were driver A. Laver, fireman P. Brown, fireman E. Harbour and engine cleaner C. Lambert. Following the withdrawal of the branch passenger services, the depot closed on Monday 22nd September, 1930, when all five staff were transferred to Cambridge travelling together on the footplate of 'F7' class 2-4-2T No. 8308, which had been stabled on the shed over the weekend.

Locomotive facilities at Ramsey East included a brick-built single-road engine shed located on the south side of the main single line, east of the station. No mess room or toilet was provided and a bucket was the only washing facilities available for footplate staff. Outside the shed on the south side of the shed road was a water crane and coaling stage.

The Ramsey High Street branch locomotive rarely travelled beyond Somersham unless sent for changeover or to St Ives for water. It invariably travelled chimney first from Somersham to Ramsey and if received the wrong way round arrangements were made, if time allowed, for the engine to be turned on the 50 ft diameter turntable at Huntingdon East.

The water supply at Ramsey High Street was regarded as hard for locomotive boilers and there was a distinct reluctance by footplatemen to use the facility.

The water was obtained from a water crane fed from a storage tank, the water from the well being pumped into the storage tank raised aloft the engine shed roof by means of a water raising cock fitted to the locomotive, and all engines working the branch services had to be equipped with this component. The pump must have been quite powerful for it was located in a small brick structure opposite the station platform and quite a distance from the engine shed. In later years the facility was totally discarded and the branch locomotive always travelled light engine to St Ives to replenish the side tanks or tender. This was considered an expensive operation and, in 1899, a water tank and water column was provided at Somersham and the light running to St Ives ceased.

The headcode carried by the branch trains during the initial years was a red light at the top of the smokebox and a white light on the buffer beam. During daylight hours, a circular red disc, with white outer rim, was carried by the chimney. Special trains carried an additional white light by night or white disc by day on the buffer beam. From 1890 a red disc with white outer rim was carried under the chimney by day and a red light under the chimney and a white light on the left-hand end of the buffer beam by night. In 1903 the single line headcode was again changed to a red disc with white outer rim under the chimney during daylight hours and a red lamp under the chimney and a green lamp on the left-hand end of the buffer beam by night. From 1910 ordinary and special trains carried the same code with a red disc with white outer rim or red lamp under the chimney and a green disc with white outer rim or green lamp over the left-hand end of the buffer beam. After Grouping the LNER phased out the green lights and discs as a possible source of danger and replaced them with purple discs and lights. By 1925 the standard stopping passenger train code of a white disc by day or a white light by night under the chimney was used on the Ramsey East branch trains and this remained in use until the withdrawal of the passenger services. Freight trains on the branch carried Railway Clearing House headcode for the appropriate class of train.

The following whistle codes were applicable to the branch when under GER control:

Somersham Junction	Main line	1 distinct sound
	To or from the Ramsey branch	3 distinct sounds
Ramsey High Street	Main line	1 distinct sound
	To or from loco siding	2 distinct sounds
	From platform line to cattle siding	3 distinct sounds
	From platform line to goods shed road	4 distinct sounds

In the event of a mishap or derailment the Cambridge breakdown crane was used to cover the Ramsey East branch. Initially GER No. 1A, a 10 ton capacity crane dating from 1885 was utilized but this was later superseded by Ransomes and Rapier 35 ton crane, LNER No. 961601 built in 1932. Latterly Cowans Sheldon 45 ton capacity steam crane LNER No. 961606 (Works No. 6873) dating from 1940, later renumbered by BR to 133 and then 330133, was used. If the above crane was not available, Ipswich 20 ton capacity steam crane and March 20 ton capacity crane No. 134 could not be used as they were restricted from the Ramsey East branch.

Coaching stock

Unlike locomotives the GER placed no weight or loading gauge restrictions on rolling stock on the Ramsey High Street branch and conventional branch line coaching stock was used. From the opening until 1896 the coaching stock was exclusively four-wheel, provided with oil lighting and equipped with the Westinghouse brake. Initially vehicles of 26 and 27 ft body lengths formed the mainstay of the coaching stock and a set of three coaches, formed of a four-compartment first/third composite to diagram 217, a five-compartment third to diagram 402 and a brake/third to diagram 504 usually sufficed for most periods of the year. On occasions a five-compartment second to diagram 302 was added to the formation. Prior to the abolition of second class accommodation outside the London Suburban area the composite would have provided first and second class accommodation.

GER diagram No.	217	302	402	504
	Four-wheel composite	Four-wheel second	Four-wheel third	Four-wheel brake/third
Length over buffers	30 ft 9 in.	30 ft 9 in.	30 ft 9 in.	30 ft 9 in.
Length over body	27 ft 0 in.	27 ft 0 ¾	27 ft 0 in.	27 ft 0 in.
Height overall	10 ft 11 in.	11 ft 2 in.	11 ft 2 in.	10 ft 11 in.
Body height	6 ft 8 in.	6 ft 10 ½ in.	6 ft 11 in.	6 ft 8 in.
Width over guard's lookout	–	–	–	9 ft 3½ in.
Width over body	8 ft 0 in.	8 ft 0 in.	8 ft 0 in.	8 ft 0 in.
Wheelbase	15 ft 3 in.	15 ft 3 in.	15 ft 3 in.	15 ft 3 in.
Seating				
1st class	16	–	–	–
2nd class	20*	50	–	–
3rd class	–	–	50	20
Luggage	–	–	–	10 cwt
Weight empty	8 tons 15 cwt	9 tons 18 cwt	9 tons 8 cwt	9 tons 12 cwt

* Also 16 x 1st, 20 x 3rd.

By the turn of the century Holden 6-wheel vehicles with a wheelbase of 20 ft, body length varying from 32 ft for a full brake to 34 ft 6 in. for a 6-compartment third were drafted to the branch as replacements for the 4-wheel vehicles.

GER diagram No.	219	404	514
	Six-wheel composite	Six-wheel third	Six-wheel brake/third
Length over buffers	35 ft 1 ½ in.	37 ft 7 ½ in.	37 ft 7½ in.
Length over body	32 ft 0 in.	34 ft 6 in.	34 ft 6 in.
Height overall	11 ft 3 in.	11 ft 3 in.	11 ft 3 in.
Body height	7 ft 0 in.	7 ft 0 in.	7 ft 0 in.
Width over guard's lookout	–	–	9 ft 3½ in.
Width over body	8 ft 0 in.	8 ft 0 in.	8 ft 0 in.
Wheelbase	20 ft 0 in.	21 ft 0 in.	21 ft 0 in.
Seating			
1st class	12	–	–
3rd class	20	60	30
Luggage	15 cwt	–	2 tons
Weight empty	12 tons 16 cwt	13 tons 3 cwt	12 tons 18 cwt

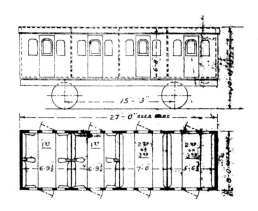

G. E. R.

4ᵀᴴ PERIOD 1876-80

—— COMPOSITE CARRIAGE ——

DIAGRAM Nº 14600-217

TO SEAT 16-1ˢᵀ & 20-2ᴺᴰ CLASS PASSENGERS
 „   16-1ˢᵀ & 20-3ᴿᴰ   „   „

TO SEAT 16-1ˢᵀ & 20-2ᴺᴰ OR
20-3ᴿᴰ CLASS PASSENGERS

TOTAL WEIGHT EMPTY 8-15-0

GER four-wheel composite to diagram 217.

G. E. R.

DIAGRAM Nº 14600-402

TO SEAT 50-3ᴿᴰ CLASS PASSENGERS
TOTAL WEIGHT EMPTY 9-8-0

THIRD CLASS CARRIAGE.

GER four-wheel third to diagram 402.

G. E. R.

4ᵀᴴ PERIOD 1876-80.

BRAKE THIRD CLASS CARRIAGE.

DIAGRAM Nº 14600-504

TO SEAT 20-3ᴿᴰ CLASS PASSENGERS
TOTAL WEIGHT EMPTY 9-12-2.

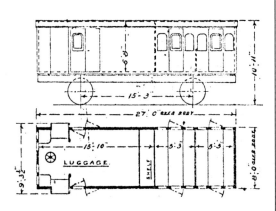

LUGGAGE.

GER four-wheel brake third to diagram 504.

GER six-wheel brake third No. 681 built in June 1895 and converted for conductor-guard working in 1922. Renumbered 62985 by the LNER she was withdrawn on 31st August, 1940 and converted to ballast brake No. 634526. Typical of the vehicles used on the Ramsey East branch, note the locked off doors with only the end door available for passengers. *J. Watling*

Interior view of a six-wheel third vehicle converted for conductor-guard working as used on the Ramsey East branch. Note the gas mantles and through end doors to enable the guard to gain access between vehicles. *Author's Collection*

In 1914 the GER fitted 'Y65' class 2-4-2T No. 1311 with compressed air auto-train equipment and coupled it to two converted bogie coaches for experimental operation on lightly-used branch lines where operational expenditure exceeded receipts. Here No. 1311 is shown with clerestory composite No. 633 and clerestory third driving trailer No. 522. The auto-train commenced trial running on the Cambridge to Mildenhall line on 5th October, 1914 and was later transferred to work the Somersham to Ramsey High Street branch, but was found unsuitable as mixed train working was well established on both lines. The train was subsequently transferred to the temporarily-restored passenger service between Cheshunt and White Hart Lane on the reopened Churchbury loop line from 1st March. 1915.   *Author's Collection*

GER auto-train driving trailer third No. 522 (to diagram 433) leads composite trailer No. 633 (to diagram 240) and propelled by 'Y65' class 2-4-2T No. 1311 forming the 2.48 pm Lower Edmonton to Cheshunt train approaching Theobalds Grove station on 20th March, 1915.
LCGB/Ken Nunn

Two coaching vehicles were provided with 'Y65' class 2-4-2T No. 1311 for the auto-train trials in 1914. The first was driving compartment third, GER No. 522. The coach was originally built in 1906 as an internal corridor lavatory third to diagram 417. When converted in 1914 to diagram 433, the lavatory was removed and the compartment became part of the corridor. The second vehicle of the set, trailer first/third composite GER No. 633 converted to diagram 240 in 1914 was originally a lavatory/luggage composite built in 1904 to diagram 212. The LNER later renumbered 522 to 61328 and 633 to 63521.

Principal dimensions of the vehicles were:

Diagram	240	433
GER No.	633	522
LNER No.	63521	61328
Type	Composite trailer	Driving trailer
Length over buffers	51 ft 4½ in.	53 ft 1½ in.
Length over body	48 ft 3 in.	50 ft 0 in.
Max. height	12 ft 8 in.	12 ft 8 in.
Body height	8 ft 5 in.	8 ft 5 in.
Max. width	8 ft 6 in.	9 ft 0 in.
Wheelbase to bogie centre	8 ft 0 in.	8 ft 0 in.
Seating		
1st class	9	–
3rd class	30	46
Total weight empty	25 tons 8 cwt	26 tons 10 cwt

The trials were inconclusive and the set proved operationally inconvenient, neither being able to take tail loads of goods traffic when booked to run as a mixed train, nor additional passenger vehicles when being propelled by the locomotive. The two-coach set together with No. 1311 was subsequently transferred to the temporarily-restored service between White Hart Lane and Cheshunt on the reopened Churchbury loop line in 1915.

Increasing competition from motorbuses in the early 1920s and the need for economy of working the unprofitable passenger services, led to the GER authorities introducing conductor-guard working on the line. Unlike other branches in East Anglia where conductor-guard working was also introduced, no new halts were opened between Somersham and Ramsey High Street. On the introduction of the new arrangements the existing rolling stock was withdrawn and replaced by specially adapted 2-coach sets comprising a brake/third and first/third composite. Each coach had a centre gangway and connecting doors at each end of the vehicle, intended for the guard's use only to enable him to gain access to the whole train to collect fares. The brake third vehicles also had retractable steps on the side of the coach for use at the low platforms but this equipment was not used when the vehicle was running on the Ramsey East branch. Direct access from station platforms was obtainable to all coaches in the usual way except that the end doors only were used, the remainder being sealed off. The carriage sets used for the conductor-guard working were converted from ordinary main line stock and appeared in the crimson livery adopted by the GER in 1919. In due course the LNER repainted the stock in the more familiar teak or brown livery. The conductor-guard sets

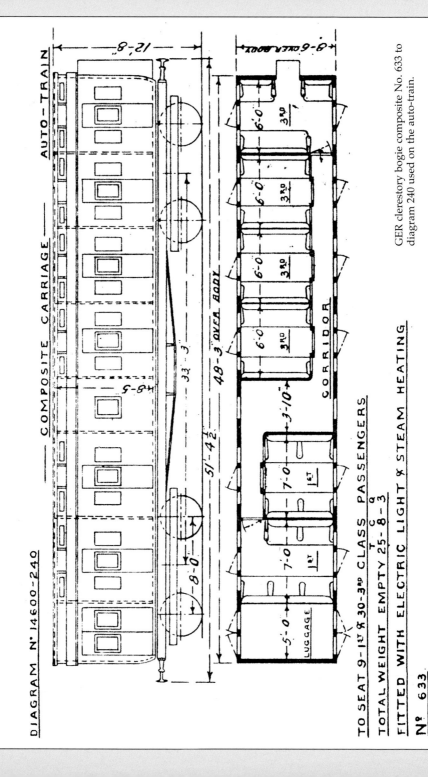

DIAGRAM Nº 14600-240

COMPOSITE CARRIAGE — AUTO-TRAIN

TO SEAT 9-1ST & 30-3RD CLASS PASSENGERS

TOTAL WEIGHT EMPTY 25-8-3 T C Q

FITTED WITH ELECTRIC LIGHT & STEAM HEATING

Nº 633

GER clerestory bogie composite No. 633 to diagram 240 used on the auto-train.

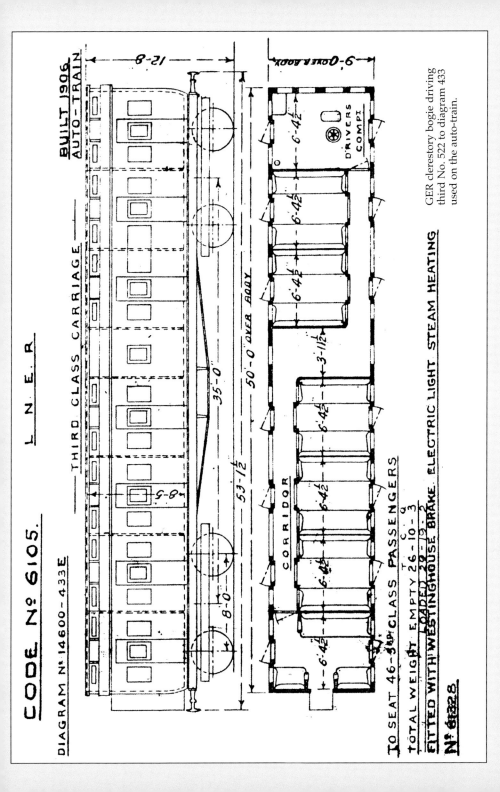

CODE Nº 6105.   L . N . E . R

DIAGRAM Nº 14600 – 433 E

THIRD CLASS CARRIAGE

BUILT 1906
AUTO-TRAIN

12-8

35-0

53-12½

50-0 OVER BODY

8-5

8-0

9-0 OVER BODY

DRIVERS COMPI

6-4½

6-4½

6-4½

3-11½

CORRIDOR

6-4½

6-4½

6-4½

6-4½

TO SEAT 46-3RD CLASS PASSENGERS

TOTAL WEIGHT EMPTY 26-10-3

LOADED 29-19-2

FITTED WITH WESTINGHOUSE BRAKE. ELECTRIC LIGHT STEAM HEATING

Nº 61328

GER clerestory bogie driving
third No. 522 to diagram 433
used on the auto-train.

used on the Somersham to Ramsey High Street branch comprised vehicles of three types: brake/third diagram 552 converted from main line stock; diagram 514 and first/third composites to diagrams 246 and 248 converted from main line vehicle diagrams 219, 404 and 422. The typical formation of each set was composite and brake third although no specific numbers of carriages used on the branch are known. Brief details of conversions are given below.

Brake third diagram 552	Converted from main line brake thirds built 1888 to 1896 to diagram 514. Eighteen vehicles converted, four in 1922, 14 in 1923, five withdrawn 1932-1933, one withdrawn in 1937 and 12 withdrawn 1940.
First/third composite diagrams 246 and 248	Two converted from composites built 1890 and 1891 diagram 219 in 1922 and withdrawn 1933 and 1935. Eighteen converted from main line thirds built in 1892 to diagram 404 and 1893/4 to diagram 422, nine converted in 1922, nine converted in 1923, two vehicles withdrawn in 1932, one withdrawn 1934 and the remaining 15 withdrawn in 1940.

The leading dimensions were:

GER diagram No.	246*	248*	552†
	Six-wheel composite	*Six-wheel composite*	*Six-wheel brake/third*
Length over buffers	35 ft 1 in.	37 ft 4½ in.	37 ft 4½ in.
Length over body	32 ft 0 in.	34 ft 6 in.	34 ft 6 in.
Height overall	11 ft 3¾ in.	11 ft 3 in.	11 ft 3 in.
Body height	6 ft 11 in.	7 ft 0 in.	7 ft 0 in.
Width over guard's lookout	–	–	9 ft 3½ in.
Width over body	8 ft 0 in.	8 ft 0 in.	8 ft 0 in.
Wheelbase	20 ft 0 in.	22 ft 6 in.	21 ft 0 in.
Seating			
1st class	12	12	–
3rd class	16	32	24
Luggage	15 cwt	–	2 tons
Weight empty	13 tons 0 cwt	13 tons 0 cwt	13 tons 0 cwt

* Converted from diagram 219, 404 or 502. † Converted from diagram 514.

If the branch train required strengthening for any reason an ordinary six-wheel third to diagram 404 or a conductor-guard converted six-wheel third to diagram 440 was utilized. The details of conversion of the full third were:

Full third diagram 440	Converted from main line thirds built 1889 to 1892 to diagram 404. Twenty-two vehicles converted, 10 in 1922, 12 in 1923, 6 withdrawn in 1932-33, 16 withdrawn in 1940.

GER diagram No.	440
	Six-wheel third
Length over buffers	37 ft 4 ½ in.
Length over body	34 ft 6 in.
Height overall	11 ft 3 in.
Body height	7 ft 0 in.
Width over body	8 ft 0 in.
Wheelbase	21 ft 0 in.
Seating	60
Weight empty	13 tons 3 cwt

None of the conductor-guard vehicles were scrapped as a result of the withdrawal of Ramsey East passenger services in 1930 and they were transferred to other lines operating under the conductor-guard method of working.

For the few excursion trains, which ran across the branch after the withdrawal of passenger services, most would have included former GER bogie corridor stock or later LNER Gresley corridor stock in the formation.

Wagon stock

When the railway opened for traffic most of the wagons used on the line would have been supplied by the GER. The company used four-plank-bodied open wagons with wooden frames, dating from 1882 for the conveyance of general merchandise and minerals. From 1887, these wagons were gradually superseded by five-plank 9 ton capacity (later 10 ton) opens, to diagram 16 with 9 ft 6 in. wheelbase and measuring 15 ft 0 in. over headstocks. Later 10 ton, 5-plank opens wagons to diagram 17, with a length of 15 ft over headstocks and 9 ft 0 in. wheelbase, were also used. Another variation was the use of 10 ton, seven-plank opens to diagram 55, measuring 17 ft 0 in. over headstocks and 9 ft 6 in. wheelbase for vegetable and root traffic. For fruit and perishable traffic 10 ton ventilated vans to diagram 15 were provided, measuring 16 ft 1 in. over headstocks, with 9 ft 0 in. wheelbase and overall height of 11 ft 0¾ in. Later covered goods vans to diagram 47 were also utilized. They measured 17 ft 3 in. over headstocks, had a wheelbase of 10 ft 6 in. and were 11 ft 2 in. in height. A third variation was the 10 ton capacity covered goods wagon to diagram 72, which measured 19 ft 0 in. over headstocks whilst maintaining a 10 ft 6 in. wheelbase.

The cattle traffic conveyed to and from St Ives, Huntingdon and Cambridge markets would have entailed the use of three types of cattle wagons on the branch. The first of 8 ton capacity was to diagram 5 and was 18 ft 7 in. over headstocks, had a 10 ft 6 in. wheelbase and was 10 ft 10¾ in. in height. The second to diagram 6 was of 9 tons capacity and measured 19 ft 0 in. over headstocks, with a 10 ft 6 in. wheelbase and overall height of 10 ft 10 ½ in. The third GER variant of cattle wagon to diagram 7 was of 10 ton capacity, 19 ft 3 in. over headstocks with 10 ft 6 in. wheelbase and overall height of 11 ft 2 in. At the tail of the train was usually a 20 ton 4-wheel brake van to GER diagram 56 measuring 17 ft 6 in. over headstocks, a 10 ft 3 in. wheelbase and 3 ft 1 in. diameter wheels. In addition many wagons owned by other railway companies were used to deliver and collect agricultural and livestock traffic, whilst coal and coke supplies came in private owner coal wagons. These fell into two categories, those belonging to collieries consigning the coal and coal factors wagons, which were loaded at the collieries. Much of the brick traffic was also conveyed in private owner wagons.

After Grouping the GER wagons continued to be utilized, but gradually LNER wagons of standard design made an appearance. The most numerous were probably the 12 ton, five-plank opens with 8 ft 0 in. wheelbase to code 2, and the 12 ton 6-plank opens with 10 ft 0 in. wheelbase to code 91 built after 1932. Later variations included 13 ton, seven-plank open wagons to code 162 measuring 16 ft 6 in. over headstocks and with a 9 ft 0 in. wheelbase. All were used on vegetable and sugar beet traffic and sometimes brick consignments. Fitted and unfitted 12 ton, 9 ft 0 in. wheelbase covered vans to code 16 conveyed perishable goods, fruit and malt, and later some were designated for fruit traffic only. From 1934 12 ton capacity vans to code 171, with steel underframe and pressed corrugated steel ends were introduced whilst at the same time the wheelbase was extended to a length of 10 ft 0 in. Specific fruit vans with both 9 ft and 10 ft wheelbase also saw service on the Ramsey East branch. Agricultural machinery destined for local farms were delivered on 12 ton 'Lowfit' wagons, with 10 ft wheelbase and overall length over headstocks of 17 ft 6 in. Larger machinery would have arrived or departed on one of the ex-GER 14 ton, 25 ft 6 in. 'Mac K2' machinery wagons to diagram 75 and later LNER builds. LNER brake vans provided for branch traffic included 20 ton 'Toad B' to code 34 and 'Toad E' to code 64 vehicles with 10 ft 6 in. wheelbase and measuring 22 ft 5 in. over buffers. Later 'Toad D' brake vans to code 61 with 16 ft 0 in. wheelbase and measuring 27 ft 5 in. over buffers were employed. Soon after Grouping several of the LNER bogie brick wagons were tested for traffic to and from Warboys brickyards but curvature of the sidings proved too severe and the wagons were banned from the line. After nationalization many of the older wooden wagons were scrapped and much of the traffic was conveyed in open wagons, usually the standard 16 ton all-steel mineral vehicles.

In GER days the body, solebars and headstocks of wagons were painted slate grey, whilst the ironwork below solebar level, buffer guides, buffers, drawbars, drawbar plates and couplings were black. The LNER wagon livery was grey for non-fitted wagons and covered vans, whilst all vehicles fitted with the automatic brake were painted oxide red, which changed to bauxite around 1940. Similar liveries were carried in BR days.

The maintenance of wagon stock used on the Ramsey East branch was carried out by wagon repair staff at Cambridge or March. In the event of the failure or defect of a wagon on the branch, a travelling wagon repairer from St Ives or March carried out repairs locally.

Appendix One

Length of Platforms, Sidings, etc.

Location	Ex-Somersham		Platforms		Loop	Sidings
			Up	Down		
	m.	c.	ft	ft	ft	
Somersham	0	00	260	260		550 ft Straight
						575 ft Middle road
						510 ft Back road
						280 ft Coal road
						225 ft Water road
						650 ft No. 1 down branch
						600 ft Up branch
						570 ft Up siding
						200 ft Up spur
						184 ft Granary No. 1
						170 ft Granary No. 2
Bateman's/Owen's Brickworks	1	22				790 ft Brickyard
						145 ft Shunting neck
						140 ft Dock
Pidley-cum-Fenton	2	20				860 ft Public siding
Warboys	4	31	320	320	580	570 ft New road
						422 ft Coal road
						290 ft Dock road
						400 ft Shed road
						660 ft Brickworks
						175 ft Brickworks dock road
						100 ft Shunting neck
						224 ft Cattle road
Cordell's	6	03				215 ft Siding
Ramsey High Street (later 'East')	6	75	330		410 later 594	330 ft Engine shed
						106 ft Cattle dock
						290 ft Shed road
						160 ft Dock road
						580 ft Back road
						420 ft Coal road
						460 ft Yard loop road

Appendix Two

Bridges

No.	Location	Mileage m. ch.	Name	Under or over	Type	Spans No.	Square span between abutments or supports ft. in.	Skew span between abutments or supports ft. in.	Depth of construction ft. in.	Distance from road or surface of water to rail ft. in.	Construction
Main line											
2301	Needingworth Jn & Somersham	11 04	Somersham	Under	Public road	1	38 0	34 4	2 7	14 0	Brick abutments, wrought iron girders. Rebuilt 1877.
2302	Somersham Station	11 06	Exchange Footbridge	Over	Exchange and public footbridge	1	38 3	– –	00 4	14 9	Cast iron columns, wrought iron girders.
Branch											
2305	Somersham & Warboys	0 39	Park Hall Road	Over	Public	1	27 10	28 0	3 0	17 9	Brick abutments, brick arch & parapets Width 25 ft 0 in. Huntingdonshire County Council from 31/10/1934.
2306	Somersham & Warboys	2 19	Pidley Drove	Under		1	6 0	6 3	2 4	10 6	Brick abutments, timber beams, cross sleeper timbers, Reconstructed concrete slabs. Ballast LR.
2306A	Somersham & Warboys	2 19	Pidley Drove	Under		1	12 6	15 0	1 6	5 6	Timber subs, main timbers, timber decking and parapets - carries yard entrance roadway over drain. Reconstructed 1936. Width 11 ft 0 in.

No.	Line	M. C.	Name	Over / Under	Road	No.	Dimension 1	Dimension 2	Dimension 3	Dimension 4	Description
2307	Somersham & Warboys	2 63	Fenton Lode	Under		1	9 0	12 6	1 10	11 6	Brick abutments, longitudinal trough girders, longitudinal running timbers, timber decking between troughs TR.
2308	Somersham & Warboys	3 11	Warboys Fen Drove	Under		1	7 6	11 0	1 10	12 3	Brick abutments, longitudinal trough girders, longitudinal running timbers, timber decking between troughs.
2309	Somersham & Warboys	3 59	Longland's Bridge	Over	Occupation	3	20 0 Over down side bank / 28 0 Over main single line / 20 0 Over up side bank		3 0	17 0	Brick abutments, brick arch & parapets. Width 12 ft 0 in.
2310	Somersham & Warboys	4 13	Warboys Road	Over	Public	3	20 0 Over down side bank / 27 9 Over main single line / 20 0 Over up side bank		3 0	17 0	Brick abutment and piers, brick arches and parapets. Width 25 ft 0 in.
2311	Warboys & Ramsey High Street	5 22	Boundary Drain	Under		1	15 0		1 10	9 6	Brick abutments, longitudinal running timbers, longitudinal trough girders, C I girder, timber decking TR.
2312	Warboys & Ramsey High Street	6 36	Bury Stream	Under	River & Occupation	2	20 2 Over river / 20 2 Over occupational cattle creep	20 9 / 20 9	3 6	10 6	Brick abutments and piers, brick arches and parapets Width 14 ft 0 in.
2313	Warboys & Ramsey High Street	6 41	Cattle Creep	Under	Occupation	1	10 0		3 6	10 6	Brick abutments, brick arch and parapets, track carried on longitudinal timbers TR. Width 14 ft 0 in.

Appendix Three

Level crossings

No.	Location	Mileage m. ch.	Local name	Status
1	Somersham & Warboys	0 30	Mason	Occupation
2	Somersham & Warboys	0 72½	Lawter	Public footpath
3	Somersham & Warboys	1 06	Meadows	Occupation
4	Somersham & Warboys	1 35	Forder's	Occupation
5	Somersham & Warboys	1 35	London Brick Co.	Occupation
6	Somersham & Warboys	1 52½	Pickwood	Occupation
7	Somersham & Warboys	1 52½	Pickwood	Occupation
8	Somersham & Warboys	1 59½	Carter	Occupation
9	Somersham & Warboys	1 59½	Carter	Occupation
10	Somersham & Warboys	2 03½	Pidley Siding	Public road
11	Somersham & Warboys	2 23	Kidman	Occupation
12	Somersham & Warboys	2 43	Green Drove	Occupation
13	Somersham & Warboys	2 62	Ashcroft	Occupation
14	Somersham & Warboys	2 73	Heading	Occupation
15	Somersham & Warboys	2 75	Fenton	Occupation
16	Somersham & Warboys	3 25	Rickard	Occupation
17	Somersham & Warboys	3 29	Heath Drove	Public road
18	Somersham & Warboys	3 53½	Longland	Occupation
19	Warboys & Ramsey East	4 37	Upchurch / London Brick Co.	Occupation
20	Warboys & Ramsey East	4 54	Hodgson	Occupation
21	Warboys & Ramsey East	4 65½	Berridge Drove	Occupation
22	Warboys & Ramsey East	5 04	Wistow Drove	Occupation
23	Warboys & Ramsey East	5 18½	Shore	Occupation
24	Warboys & Ramsey East	5 38	Jack's Corner	Public road
25	Warboys & Ramsey East	5 74	Cordell	Occupation
26	Warboys & Ramsey East	6 11½	Bury Drove	Public footpath
27	Warboys & Ramsey East	6 23		Public footpath
28	Warboys & Ramsey East	6 46		Occupation

G. E. R.

Somersham

Acknowledgements

The publication of this history would not have been possible without the help of many people who have been kind enough to assist in many ways. In particular I should like to thank the late A.R. Cox, the late W. Fenton, Alan Keeler, Ray Debenham, John Watling, the late Bernard Walsh, the late John Mott, the late Dr I.C. Allen, the late George Woodcock, Dave Taylor, Dave Hoser, the late Peter Proud, the late C.A. Lambert, A.E. Clarke, G. Robinson, Mike Brooks, the late Geoff Pember, Colin Holmes, the late Canon Charles Bayes, John Petrie, Peter Webber, Michael Back and the many other active and retired railway staff, especially of the motive power depots, operating, civil engineering and signalling functions at Cambridge, March and Peterborough, some of whom worked on the line. I am also extremely grateful to Robert Powell who read through the draft of the manuscript and made many useful comments.

Thanks are also due to the National Archives, Kew, British Railways Eastern Region, House of Lords Record Office, the British Library Newspaper Library, Huntingdon County Record Office, Cambridge County Record Office, Cambridge Library, Peterborough Library and members of the Great Eastern Railway Society and Great Northern Railway Society.

Bibliography

General works

Allen C.J.	*The Great Eastern Railway*, Ian Allan
Gordon D.I.	*Regional History of the Railways of Great Britain Vol. V* (David & Charles)
Gordon W.J.	*Our Home Railways*
Tatford B.	*Story of British Railways*
RCTS	*Locomotives of the LNER* - various volumes
Aldrich C.L.	*GER Locomotives*
Wrottesley J.	*The Great Northern Railway* - 3 volumes (Batsford)

Periodicals

Bradshaw's Railway Guide
Bradshaw's Railway Manual
British Railways Eastern Region Magazine
Buses
Great Eastern Railway Magazine
Herapath's Journal
Huntingdon Life
Locomotive Carriage & Wagon Review

Locomotive Magazine
LNER Magazine
Railway Magazine
Railway Times
Railway World
Railway Year Book
Trains Illustrated

Newspapers

Cambridge Chronicle   *Hunts County Guardian*   *Huntingdon Post*

Also the Minute books of Ramsey & Somersham Junction Railway, Eastern Counties Railway, East Anglian Railway, Great Eastern Railway, Great Northern Railway, Great Northern & Great Eastern Joint Committee, London & North Eastern Railway

Working and public timetables of the GER, GNR, GN&GE Joint Committee, LNER and BR (ER).

Appendices to working timetables of the GER, GNR, LNER and BR (ER).

Index

Accidents, 20, 35, 37

Acts of Parliament, 8, 9, 11 *et seq.*, 18, 19, 21, 45, 47

Auto-train trial, 55, 147, 173

Bateman's siding (later Owen's sdg), 49, 77, 85, 87, 111 *et seq.*, 118, 121 *et seq.*, 133, 134, 156, 179

Beeching Report, 75

Benwick branch, 47, 75

Billup's siding, 118, 166

Birt, William, 16, 18, 20, 23, 29, 37, 39, 41

Board of Trade (including inspections), 18, 21-3, 25, 29, 43, 49, 51, 64

British Railways, 71, 75, 77, 105, 139, 161, 164, 168, 178

Burt, George, 27

Bus services, competition, 57, 59, 60, 65, 173

Bus services, replacement, 61, 63, 65, 71, 75

Cambridge, 7, 20, 37, 63, 68, 99, 104, 110, 117, 118, 121, 129 *et seq.*, 139 *et seq.*, 159, 161, 165 *et seq.*, 177, 178

Campion, George, 15, 45

Capel, Reginald, 43

Chatteris, 7, 9, 10, 99, 105, 121, 123, 166

Closure of branch, 5, 75

Closure of shed, 167

Conductor-guard working, 57, 59, 105-6, 173, 176, 177

Cordell's siding, 71, 95, 125, 179

Darby, J., 43

Diesels introduced, 75

Eastern Counties Railway, 7 *et seq.*

Eastern Counties Extension Rly, 7

Ely, 7, 11, 13, 61, 64, 65, 98, 111, 113, 121, 129, 130, 133, 134, 140

Ely & Huntingdon Railway, 7

Engine loads (summary), 135-7

Excursions after 1930, 65, 67, 71, 130, 153, 177

Fairbairn, Andrew, 25

Fellowes, Edward, 10, 13, 18

First train, 24

Fitch, A., 17

Flooding of line, 51

Fox, Sir Charles, 9, 10

Freeman, J.J., 27, 43

Fuller, Alfred, 15, 18, 24, 27, 36, 45, 89, 133

Goods facilities (summary), 134-5

Gradient diagram, 28

Great Eastern Railway, 5, 9 *et seq.*, 18 *et seq.*, 22 *et seq.*, 27, 29, 35 *et seq.*, 47, 50, 51, 55, 98, 105 *et seq.*, 109, 110, 113, 129 *et seq.*, 135, 139, 147 *et seq.*, 166 *et seq.*, 173, 177, 178

Great Northern & Great Eastern Jt Line (incl. Committee), 5, 17, 19 *et seq.*, 23 *et seq.*, 39, 41 *et seq.*, 47 *et seq.*, 59, 81, 85, 87, 93, 99, 105, 109, 133 *et seq.*, 139

Great Northern Railway, 5 *et seq.*, 20, 22, 23, 37 *et seq.*, 51, 106, 129, 130, 161

Hawkshaw, Sir John, 16

Headlamp codes, 168

Holden, James, 40, 41, 145, 149, 151, 155, 169

Holme, 5, 7, 8, 10, 13, 15, 18, 22, 60, 130

Hopkins, George, 15, 20, 23

Huntingdon, 6, 7, 17, 60, 63, 75, 130, 165, 167, 177

Last passenger train, 63

London & North Eastern Rly, 5, 59 *et seq.*, 87, 88, 98, 105, 106, 119, 130, 139, 149, 151, 155, 156, 159, 161, 166, 168, 173, 177, 178

March, 7, 9, 15, 17, 63, 75, 124, 125, 129, 131, 140, 152, 153, 156, 159, 163, 165 *et seq.*, 178

Mawdesley, Thomas Smith, 15, 45

Mowlem, John (contractor), 19, 20, 23, 98

Needingworth Jn, 17

Northern & Eastern Rly, 7

Oakley, Sir Henry, 16, 18, 20, 23, 37, 39 *et seq.*

One Engine in Steam working, 65, 69, 104

Opening of line, 25, 27, 29

Owen's siding *see* Bateman's siding

Parkes, Charles, 16, 17

Passenger services withdrawn, 61, 167, 177

Peterborough, 6, 7, 16, 59, 98, 130, 131, 133, 163, 167

Pidley cum Fenton, 8, 11, 15, 21 *et seq.*, 35, 37, 38, 45, 47, 50, 65, 68, 75, 99, 103, 107, 109 *et seq.*, 179

Ramsey & St Ives Rly, 9, 10

Ramsey & Somersham Jn Rly, 5, 15 *et seq.*, 22 *et seq.*, 29, 31, 36, 37, 39 *et seq.*, 49 *et seq.*, 98, 99, 105, 109, 130

Purchase of, 45

Ramsey High St (later East), 5, 20 *et seq.*, 38, 39, 47, 49, 51, 55 *et seq.*, 65, 68 *et seq.*, 77, 95, 97 *et seq.*, 103 *et seq.*, 109 *et seq.*, 145 *et seq.*, 153, 156, 165 *et seq.*, 179

Closure to goods, 71, 125

Ramsey North, 5, 10, 13, 15, 22, 59 *et seq.*, 68 *et seq.*, 106, 119, 133

Closure to passengers, 71

Ramsey Railway, 5, 9 *et seq.*, 17, 20, 22, 37, 39, 43, 109

Opening, 10

Road C&D service, 134, 135

Route availability, 139

St Ives, 5, 6, 7, 9 *et seq.*, 16 *et seq.*, 24, 25, 38 *et seq.*, 49, 59 *et seq.*, 75, 99, 109 *et seq.*, 140, 165 *et seq.*, 177, 178

Scotter, Sir Charles, 41

Serjeant, Frederick, 15, 16, 18 *et seq.*, 24 *et seq.*

Shareholders' meetings, 24, 36

Snow blocking line, 68

Somersham, 5, 7, 10, 13 *et seq.*, 18 *et seq.*, 27 *et seq.*, 31, 35, 36, 38 *et seq.*, 47 *et seq.*, 55 *et seq.*, 64 *et seq.*, 75, 77, 81, 85, 98, 99, 103 *et seq.*, 109 *et seq.*, 139, 164, 167, 168, 178 *et seq.*, 182

Somersham, Ramsey & Holme Rly, 8, 11, 13

Stirling, Patrick, 40, 41

Strikes, 57, 59, 117

Train Staff & Ticket working, 25, 69, 99, 104

Warboys, 5, 7 *et seq.*, 15, 16, 21 *et seq.*, 25, 27, 36, 38, 41, 43, 47 *et seq.*, 55 *et seq.*, 65, 68 *et seq.*, 71, 75, 77, 89, 93, 98, 99, 103 *et seq.*, 139, 156, 163 *et seq.*, 178, 179

Whistle codes, 169

Whitemoor Yard, 121 *et seq.*, 133, 155

Whittlesea, 59, 105, 107

Wisbech, St Ives & Cambridge Jn Rly, 7

Withdrawal of passenger services, 61, 167, 177

World War I, 51, 55, 68, 113, 131, 151

World War II, 65, 68, 123, 130 *et seq.*, 137